Working with Māori children with special education needs

He mahi whakahirahira

NZCER PRESS
New Zealand Council for Educational Research
PO Box 3237
Wellington
New Zealand

ISBN 978-1-927231-43-2

Designed by Book Design Ltd (www.bookdesign.co.nz)
Distributed by NZCER Distribution Services
PO Box 3237
Wellington
New Zealand
www.nzcer.org.nz

Cover artwork: The cover features a painting by artist Donn Ratana of Ngāi Tūhoe.
Donn's painting depicts a contemporary view of whānau inclusiveness. In this context,
everyone, including tamariki, are involved in the everyday discussions or important
decision-making around the wellbeing of any and all members of the whānau.
Beginning from a relational and cultural position of connectedness, our collective
questions and sense making can bring greater understanding and inclusion.
He aha te mea nui i te ao? Māku e kī atu, he tangata, he tangata, he tangata.
What is the greatest thing in the world? I say it is people, it is people, it is people.

Working with Māori children
with special education needs

He mahi whakahirahira

Jill Bevan-Brown, Mere Berryman, Huhana Hickey,
Sonja Macfarlane, Kirsten Smiler and Tai Walker

NZCER PRESS

Contents

Foreword

Let me begin by acknowledging Tai Walker, my first cousin, whose contribution to the book was completed before her death in 2013. I firstly remember Tai as an older cousin who lived this fiercely independent life in Ruatoria and who always had a unique view on everything and opinion on everyone. Then I remember her as a doctoral student who would read her material word by word, size 38 font or higher, with immense patience and focus. No one who knew her would ever doubt her determination to be known by her abilities rather than her disabilities. In fact, if you knew Tai you knew her for her personality which could come across as sharp, opinionated, and scary, and then as you came to know her you found this funny, kind, generous, and engaged woman. I am proud that her work is in this book and acknowledge her contribution to the field of disabilities studies.

Working with Māori Children with Special Education Needs: He Mahi Whakahirahira is a book that is long overdue. I know adults who are now in their 60s whose special or not-so-special educational experiences were devoid of any connection to Māori cultural values and experiences. Some were removed from their families to get specialist help, while others attended their local schools. The disconnection between their cultural and schooling lives has had a huge impact on their adult lives. Culture exists wherever people live, so the absence of Māori culture from programmes and practices means a substitution by default of other cultural values, meanings, symbols, and practices. Not only are these 'other' practices and values an assimilation of culture, but they are often an assimilation by a 'special educational needs' culture that, in my view, while well intended can only ever be partial and inadequate as a way to live an adult life in their cultural community.

This book addresses a significant gap in knowledge about how Māori cultural perspectives and strategies can be incorporated into professional practice. It is timely because as the authors argue it is urgent. It is urgent because the needs and rights of many Māori children are being neglected, and because the barriers these children and their families face are unacceptable and unjust. Failure to address their needs in schooling exacerbates the challenges that they, their families, and society will face later.

The book brings together research and insights from Māori experts in the field held together by the significant research of Jill Bevan-Brown who is an undoubted leader in this arena. More importantly, the book offers different strategies, perspectives, and models for practising culturally responsive pedagogies. The chapters bring together a body of knowledge about Māori education more broadly, not just as it applies to special needs education. It should be read by all educators interested in supporting students with special needs and interested in the needs of Māori learners.

Linda Tuhiwai Smith

Acknowledgements

The authors wish to thank Annie Siope and Donna Fengewisch for their support with the formatting of this book, the transcribing, and the checking of references. We also wish to thank Hinepukohurangi Day for her technical support and work in researching the glossary of Māori terms and abbreviations. We appreciate that our role as writers was more easily achieved with your skills, enthusiasm and willingness to support us in any way you were able.

Finally, we wish to acknowledge the contributions of the very many children, young people, whānau members and professionals who worked with us and participated in our research activities over the years, and from whom we learned so much. The frank and open sharing of your experiences, the frustration, the humour and the joy—without your contributions this book would not have been possible.

He mihi maioha ki a koutou.

Dedications

This book is dedicated both to all the participants of the research reported in this book, and to the authors' whānau members, who have provided the encouragement and support that has enabled them to complete their various research projects.

Chapter 2 is dedicated to the memory of Roslyn Ayrton (Roseann), Ngāi Tuhoe, who died in December 2013. Roseann worked tirelessly for many years as a kaitakawaenga within the Ministry of Education, Special Education. She was passionate about enhancing the social, cultural and educational outcomes for tamariki and rangatahi Māori who were referred for special education support. Roseann always put the whānau at the centre of her work, and had a unique way of bringing people together for a shared purpose. She always worked from a position of strength, opportunity and potential. A woman of dignity, grace and humility, Roseann will be remembered for the positive difference she made for so many people. Ahakoa i ngaro ai, ka tū tonu ngā hua o tou mahi.

Chapter 3 and **Chapter 10** are dedicated to Rangiwhakaehu Walker (Ngāti Ranginui, Ngāi Te Rangi) and Mate Reweti (Ngāti Porou), who, over a period of 20 years, provided researchers from Poutama Pounamu with the cultural leadership and expertise to work confidently and competently within many different Māori and school communities. Without the guidance and advice of these wahine toa, the research in these chapters would not have been undertaken, nor would the messages have been so clearly received and understood.

Tauwhare ana mai te pūkohu ki te take o Mauao.
Hoki atu ra korua ki te kapunipunitanga o ngā wairua,
ki te mūrau o te tini,
ki te wenerau o te manu.
E kore e wareware.

The mist hangs over the roots of Mauao.
Return to the resting place of the spirits,
to the resting place of those who have gone before.
This is a better place.

You will not be forgotten.

Chapter 4 is dedicated to our atua with disabilities, who guide us and remind us of our humanity and our own identity that we can be proud of. I (Huhana Hickey) also dedicate this chapter to my tīpuna, who, in their own journeys, have moulded me to be who I am; and also to those with disabilities who have worked hard for the disability community to bring about change and have passed on, in particular Agnes Snedden and Rosa, both gone before their time, and yet both began a journey of change as yet still only in its infancy. All of these influences have had an important impact on bringing the identity of Māori with disabilities to the fore. While we have a long journey ahead, the path has been laid by all of these past influences.

Chapter 5 is dedicated to the late Patrick Wikiriwhi Thompson (Ngāti Paoa, Ngāti Whanaunga, Ngāti Turi), whose tireless advocacy for deaf people, whānau hauā (Māori disabled people) Ngāti Turi (Māori deaf people and their whānau) was recognised when he was awarded the Queen's Service Medal (QSM) in 2013. Patrick's wisdom about deaf people, their families and whānau was vast. Reflecting on his own life experiences and the narratives of others, Patrick was able to synthesise these multiple narratives to develop a sophisticated lens through which he would educate, question, explain, theorise, empathise and challenge. His presence will be missed.

Chapter 6 is dedicated to Taingunguru Whangapirita Walker, who died in 2013. As reported in this chapter, Tai was involved in the research on which it is based. Despite being ill at the time the chapter was written, she willingly contributed her support and feedback. She was an amazingly strong, uncompromising Ngāti Porou woman who was outspoken and unswerving in her advocacy for the causes she supported and determined to overcome any barriers she encountered. A loyal friend, she was a dedicated scholar and an inspiration to many people with whom she was associated: kua ngaro ki te pō, e kore e mimiti te aroha.

Chapter 7 is dedicated to my (Huhana Hickey's) birth mother, Pamela McVicker, who I barely knew, yet, she had a big impact on my life as I am sure all mums do. I wish she had the chance to know me more, but she passed at the age of 63 and did not have the opportunity to know me more than the brief encounters we managed to have. I also dedicate this chapter to my two sons, each special in their own ways and each giving me such beautiful moments to treasure in life. One of these taonga is my grandson, Zavier: a special dedication is for him with the hope he grows into a fine young man, just as his father and uncle have done. Disability is not a limitation. It did not stop me being a mother and a grandmother, nor did it stop me following a path for change, and I hope in reading my story others will have that same determination.

Chapter 8 is dedicated to Fay and Vince Bevan. Vince was one of the participants in the research reported in this chapter. I (Jill Bevan-Brown) could not have wished for better parents. Their humility, work ethic, humour, aroha, generosity, love of learning, sense of fun, strong whānau focus and unconditional support of their children provided an indelible model that continues to influence and inspire their descendants. Aroha mai, aroha atu.

Chapter 9 is dedicated to Joanna Curson, who was instrumental in bringing about the research reported in this chapter. Joanna was Aotearoa / New Zealand's champion for autism spectrum disorder (ASD) and drove many of the major initiatives that have contributed to improvements for people with ASD and their whānau. In particular, we principally have her to thank for the *New Zealand Autism Spectrum Disorder Guideline* (2008), which is having a major influence in this country and has been heralded internationally as a ground-breaking publication. It would be difficult to find a more hard working, friendly and caring person. Her drive and dedication to the ASD cause, her sparkle and her aroha are sadly missed.

Chapter 11 is dedicated to my (Jill Bevan-Brown's) children: Meriana, Nathan, Taramea and Mahaki. Meriana and Nathan assisted in transcribing the interview tapes for the research reported in this chapter. My children's gifts and talents lay in the joy, pride, and love they have given to their parents over the years and the mokopuna they have produced: Raukura, Kotuku, Rawhiti, Harper, Awatea and Te Hiringa, who are an unending source of delight to their Nana and Koro. Kia whakapapa pounamu te moana, kia teretere te kārohirohi e.

Author profiles

Jill Bevan-Brown (PhD), Ngāti Raukawa, Ngāti Wehiwehi, Ngāi Te Rangi and Ngāti Awa ki Waikanae. Jill is the mother of four children and nana of six mokopuna. She lives with her husband, Rawhiti, in Palmerston North, where she teaches at the Institute of Education at Massey University. She is an associate professor, who has taught overseas and in Aotearoa / New Zealand for over 40 years. Jill has a particular interest in culturally effective provisions for Māori children with special needs, inclusive education, gifted education, the education of learners with ASD, and parent voice, and she has researched extensively in these areas. Jill is also on a number of national advisory committees.

Mere Berryman (PhD), Ngāi Tūhoe, Ngāti Awa and Ngāti Whare. Mere is the mother of three sons and nanny to six mokopuna. She has advanced along a career pathway that has both challenged and enabled her to focus on finding new ways to improve educational outcomes for Māori students and families in both Māori-medium and English-medium educational settings. As a researcher she has collaborated extensively with other academics, school leaders, classroom practitioners, families, communities and other professionals to bring about educational reform. She has worked with educators in New Zealand and also in parts of Canada and the United States. Mere is currently an associate professor in the Faculty of Education at the University of Waikato in Hamilton, Aotearoa / New Zealand.

Huhana Hickey (PhD), Ngāti-tahinga and Ngai Tai; also Aboriginal, Sami, Scots and Native American. Huhana has a lived experience of disability and has always maintained that it is her role within her whānau that counts, not her disabilities, which has meant she uses a power chair for her mobility. Huhana is currently working as a post-doctoral fellow at AUT University in the Taupua Waiora unit, where she is looking at whānau hauā and what that means in the context of health and wellbeing. Huhana is a mother, a partner and a grandmother, and she spends her spare time writing poetry, short stories and delving into art projects. Huhana has in the past worked as a lawyer, an advocate and a voice for the disability sector, representing locally, nationally and internationally the voice of disability from an indigenous paradigm, which has been her passion for many years. Huhana continues to work with the community to try to evoke positive change, particularly for whānau hauā and those closest to them.

Sonja Herahine Macfarlane (PhD), Ngāi Tahu, Ngāti Waewae. Sonja is an experienced educationalist, whose conviction for improving outcomes for students at risk of educational failure has seen her move from classroom teacher, to resource teacher of learning and behaviour (RTLB), to special education advisor, to national professional practice leader: services to Māori (pouhikiahurea) in the Ministry of Education, Special Education. In 2011 she took up a senior lectureship in the School of Health Sciences at Canterbury University, Christchurch, a position that focuses on Māori health and wellbeing, psychology, counselling and special education. Sonja's teaching and research concentrates on enhancing the social, cultural and educational outcomes for Māori learners by strengthening specialists' professional practice. Her research focuses on culturally responsive, evidence-based practice.

Kirsten Smiler (PhD), Te Aitanga-a-Māhaki, Rongowhakaata, Whakatōhea. Kirsten is a mother to her two energetic boys, Wairongo and Raukura. She lives in Wellington, where she is currently working at Victoria University of Wellington at the Health Services Research Centre on a post-doctoral research fellowship funded by the Health Research Council. Kirsten has an interest in deaf people, their families and whānau, as well as Māori health and disability-related research.

PART I
Principles, Policies, Programmes, Practices and Issues

Chapter 1

Introduction

Jill Bevan-Brown

He kura ngā tāngata

People are precious[1]

The need for this book

This book is long overdue.[2] I identified a need for it many years ago when research-based information about Māori children with special education needs was scarce. Over the years, research on this topic has grown, but articles reporting it are spread over many publications and can be difficult to locate. The intention of this book, therefore, is to bring some of this research together for ease of access and to facilitate its use. All the authors are passionate about helping Māori children with special educational needs and their whānau. We hope this book will contribute to the provision of culturally responsive, effective education that will provide even greater benefits to all concerned.

1   Mead and Grove (2003) explain that this pepeha "attests to the regard of the Māori both for the intrinsic value of a human being and for the contribution of each person to the well-being of the group" (p. 91). The word *kura* means both education and treasure/precious. In this pepeha the meaning is the latter, but the pun on the word is appropriate given the nature of this book.

2   This chapter draws substantially on the author's publications listed in the references section.

Overview

The chapters in this book report on research the authors have conducted in their respective areas. They include suggestions for practically applying lessons from their research findings and personal experiences and conclude with study questions aimed at getting readers to reflect on what they have read.

The book is divided into two parts. Part I covers principles, policies, programmes, practices and issues, and it contains the following chapters.

Chapter 1, the introduction by Jill Bevan-Brown, presents a Māori perspective of special education needs; highlights the influential role culture plays in the perception and management of these needs; discusses terminology, differing discourses, barriers, helpful programmes and strategies; and emphasises the importance of learning from the past and listening to Māori children with special education needs, their parents and wider whānau.

Chapter 2, by Sonja Macfarlane, explores the key components of culturally responsive, evidence-based, special education practice from the perspectives of Māori. From the voices of Māori researchers, special education practitioners and whānau, six key imperatives emerge that can inform practice approaches and policy development.

Chapter 3, by Mere Berryman, describes how staff and whānau in four kura rumaki consistently identified the need for holistic and inclusive responses to educating all tamariki, especially those with identified special education needs. It presents a model that emerged from this research and considers some of the implications for others.

Chapter 4, by Huhana Hickey, explores a paradigm for Māori disability identity and introduces and unpacks the term *whānau hauā*. It examines a number of Māori and non-Māori wellbeing/disability models, discussing their sustainability as models of wellbeing for whānau hauā. Finally, the tātau tātau framework, which recognises te ao Māori as the foundation for whānau hauā identity, is introduced and explained.

Part II discusses disability categories.[3] It contains the following chapters.

---

3 These categories are used for the sake of convenience. It is acknowledged that a child's special education needs are unique, and that while categorial information is useful for alerting professionals to factors that should be considered, it must not be used to stereotype individuals.

Chapter 5, by Kirsten Smiler, reports on a doctoral study which examines the early intervention experiences of the whānau of deaf children, discusses how these experiences contribute to whānau constructions of the meaning of deafness, and explores whether the current system design and delivery of early intervention supports need to be adapted to be more effective for Māori.

Chapter 6, by Jill Bevan-Brown and Tai Walker, discusses the prevalence of blindness and vision impairment among Māori today and in pre-European times. It then reports on a small study of kāpō Māori. General, educational and cultural barriers are outlined, as are suggestions for overcoming them. Findings in common with three other studies are discussed and their implications presented.

Chapter 7, by Huhana Hickey and Jill Bevan-Brown, consists of an interview with Huhana Hickey (affectionately known as 'Dr Hu'). In it she discusses her physical disability, the barriers she has faced both in childhood and as an adult, what she has found helpful and unhelpful, her future dreams, and her advice to professionals who work with Māori children who have physical disabilities.

Chapter 8, by Jill Bevan-Brown, reports on the findings of a small study that investigated pre-European and contemporary Māori concepts of intellectual disability and opinions about the care and education of intellectually disabled Māori children. Subsequent research in the health and education sectors is considered, and the implications of concurring findings for people who work with intellectually disabled Māori and their whānau are outlined.

Chapter 9, by Jill Bevan-Brown, briefly introduces autism spectrum disorder (ASD) and then reports on a study in which parents and whānau shared their experiences of raising a Māori child with ASD. Similarities between subsequent research studies are discussed, as are the implications for professionals who work with Māori children with ASD and their whānau.

Chapter 10, by Mere Berryman, discusses research that has sought to capitalise on the strengths and knowledge available within teachers and whānau in order to take joint responsibility for students' learning and behaviour. What emerged is a clear reminder of the strengths to be found in the students themselves.

Chapter 11, by Jill Bevan-Brown, presents a brief discussion of the concept of giftedness, and giftedness in pre-European times. It then reports the results of a study into giftedness from a Māori perspective. Subsequent research, writing, and gifted initiatives are discussed, and the chapter concludes with a section on how professionals can nurture gifted Māori children.

Chapter 12, the conclusion, by Mere Berryman, reflects on what the authors have identified and presented through their chapters, reiterating their main points. It discusses the power and use of metaphor, and the messages inherent in the whakataukī used to preface each chapter.

Working with children with special education needs

Introduction

The title of this book, *Working with Māori Children with Special Education Needs: He Mahi Whakahirahira*, raises three immediate questions:

- Who are Māori children with special education needs?
- Why would working with them be any different to working with other children with special education needs?
- Why is this a highly important job—he mahi whakahirahira?

This chapter answers these three questions and discusses themes and issues associated with them.

However, from the outset an important point must be made. This book does not claim to represent *the* Māori view of special education needs, or of any particular category of need. Māori, like other people, are a diverse group. They differ in lifestyle, beliefs, values, socioeconomic circumstances, religious and tribal affiliation, geographic location, degree of acculturation and Māori identification, knowledge and practice of Māori culture, and in many other ways. As Durie (1995) reminds us, Māori experience diverse realities, and so there can never be a single Māori viewpoint on special education needs, nor on anything for that matter!

Instead, this book presents many snapshots of Māori opinion and experiences for you to consider. Lynch and Hanson (1992/1998) offer pertinent advice in this context:

Each individual and each family is different and culture-specific information cannot be assumed to apply in every situation. Its value is that it raises issues that should be considered, poses questions that may need to be answered and underscores the interventionist's desire to respond sensitively to each family and each family member … Although [families and individuals] are influenced by their ethnic, cultural and language backgrounds, they are not fully defined by them. Therefore differences in these areas should be used to enhance our interactions rather than to stereotype or to serve as the sole determiner of our approach to intervention. (pp. xiii, 359)

Professionals must never make assumptions about the degree to which cultural values and practices apply to the children they work with. My research (Bevan-Brown, 2002) has shown that when professionals make these assumptions they are often completely wrong. Instead, they should consult with the child with special education needs, and with the child's parents and whānau. Maintaining ongoing discussions about cultural and special educational needs, preferences and aspirations will provide accurate and up-to-date information that can guide present and future provision.

Who are Māori children with special education needs?

In my research (Bevan-Brown, 2002; Cullen & Bevan-Brown, 1999) I asked participants this very question. They described a wide variety of special needs, which can be grouped into the following 10 categories.

1. Physical and health needs: children with significantly restricted mobility or physical function due to some type of physical impairment, condition or health-related problem.

2. Sensory needs: children with significantly restricted sensory function, such as those with vision and hearing impairments.

3. Communication needs: children who have difficulty communicating because of delayed language development or some type of disorder or speech impediment.

4. Learning needs: children whose learning is significantly impaired for a variety of reasons; for example, those with intellectual disability associated with Down syndrome or brain damage, as well as those with more school-specific learning problems such as attention deficit hyperactivity disorder (ADHD) or dyslexia.

5. Social and emotional needs: children who have difficulty relating to others: for example, children with autism spectrum disorder; those with long-term depression or unhappiness; abused and neglected children; and those affected by family violence, discord or specific trauma.

6. Behavioural needs: children with extreme disruptive, aggressive, non-compliant or anti-social behaviour.

7. Needs associated with giftedness: these are the result of the lack/absence of the processes, services, expertise and resources needed to challenge and extend gifted children.

8. Needs associated with socioeconomic circumstances, or geographical location, or both: poverty and rural location can create special education needs for many Māori children. The common factor is an absence of resources and services, which has a negative impact on children's progress and development. This can be a primary or secondary influence. An example of a primary influence is where children fail to progress at school because they cannot afford books, calculators, lunches, school trips and other necessities to facilitate and support learning. An example of a secondary influence is children with glue ear whose language development is further delayed because of the time and cost involved in accessing the required support (e.g. getting grommets fitted).

9. Needs associated with the perceptions of, attitudes towards and treatment of people with disability: special education needs arising from a child's disability, condition or circumstances can be exacerbated by people's reactions to them. For example, low expectations and demands can result in fewer learning opportunities, which in turn limit a child's developmental progress and compound the child's special education need.

10. Needs associated with being Māori: these stem from three principal causes.

(a) Societal and individual practices and attitudes that disadvantage Māori learners

At the societal level, Māori learners are disadvantaged by assimilative policies and practices, and by the limited acknowledgement their cultural capital receives within a Pākehā-dominated education system (Bishop & Glynn, 1999). At an individual level, a wide range of negative, stereotypical attitudes and behaviours disadvantage Māori children.

(b) Certain cultural traits and behaviours that put Māori at a disadvantage
Participants gave examples of the unwillingness of many Māori to "speak up", a tendency to "go with the flow" and be whakamā in unfamiliar or uncomfortable situations; and a lack of confidence or ability to "hassle" with Pākehā institutions to receive services. While it can be debated whether these traits and behaviours are in fact cultural in nature, they were certainly evident in participants' experiences; for example, children who were "too whakamā" to ask for clarification when lessons were not understood.

(c) Needs related to te reo Māori
Some participants viewed the inability of Māori to speak their own language as being a special need. Others believed that special education needs could be exacerbated by involvement in total immersion education. Examples are children with special education needs who are unable to receive assistance because of the shortage of special education professionals with the prerequisite cultural and te reo Māori expertise, and children without a "special education label" who struggle to learn te reo Māori but are not eligible for assistance because problems associated with learning a second language do not meet special education funding criteria.

Interestingly, the broad, inclusive concept of special needs described by the research participants is in accord with the Whare Tapa Whā concept of Māori wellbeing outlined by Durie (1985), and with Kingi and Bray's (2000) Māori concepts of disability. The latter argue that colonisation has resulted in Māori being disabled by a disconnection from their land, their culture and their language, a position supported by Huirangi Waikerepuru (cited in Kingi, 1995).

The 10 categories of special education need mentioned above are discussed in this book to a greater or lesser degree.

Why is working with Māori children with special education needs any different to working with other children with special education needs?

Research conducted by Massey University (1999, 2002) showed that 11 percent of the 369 educators interviewed in the first phase of the SE2000 evaluation[4] believed that the needs of Māori and Pākehā students with special education needs are identical. Indicative comments were:

> Māori don't need to be encouraged to be different. They need to be treated as New Zealanders. After all we are all one race.

> I don't treat him differently. He's just another child. You have to look at a child's personality and interests, not their race.

> Each child has an IEP [individual education plan] and so each child's needs are individually met. We feel that culture is irrelevant. (Bevan-Brown, 2003, p. 21)

These opinions are not supported by research. There is substantial evidence, from Aotearoa / New Zealand and overseas, showing that culture plays a major role in a child's education. Gay (1997) goes as far as saying, "Culture is a crucial, if not the ultimate, mediating factor in academic achievement" (p. 223).

The influence of culture

As can be seen from the previous 10 categories, 'special education needs' is a concept that is culturally defined. What is perceived as a special education need for one group may not be considered so for another. Similarly, the degree of disability needed to warrant recognition of a special education need can vary from group to group, as can attitudes towards disability, causal attributions, and preferred assessment and 'treatment' methods.

Culture is a broad and complex concept. Many thousands of books have been written about the differing definitions and permutations of culture, ranging from culture as the arts, to culture as "ways of ordering life which collectively distinguish humankind from other species" (Metge, 1990, p. 6). *Culture*, in the sense that underpins this book, is

---

4   Massey University was commissioned and funded by the Ministry of Education to evaluate and monitor the SE2000 policy over 3 years from 1999 to 2001 inclusive. The research was conducted in three phases—Phase 1 in 1999, Phase 2 in 2000 and Phase 3 in 2001.

the system of symbols, meanings, behaviours and values by which a particular group of people share and make sense of their world (Metge, 1990). The particular group in this instance is, obviously, Māori, but it should be noted that every person belongs to multiple cultural groups, not only the culture associated with their ethnicity. Other cultural groups include those associated with people's gender, age, religion, social class, exceptionality, sexuality and nationality at one level, and their education, workplace, interests and so forth at another level. The membership and influence of these various cultural groups can wax and wane depending on a person's circumstances and life journey.

Culture provides a blueprint for how people think, feel and behave. A myriad of culturally related factors can influence the perception and management of special education needs. These include:

- world view, and the beliefs, values, attitudes and practices that emanate from it
- cultural norms, expectations and lifestyle
- beliefs about the cause and nature of disability
- child-rearing practices
- family structure and interpersonal relationships, communication and interaction styles
- differential gender roles
- spiritual beliefs
- historical and geographical origins
- economic and political circumstances
- majority or minority status
- language
- degree of acculturation.

To work effectively with Māori children with special education needs and their whānau, professionals must have an understanding of Māori perspectives and practices relating to the factors listed above and be able to incorporate this cultural knowledge into their daily practice. Just as importantly, they must also have an understanding of their *own* cultures, how these influence their beliefs and practices, and how these beliefs and practices affect the people they interact with. Speaking specifically of ethnic culture, Metge (1990) explains that cultural competence is acquired unconsciously, and that "people live in their culture as a fish lives in water, taking it for granted as natural and right" (p. 10). She adds that this is particularly applicable to Pākehā, who do not have their ways thrown into relief in their encounters with others as minority groups do. Being in the majority, Pākehā perceive the water they swim in as "the norm. (It is always other people who have an accent)" (p. 15).

With increased understanding of their own culture, professionals are in a better position to recognise that many so-called truths, facts and values are not 'right' or 'universally held' but are expressions of their own cultural beliefs:

> All cultures have built-in biases, and there are no right or wrong cultural beliefs: however, there are differences that must be acknowledged. Cultural self-awareness is the bridge to learning about other cultures. It is not possible to be truly sensitive to someone else's culture until you are sensitive to your own culture and the impact that cultural customs, values, beliefs, and behaviours have on practice. (Lynch & Hanson, 1998, p. 3)

In Aotearoa / New Zealand past educational policies and legislation sought to assimilate Māori into Pākehā culture as quickly as possible by discouraging, ignoring or outlawing their cultural practices and language. This assimilative approach was based on notions of cultural superiority and inferiority, with compensatory programmes being introduced to overcome learners' 'cultural disadvantages'. Fortunately, the cultural deficit mentality and assimilative approaches have been thoroughly discredited by research that has shown that compensatory programmes were ineffective (e.g. Currie, 1962; Hunn, 1961), and that having a strong cultural base actually advantages learners from ethnic minority cultures (Altschul, Oyserman, & Bybee, 2006; Chavous et al., 2003; Wong, Eccles, & Sameroff, 2003).

Over the years there has been increasing acknowledgement of the importance of culturally responsive provisions for Māori children with special education needs, and many worthwhile initiatives have been introduced. However, the fact remains that the Aotearoa / New Zealand education system is still firmly based on middle-class Pākehā values and the majority of professionals involved in the system come from a middle-class, Pākehā background. Consequently, professionals are challenged to discover and change ways that Pākehā cultural values, attitudes, beliefs and assumptions inherent in the education system are disadvantaging Māori students, both with and without special education needs. This will necessitate them looking critically at such factors as:

- curriculum content
- teaching and learning styles
- methods of assessment and evaluation
- school/ early childhood education facility (ECEF) climate and organisation
- teacher expectations inherent in teaching practices and goals set
- methods of interaction between the school/ECEF and community, including reporting procedures
- resources used
- external appearance of the school/ECEF environment
- values that permeate the educational environment
- oral and body language used
- methods of, and reasons for, discipline and reinforcement
- types of teacher–student and student–student relationships that are encouraged and discouraged.

There is no such thing as a culturally free or culturally neutral teaching activity!

Why is working with Māori children with special education needs a highly important job (he mahi whakahirahira)?

Upholding rights

Working with *all* children with special education needs is a highly important job. These children have the same rights to an inclusive, effective education as their peers. These rights are enshrined in a plethora of legislation and documentation, including the Human Rights Act 1993, Article 23 of the United Nations Convention on the Rights of the Child, *The New Zealand Disability Strategy* (Ministry of Health, 2001), the *Special Education Policy Guidelines* (Ministry of Education,

1999), the *Specialist Service Standards* (Ministry of Education, 2013a), and various goals and principles in the *National Education Guidelines* and the *New Zealand Curriculum Framework.*[5] Particularly relevant to Māori children with special education needs is principle 6 of the *Special Education Policy Guidelines*, which states that children's

> language and culture comprise a vital context for learning and development and must be taken into consideration in planning and programmes. This principle will be visible in practice when: 1. Special education is responsive to the needs and preferences of the tangata whenua. (Ministry of Education, 1999)

Similarly, the culture section of the *Specialist Service Standards* set for Ministry of Education-funded special education specialists states:

> We recognise and value the role of culture in the lives of our children and young people, their families and whānau through: recognition of Māori as tangata whenua ... culturally appropriate, collaborative ways of working ... interventions that are culturally and contextually evidence-based for the New Zealand context. (Ministry of Education, 2013a, p. 5)

Professionals have the important task of ensuring these rights, standards and principles are not merely words on paper but are a living reality.

Treaty of Waitangi

For Māori children with special education needs, these rights are further supported by the Treaty of Waitangi. Regardless of whether a principles or articles approach is taken to interpreting the Treaty, it contains obligations relevant to Māori children with special education needs and their whānau. For example, "equal rights and privileges" means that children in kura kaupapa Māori are entitled to the same special education services as children with special education needs in the mainstream. The shortage of professionals conversant in te reo is not an acceptable excuse for them missing out. Proactive measures must be taken to enable the provision of these services. Similarly, "partnership" does not mean seeking approval from Māori parents of

---

5   Principles 6 and 7 of the *New Zealand Curriculum Framework* (Ministry of Education, 1993); Goals 2, 7, 9 and 10 of the National Education Guidelines; and Section 8 of the Education Act 1989.

children with sensory impairments after placement and programme decisions have already been made. To honour Treaty obligations in special education, professionals have a responsibility to consult with Māori from the outset; involve them in meaningful decisions relating to the planning and development of programmes and services; enable participation; empower Māori to provide their own services; and, where there are disparities that have a negative impact on Māori children's health and education, introduce measures to rectify these circumstances.[6]

Overcoming barriers: A matter of urgency

The urgency of the mahi whakahirahira is highlighted by statistics and research showing that, despite being over-represented in special education, Māori children with special education needs are often being neglected, overlooked, inadequately provided for, and even excluded. An examination of research evaluating SE2000 policy (Massey University, 2002) revealed over 60 different barriers to culturally responsive educational provisions. Prominent among these were a lack of culturally appropriate services, programmes, assessment measures and resources, and detrimental individual and societal beliefs, attitudes and practices (Bevan-Brown, 2006a).

In the years since the SE2000 evaluation was conducted, a range of promising initiatives have been introduced. These include national initiatives targeting the education of Māori children in general, and particular special education programmes focusing on Māori children with special education needs. While space precludes discussing all these initiatives, of particular significance are many of the programmes and resources introduced under the auspices of *Ka Hikitia: Managing for Success—Māori Education Strategy 2008–2012* (Ministry of Education, 2008a) and the updated *Māori Education Strategy: Ka Hikitia: Accelerating Success, 2013–2017* (Ministry of Education, 2013b). These include:

---

6   The Treaty of Waitangi principles are used as the basis for a cultural self-review (CSR) I developed as part of my PhD. The CSR provides a user-friendly structure, process and products that can be used by educators at all levels to explore how well they provide for Māori learners in general, and those with special education needs in particular. It focuses on celebrating and building on strengths and identifying and working on weaknesses (see Bevan-Brown, 2003). A shortened version of the CSR aimed at assessing programmes and services is accessible at http://www.massey.ac.nz/massey/fms/Colleges/Institute%20of%20Education/Documents/ 2013/Volume%2012_Issue%202_2011.pdf

- Te Kotahitanga, which is experiencing great success in providing professional development for secondary school leaders and teachers, moving them from deficit theorising towards prioritising the need to build relationships of trust and respect with Māori students in order to engage them in learning (Bishop, Berryman, & Wearmouth, 2014)

- *Tataiako: Cultural Competencies for Teachers of Māori Learners* (Ministry of Education, 2011)

- the *Tātai Pou Competency Matrix*, a rubric that contributes to the Measureable Gains Framework (see http://www.minedu.govt.nz/theMinistry/PolicyandStrategy/KaHikitia/MeasuringandReportingProgress.aspx)

- *Te Hikoitanga* (Ministry of Education, 2008b), a framework to assist special education practitioners and service teams to understand their own roles in delivering culturally responsive services.

Together, these initiatives are increasing people's understanding of the role they play in providing more culturally responsive services. They are also helping to equip them to develop and provide Māori-relevant programmes, services, assessment measures and resources.

Associated themes and issues

Terminology and differing discourses.

This book refers to *children with special education needs*. This term was chosen because it is the one preferred by the Ministry of Education and is used regularly in schools and early childhood education providers, although in these contexts it is frequently abbreviated to 'special needs'. While these two terms are often used interchangeably in practice, strictly speaking they represent different ideological viewpoints. 'Special education needs' places emphasis on the requirements needed to cater for the child, while 'special needs' places the problem within the child.[7]

The Ministry of Education also refers to 'children and young people with special education needs', which is appropriate given that their services extend to young people aged 21 who are still at school. The content of this book also applies to young people still at school, and in

---

7   A further interpretation of "special" is "unique" This interpretation is preferred by the authors.

fact many of the principles, strategies and issues discussed apply equally to adults. However, for ease of expression, we have used *children* as a generic term to encompass all applicable individuals.

A number of participants in my research (Bevan-Brown, 2002; Cullen & Bevan-Brown, 1999) did not like the term *special needs* because it could be interpreted as meaning some children are more 'special' than others, or that some children's needs are more important than other children's needs. As all children are special and all have important needs, it was felt a different term was preferable. One participant questioned the whole concept of 'special education', saying that it was not based on Māori values. She pointed out that as the needs of all children are special, there should not be any separate system of funding for 'special' education:

> If in Māori, he mana ko te tamaiti (each child has mana), then no matter what, we would look at each child and we would gear our learning and programme, we would design a learning environment for each child. I think we would be at fault to follow, to continue to follow, the Pākehā way of dealing with all kids, of slicing it all up and having an add-on approach to resourcing in a way that, the context from which this has come, i.e. more resources for kids with disabilities because they are special. Okay so coming back to me, a Māori perspective, I would rather it be viewed as, 'What is the Māori perspective on catering for children's learning needs?' and build our education around that and I don't believe it happens in the current system. I believe we have to be given the resources with Māori to devise our own systems ... The way to go about addressing conditions is to go back to the drawing board and not take the Pākehā model that you have asked us to consider. If I were to turn it around I would therefore look at how a whānau embraces children who are regarded by the system as disabled, but I would also look at each child ... in whatever their needs are in ... For those of us in kōhanga and kura we ought to be aware of and watching for and receiving, warming, nurturing and down the track being resourceful so that we wipe away any notion of negativity because the word 'disability' and the word 'behavioural difficulty' really starts us out with a negative focus. Whereas the Māori whānau, with the so-called disabled child, looks at the child lovingly and raises it. This

is idyllic of course, but in terms of our values, it guides us in nurturing and awhi. If they are still going to be fed the same amount of kai at the whare kai then it will be up to them to choose how much they partake of. They will still be part of the wānanga and if they fall asleep or if they aren't able to sit in class they're not going to be pushed out of the whare tupuna. (Bevan-Brown, 2002, p. 309)

This opinion aligns with Tau's (1999) objection to "massaging" one culture's perceptions into another culture's framework. It would also find favour with many inclusionists, who argue that special education and inclusive education cannot co-exist because they are from incompatible ideological bases: special education is underpinned by a pedagogical discourse of deviance, viewing children with disabilities and disorders as deviating from the norm and requiring additional teaching, equipment and other resources to accommodate their difference. Inclusive education, on the other hand, has the discourse of inclusion at its foundation. *All* children are valued members of the ECEF/school and wider community, and it is the responsibility of the regular system to address their diverse needs (Skidmore, 2002; UNESCO, 2005). The authors of this book all favour this inclusive education discourse, and our support for inclusion is found throughout the various chapters. It may appear contradictory, therefore, that this book is about "working with children with special education needs." In an ideal world Māori children who require additional assistance would not be singled out and their educational needs categorised as "special." Instead, they would be provided for in an inclusive system where all children are equally valued and equitably provided for as a matter of course. Unfortunately, we do not live in an ideal world. Consequently, we have grounded this book in the context of our present reality, but are hopeful that it will contribute to building a truly inclusive education system in Aotearoa New Zealand.

Another frequently used term warranting definition is *culturally responsive*. Simply put, being culturally responsive involves valuing, affirming and developing the child's culture. In a culturally responsive environment the child's self-esteem is enhanced: the child feels psychologically secure and motivated to learn because the educational and home environments are culturally compatible. Four essential ingredients of a culturally responsive environment are:

- teachers who value and support cultural diversity in general, and Māori culture in particular
- programmes and services that incorporate cultural content, including cultural knowledge, skills, practices, customs and traditions
- programmes and services that incorporate cultural values, beliefs, attitudes, behaviours and dispositions
- teaching and assessment that utilise culturally preferred ways of learning.

Learning from the past

"Kia anga whakamua me hoki whakamuri" (Look to the past to shape the future.) This whakataukī embodies the philosophy underpinning this book. For Māori, a true understanding of the present can only be gained through consideration of the past (Ihimaera, 1993; Reid, 1986). While acknowledging the vastly differing lifestyles and social, political and economic circumstances of pre-European times and today, there are many valuable lessons from the past that can guide our thinking and practice into the future and ensure that it is grounded in Māori values and knowledge.

Paul Gibson, the Disability Rights Commissioner (2011–), refers to this in his *Matariki* newsletter. He notes that there are "many mana enhancing narratives of disability in te ao Māori … and … almost forgotten disability wisdom" that needs to be recovered and applied "to the issues of today for the benefit and inspiration of the whānau hauā". He goes on to ask,

> Would Māui be able to express his rebelliousness and defiance through creativity, and achieve all he did, or would he be representative of the education system's 'tail of underachievement' and be given a label of ADHD and a dose of Ritalin? Would someone hearing the voices of ancestors be listened to, supported? Or would we first discourage, constrain, and medicate? Would someone walking in the footsteps of Hape still be left out of the waka? Would his use of the modern day equivalent of the supporting stingray, a support dog … be accepted on marae? (Gibson, 2012)

Pertinent questions indeed! People with disabilities existed in pre-European Māori society, but it is possible that the concept of disability did not. The dominant Western disability discourse is based on acceptance of biological and psychological constructs of wellness, normality and deviance. If these constructs did not exist in pre-European times, or if the practice of making comparisons to a group norm did not exist (as Green, cited in Smith, 1998, reports for certain Native American cultures), then medical model concepts of handicap, disability and special needs would have little if any meaning. If a concept of disability did exist, it would have been very different to today's Western concepts.

Irrespective of this, as Gibson notes, traditional practices and the beliefs and values on which they are based can be examined for relevance and potential guidance in the 21st century. This is further supported by Hemara (2000), who, after an extensive investigation of traditional and contemporary Māori pedagogies, concluded:

> The way Māori educated themselves and their young appears to be applicable today. Many of the hallmarks of Māori education prove that traditional values and operating standards can be translated into contemporary contexts. (p. 81)

So, how were children with 'special education needs' treated in pre-European times? Opinions vary, but the weight of historical evidence indicates that they were accepted and valued as an integral part of the community (Bevan-Brown, 1989). This being the case, they would have received the same care and education as their siblings. This involved parents, whānau and kaumātua teaching them practical survival skills and tribal knowledge using methods that focused on learning through observation, listening, imitation and repetition (Metge, 1984). They were taught the skills needed to play a useful role in society and given tasks to perform that befitted their particular capabilities.

While learning informally in an inclusive environment alongside their peers was the norm, some children who demonstrated particular aptitude and interest were selected to receive specialist knowledge in a whare wānanga or in a mentor-like relationship with a tohunga or kaumātua. Kaumātua were also reported as having additional responsibility for particular children with physical and intellectual disabilities. Treatments of physical disability used karakia and environmental healing resources (especially water) and were holistic in nature, focusing on the whole child, including the child's hinengaro and wairua (Kana

& Harawira, 1995). The relevance of these practices for educating Māori children with special education needs today warrants careful consideration.

The voices of parents and whānau

A dominant theme throughout this book is the importance of listening to and involving Māori parents and whānau. As mentioned earlier, they should be consulted from the outset and on an ongoing basis. In my experience, professionals often report wanting to involve Māori parents and whānau, but getting no response to their invitations and requests. Unfortunately, this is sometimes interpreted as a lack of caring about their children's education, and consequently efforts to involve parents and whānau are abandoned. It is extremely rare, if ever, the case that parents and whānau simply "don't care". The reasons for no or limited involvement in special education are multiple, complex and inter-related. The following research-based list of personal, cultural and contextual reasons provides possibilities professionals should consider.

Personal reasons reported by parents include:

- not feeling valued and respected by professionals
- past experiences of being blamed for their child's difficulties and their requests for information being ignored
- feeling uncomfortable in the school environment due to their own negative schooling experiences
- mistrust of professionals
- feeling embarrassed about their lack of knowledge about rights, entitlements, special education policies, procedures and services
- lack of confidence, or feeling whakamā when interacting with professionals
- feeling disheartened by the ever-present focus on their child's bad behaviour, weaknesses and label
- professionals' negative attitudes, treatment and low expectations of their children
- feeling disenfranchised by ineffective home–school communication methods and not knowing how they can help.

This last reason is further explained by a Māori parent who was also a teacher aide. Her job included visiting parents to explain their child's special education programme:

> When the child goes home you are expecting that child to communicate with the family if they want help. Sometimes it's not that parents don't want to help, it's that they don't know they can help or how they can help ... I didn't learn [what to do] until I was a teacher aide. (Bevan-Brown, 2002, p. 291)

Cultural reasons reported by parents include:

- being reluctant to engage with professionals because of majority-culture ethnocentrism
- differing cultural concepts and practices relating to disability, leading to cultural conflict, misinterpretation and mislabelling
- conflicting cultural values that underpin special education programmes and interventions
- differing cultural communication styles and expectations about involvement in their child's education
- negative cultural stereotyping and deficit thinking
- insensitivity to cultural beliefs and traditions
- discriminatory practices and problematising being Māori
- professionals having limited or no knowledge of Māori culture and not valuing or ignoring its importance.

Contextual reasons for limited involvement include:

- lack of time, transportation or child-care support
- unfriendly or intimidating meeting and service venues
- heavy work commitments
- fatigue
- conflicting family responsibilities
- the child acting negatively when the parent comes to the school/ ECEF
- lack of resources
- poor health
- inconvenient, inflexible scheduling of services and meetings.

While the personal and contextual reasons listed above can apply to any parent regardless of ethnicity, many of these barriers are experienced to a greater degree by Māori because of their geographical location and/or socioeconomic factors.

A wide range of strategies are being used by professionals to overcome these barriers. For example, individual education plan (IEP) meeting attendance is being facilitated by:

- providing parents with user-friendly preparatory notes
- inviting them to bring extended family, siblings or community members for support
- holding meetings in culturally appropriate, family-friendly venues, or inviting parents to choose meeting venues and times
- making meetings more informal by including time for small talk
- including opening and closing karakia and kai
- providing transportation and child-care facilities
- having flexible time schedules
- including both home and ECEF/school priorities and suggestions in goal setting and intervention plans
- recording meetings for absent members for later consideration.

Similarly, a variety of ECEF/school-wide strategies are being used in efforts to empower parents and whānau and build positive home–ECEF/school relationships. These include:

- having an ECEF/school kaumātua and whānau committee
- whanau-driven bilingual and bicultural policies
- regular ECEF/school cultural self-reviews
- pōwhiri and poroporoaki for welcoming and farewelling children and staff
- celebrating important cultural events, such as Matariki
- bilingual signage
- kapa haka performances
- making home visits

- attending Māori community events.[8]

Involving parents and whānau should not be about 'fulfilling require-ments' or an exercise in how they can be 'used'. Rather it should be about genuine power-sharing and partnership. If the ECEF/school is perceived as being a culturally responsive and welcoming place and professionals as caring individuals who want the best for their children, then parents and whānau will feel more motivated and empowered to become involved in their child's education. However, an important caveat must be added: parents and whānau should never feel coerced into participation or made to feel guilty if they opt out. Raising a child with special education needs can be incredibly demanding. A request to attend another meeting or be involved in another activity might be the straw that breaks the camel's back. Sensitivity, understanding and support from professionals are crucial at times like this.

Children's voice

A further message in this book is the importance of listening to, and heeding the thoughts, opinions, suggestions, requests and aspirations of children with special education needs and disabled adults, both Māori and non-Māori. Children, in particular, are in grave danger of being overlooked, especially if their special education need includes commu-nication difficulties. While acknowledging that communication will often be challenging and time consuming, in this day of advanced aug-mentative communication devices, computer-assisted communication, high-tech visual schedules and so forth, gaining children's input can no longer be relegated to the too-hard basket.

In an examination of two projects, Te Kotahitanga (Bishop, Berryman, Cavanagh, & Teddy, 2007) and AIMHI (Hill & Hawk, 2000), as part of which hundreds of Māori and Pasifika students were interviewed,[9] I identified four principal messages. Firstly, students

---

8   These are just a few suggestions, and many more can be found in the literature and education web sites. A good starting point is http://www.educationalleaders.govt.nz/Partnerships-and-net-works/Building-community-relationships/Involving-parents-families-and-whānau, and http://www.educate.ece.govt.nz/learning/curriculumAndLearning/Assessmentforlearning/KeiTuaotePae/Book5/DevelopingLearningCommunities.aspx.

9   It is acknowledged that these two studies consulted mainly students without special education needs, but I would argue that the messages would be the same if the samples consisted entirely of Māori students with special education needs. Certainly, the messages have been the same for the relatively small number of these children I have interviewed in my various research projects. Unfor-tunately, no research presently exists where large numbers of Māori children with special education needs have been interviewed.

emphasised the importance of caring teachers who encouraged and had high expectations of them. Secondly, they wanted their culture valued and affirmed. Thirdly, they wanted: well-organised teachers who make learning understandable, interesting and fun; to be actively involved in their own learning; and a classroom environment where it is okay to make mistakes. Finally, students wanted the support of their parents, family and friends (Bevan-Brown, 2006b).

Chapter 4 discusses the issue of self-advocacy for disabled Māori adults in some depth. Suffice to add here a message delivered by Tariana Turia (2010) at the National Māori Disability Network's annual conference:

> We need to be cautious that we do not fall into thinking that it will be us that will change the world. We may well hope to have a generous, motivating, thoughtful and helpful presence alongside people, however, their world shouldn't have us at its centre, nor should it crumble without us. In the long run, our success can only ever be measured by the security, intimacy and embrace that the people we serve find amongst their own family and friends and in their own lives in our community. (n.p.)

Conclusion

In conclusion,[10] it must be emphasised that while the importance of a culturally responsive educational environment and consultation with parents and whānau are highlighted throughout this book, these factors alone are not enough to ensure the success of Māori children with special education needs. As the students in the section above have outlined, there are other equally important ingredients in their education. A similar message is given by parents and whānau: consulting with them and including cultural input must be done by skilful educators who care for their children, have high expectations of them and can

---

10   While it is beyond the scope of this book to make comparisons with and discuss the situation for minority group students with special education needs internationally, it warrants mentioning that it is very similar to the situation for Māori children with special education needs. Consequently, lessons can be learned from considering successful overseas initiatives, just as Aotearoa / New Zealand literature can make a valuable contribution to special education provisions for minority group students in other countries.

deliver a high-quality, well-resourced programme.[11] To these ingredients the research adds: a variety of evidence-based successful teaching practices; positive teacher–child and home–ECEF/school relationships; and professionals who are positively focused, hard-working, motivated, knowledgeable, fair, respectful, patient, humorous, persevering, reflective practitioners. We have all the answers—the challenge is putting them into practice!

Study questions

1. In what ways does culture have an impact on provisions for Māori children with special education needs?

2. In your opinion, what are the three major barriers to providing culturally responsive, effective education for Māori children with special education needs, and how can they be overcome?

3. Why is 'learning from the past' considered an important aspect of special education provision for Māori? What messages from pre-European times can be deduced from the information in this chapter?

4. How are the voices of Māori children, their parents and whānau listened to and incorporated into your own special education practices? What element of empowerment is involved?

References

Altschul, I., Oyserman, D., & Bybee, D. (2006). Racial-ethnic identity in mid-adolescence: Content and change as predictors of academic achievement. *Child Development, 77*(5), 1155–1169.

Bevan-Brown, J. (1989). *Intellectual disability: A Māori perspective.* Unpublished master's project, Massey University [Palmerston North].

Bevan-Brown, J. (2002). *Culturally appropriate, effective provision for Māori learners with special needs: He waka tino whakarawea.* Unpublished doctoral thesis, Massey University [Palmerston North].

Bevan-Brown, J. (2003). *The cultural self-review. Providing culturally effective, inclusive education for Māori learners.* Wellington: NZCER Press.

Bevan-Brown, J. (2006a). Beyond policy and good intentions. *International Journal of Inclusive Education, 10*(2–3), 221–234.

---

11   See also the 17 personal and service requirements of culturally appropriate, effective service provision identified by parents in my PhD research (Bevan-Brown, 2002, pp. 278–310).

Bevan-Brown, J. (2006b). Teaching Māori children with special education needs: Getting rid of the too hard basket. *Kairaranga*, *7*, 14–23.

Bishop, R., Berryman, M., Cavanagh, T., & Teddy, L. (2007). *Te Kotahitanga: Phase 3 whanaungatanga: Establishing a culturally responsive pedagogy of relations in mainstream secondary school classrooms*. Report to the Minister of Education. Wellington: Ministry of Education.

Bishop, R., Berryman, M., & Wearmouth, J. (2014). *Te Kotahitanga: Towards effective education reform for indigenous and other minoritised students*. Wellington: NZCER Press.

Bishop, T., & Glynn, T. (1999). *Culture counts: Changing power relations in education*. Palmerston North: Dunmore Press.

Chavous, T. M., Bernat, D., Schmeelk-Cone, K., Caldwell, C., Kohn-Wood, L. P., & Zimmerman, M. A. (2003). Racial identity and academic attainment among African American adolescents. *Child Development*, *74*(4), 1076–1091.

Cullen, J., & Bevan-Brown, J. (1999). *Resourcing special education in early childhood: Database and best practice validation*. Final report to the Ministry of Education. Palmerston North: Institute for Professional Development and Educational Research, Massey University.

Currie, G. (1962). *Report of the Commission on Education in New Zealand*. Wellington: Government Printer.

Durie, M. H. (1985). A Māori perspective of health. *Social Science Medical*, *20*(5), 483–486.

Durie, M. H. (1995). *Ngā matatini Māori: Diverse Māori realities*. Report to the Ministry of Health. Palmerston North: Te Pūmanawa Hauora, Department of Māori Studies, Massey University.

Gay, G. (1997). Educational equality for students of color. In J. A. Banks & C. A. McGee Banks (Eds.), *Multicultural education: Issues and perspectives* (3rd ed., pp. 195–228). Boston, MA: Allyn & Bacon.

Gibson, P. (2012). *Manahau, mana hauā, and Matariki*. Retrieved from: http://www.hrc.co.nz/newsletters/manahau/2012/06/manahau-mana-haua-and-matariki

Hemara, W. (2000). *Māori pedagogies: A view from the literature*. Wellington: NZCER Press.

Hill, J., & Hawk, K. (2000). *Making a difference in the classroom: Effective teaching practice in low decile, multicultural schools*. Wellington: Research Division, Ministry of Education.

Hunn, J. K. (1961). *Report on the Department of Māori Affairs: With statistical supplement.* Wellington: Government Printer.

Ihimaera, W. (Ed.). (1993). *Te ao mārama: Regaining Aotearoa:* Māori writers speak out. Auckland: Reed.

Kana, P., & Harawira, W. (1995). Special Education Services (SES) policies and practices: Services to tāngata whenua: Special needs (reo and tikanga Māori). In: D. Fraser, R. Moltzen, & K. Tyba (Eds.), *Learners with special needs in Aotearoa / New Zealand* (pp. 33–51; 390–405). Palmerston North: Dunmore Press.

Kingi, J. (1995, 4 March). Arts award winner sees language value. *Evening Post,* p. 5.

Kingi, J., & Bray, A. (2000). *Māori concepts of disability.* Dunedin: Donald Beasley Institute.

Lynch, E., & Hanson, M. (1992/1998). *Developing cross-cultural competence: A guide for working with young children and their families.* Baltimore, MD: Paul H. Brookes.

Massey University. (1999). *Special Education 2000: Monitoring and evaluation of the policy: Phase One final report to the Ministry of Education.* Wellington: Ministry of Education; Palmerston North: Institute for Professional Development and Educational Research, Massey University.

Massey University. (2002). *Special Education 2000: Monitoring and evaluation of the policy: Final report to the Ministry of Education.* Wellington: Ministry of Education; Palmerston North: Institute for Professional Development and Educational Research, Massey University.

Mead, H. M., & Grove, N. (2003). *Ngā pēpeha a ngā tīpuna.* Wellington: Victoria University Press.

Metge, J. (1984). *Learning and teaching: He tikanga Māori.* Wellington: Department of Education, Māori and Island Division.

Metge, J. (1990). *Te kohao o te ngira: Culture and learning.* Wellington: Learning Media.

Ministry of Education. (1993). *The New Zealand curriculum framework: Te anga mātauranga o Aotearoa.* Wellington: Learning Media.

Ministry of Education. (1996). *Te whāriki: He whāriki mātauranga mō ngā mokopuna o Aotearoa: Early childhood curriculum.* Wellington: Learning Media.

Ministry of Education. (1999). *Special education policy guidelines.* Retrieved from http://www.minedu.govt.nz/NZEducation/

EducationPolicies/SpecialEducation/AboutUs/ContextOfOurWork/
SpecialEducationPolicyGuidelines.aspx

Ministry of Education. (2008a). *Ka hikitia—Managing for success:* Māori *education strategy, 2008–2012.* Wellington: Author.

Ministry of Education. (2008b). *Te hikoitanga: Māori cultural responsivity.* Retrieved from http://www.minedu.govt.nz/NZEducation/ EducationPolicies/SpecialEducation/OurWorkProgramme/ GettingItRightForMāori/TeHikoitangaMāoriCulturalResponsivity.aspx

Ministry of Education. (2011). *Tātaiako: Cultural competencies for teachers of Māori learners.* Retrieved from http://www.minedu.govt.nz/~/media/MinEdu/ Files/TheMinistry/EducationInitiatives/Tataiako/TataiakoWEB.pdf

Ministry of Education. (2013a). *Specialist service standards.* Retrieved from http://www.minedu.govt.nz/NZEducation/EducationPolicies/ SpecialEducation/AboutUs/SpecialistServiceStandards.aspx

Ministry of Education. (2013b). *The Māori education strategy—Ka hikitia: Accelerating success, 2013–2017.* Retrieved from http://www.minedu.govt.nz/ theMinistry/PolicyandStrategy/KaHikitia.aspx

Ministry of Health. (2001). *The New Zealand disability strategy: Making a world of difference: Whakanui oranga.* Wellington: Ministry of Health.

Reid, P. (1986). Te waiora. In: M. Abbott & M. Durie (Eds.), *The future of mental health services in New Zealand: Māori perspectives* (pp. 13–18). Auckland: Mental Health Foundation of New Zealand.

Skidmore, D. (2002). A theoretical model of pedagogical discourse. *Disability, Culture and Education, 1*(2), 119–131.

Smith, D. D. (1998). *Introduction to special education: Teaching in an age of challenge* (3rd ed.). Boston, MA: Allyn & Bacon.

Tau, T. M. (1999). Mātauranga Māori as an epistemology. *Te Pouhere Kōrero, 1*(1), 10–23.

Turia, T. (2010). Speech given to the National Māori Disability Network's Annual Conference, Kairau Marae, Taranaki. Retrieved from http://www. voxy.co.nz/politics/speech-turia-hui-taumata-te-piringa-national-maori- disability-network039s-annual/5/52176

UNESCO. (2005). *Guidelines for inclusion: Ensuring access to education for all.* Paris, France: UNESCO.

Wong, C. A., Eccles, J. S., & Sameroff, A. (2003). The influence of ethnic discrimination and ethnic identification on African American adolescents' school and socioemotional adjustment. *Journal of Personality, 71*(6), 1197–123.

Chapter 2

In pursuit of culturally responsive evidence-based special education pathways for Māori: Whaia ki te ara tika

Sonja Macfarlane

> Whaia te kotahitanga o te wairua,
> Mā te rangimārie me te aroha e paihere.
>
> *Pursue unity of spirit,*
> *Which is bound together by peace and compassion.*

Introduction

What are the key components of culturally responsive, evidence-based special education practice for the indigenous Māori people of Aotearoa / New Zealand? An underlying debate is the contention that conventional perspectives are incongruent with perspectives that are commonly held by Māori. Competing discourses about what constitutes 'evidence' and what comprises 'cultural responsiveness' effectively stultify concerted efforts to address the educational inequities that continue for

Māori. Divergent perspectives, hegemonic policies and processes, and the privileging of Western over indigenous Māori knowledge create a default setting that relegates cultural evidences to the margins, despite their relevance or potential to inform (Tooley, 2000).

This chapter reports on research that explored two questions:

• What are the key components of culturally responsive special education practice for Māori?

• What are the key components of evidence-based special education practice for Māori?

Influences and realities

Māori students and whānau are entitled to receive effective special education (SE) services. Their entitlement is enshrined within our nation's founding document, Te Tiriti o Waitangi, and espoused within an array of policy documents. While the nature of the Treaty partnership continues to be keenly debated, there have been many educational initiatives since the signing of that historic document in 1840. Notwithstanding recommendation after recommendation and report after report throughout the years, education policies and practices have continued to marginalise Māori customs, language and 'ways of knowing'. Evidence continues to mount which shows that disparities and inequities for Māori learners in all spheres of education continue.

In comparison to education systems globally, the top 80 percent of Aotearoa / New Zealand students are performing at world-class standards (Hattie, 2003). However, the bottom 20 percent (the 'tail') are falling behind at a rate greater than any other country in the world. In essence, we have one of the greatest rates of disparity between those who achieve and those who languish. Hattie expresses particular concern with regard to the educational experiences and opportunities of those students who are most likely to be accessing special education services. Māori are disproportionately overrepresented in this cohort (Ministry of Education, 2011).

The interests of those described as the 'tail' must be at the forefront of educational research initiatives. According to Salmond (2003), part of the solution hinges on the questions that are posed at the outset of research pursuits, along with the meaning-making of information that has been gathered. Salmond believes that research should illuminate

Māori learners' educational aspirations and performance, and researchers should search for approaches that enable these to be actualised.

The Information Age has provided educators with greater access to research and literature. This has coincided with increasing pressure being asserted on government organisations to provide services that draw on the most effective research, and that are timely, responsive, outcomes focused and accountable (Mayne & Zapico-Goni, 1997). Within the Ministry of Education, Special Education (SE), increasing onus is being placed on practitioners to become critical consumers of research; to discerningly evaluate the best available information—tempered with skill and experience—on any given topic relevant to their practice (Ministry of Education, 2005). It is also incumbent on them to consider the context within which the research evidence was gathered, as well as the context within which the research will be applied.

Informing and being informed: *Evidence that counts*

In recent years these latter contexts have demanded that a more authentic awareness of Māori knowledge and values be drawn on (Ministry of Education, 2008). Māori epistemology and pedagogy have been acknowledged by researchers and educators as having integrity and reliability (Durie, 1997). Kaupapa Māori philosophies have informed and transformed initiatives in health and education. At the forefront have been Māori whānau, hapū and iwi, each intent on revitalising and retaining control over their own knowledge and research (Smith, 1995, 1999). This renaissance has resulted in a growing societal acceptance that change must occur and be owned by everyone. Given that SE professionals are tasked with determining the needs of tamariki and whānau in order to shape responsive programmes, then the expectation that they understand more about kaupapa Māori is not at all unreasonable.

Enter evidence-based practice (EBP). Originating in medicine, EBP spread through the health sector in the early 1990s to augment clinical expertise with the best research evidence, providing a judicious method for approaching casework (Holm, 2000). In the mid-2000s EBP permeated the education sector in Aotearoa / New Zealand. The challenge for SE practitioners is to ensure that the best evidence is considered, by drawing on three types of evidence: research, practitioner expertise and client participation.

EBP is intended to strengthen the link between research and practice, not to promote a prescriptive 'one-size-fits-all' tool. However, ongoing concern continues to be expressed that no agreed definition has been applied to the term *evidence*. A question that continually arises is: 'What constitutes evidence, and who decides?' The fear is that, until greater clarity is provided, there are inherent risks in terms of the responsiveness of assessment, analysis and programme planning for Māori. The argument is that 'evidence' means different things to different people, and that these interpretations are influenced by a range of factors, including ethnicity, world view and life experiences.

So what are these competing perspectives? There are those who propose that a more prescriptive view of what constitutes evidence is essential (Davies, Nutley, & Smith, 2000). These proponents place greater emphasis on research evidence as providing the exclusive foundation for EBP. They claim that research is the most accurate and valid form of evidence, able to be assessed and interrogated objectively. Conversely, there are those who declare that a more descriptive interpretation—one that acknowledges client voice and world-view perspectives, as well as practitioner judgement, experience and intuition (Hammersley, 2001)—needs to be adopted. They declare that the effectiveness of any practical action not only depends on *what* is done, but also on *how* it is done, *by whom*, *with whom* and *when*.

Holm (2000) contends that research evidence must augment (not replace) the many other forms of evidence that comprise professional decision-making. Other indigenous scholars suggest that subjective action and thought are also relevant forms of evidence (Aluli-Meyer, 2008; Cajete, 2000; Kawagley & Barnhardt, 1997; Marsden, 2003; Smith, 1999). This is succinctly encapsulated by Hammersley (2001), who believes that the process of defining what constitutes evidence will be forever fraught with difficulty if particular research evidence is privileged over evidence from other sources.

These EBP debates may emanate from belief systems that are talking past each other (Metge & Kinloch, 1984). This highlights the power and influence of the particular terminology that is used in zones where knowledge, research, policy and practice intersect. Slee (2001) draws attention to the dangers of government organisations using default vocabulary, such that public discussion is reduced to co-opted terms which (incorrectly) assume an agreed meaning. The power of the word is profound. Particular phrases are often adopted to drive new initiatives and strategic directions. It may therefore be useful for researchers and policy makers to reflect on the following questions:

- What concept does this term impart?
- Is this understanding shared?
- How might interpretations vary?
- How can we ensure that we are not subjugating Māori knowledge?

The research premise

In 2003, Cashmore undertook research that explored the significance and interconnectedness of three key drivers of EBP; research, policy and practice. Cashmore's research lead her to contend that the overall aim of educational research should be to inform policy and practice so as to improve the education outcomes for children and their families. In 1984 Elliot Eisner declared, somewhat fortuitously, that: "If educational research is truly to inform practice, we must construct our own conceptual apparatus and research methods" (p. 450). Kaupapa Māori research methodology emerged, and has been validated, during almost the same 30-year time span, and this has emancipated a range of Māori cultural constructs—constructs that have guided the approaches adopted in this study.

The EBP framework developed by Bourke, Holden and Curzon (2005) is recognised as being a robust lens through which SE practitioners and policy makers are able to moderate three forms of evidence in order to shape the quality of special education services (Figure 2.1). This framework was used to guide the selection of participants for the research study that is being reported on in this chapter. The selection process sought to target the discrete perspective that each participant would espouse, specific to the evidence domain with which they were most familiar.

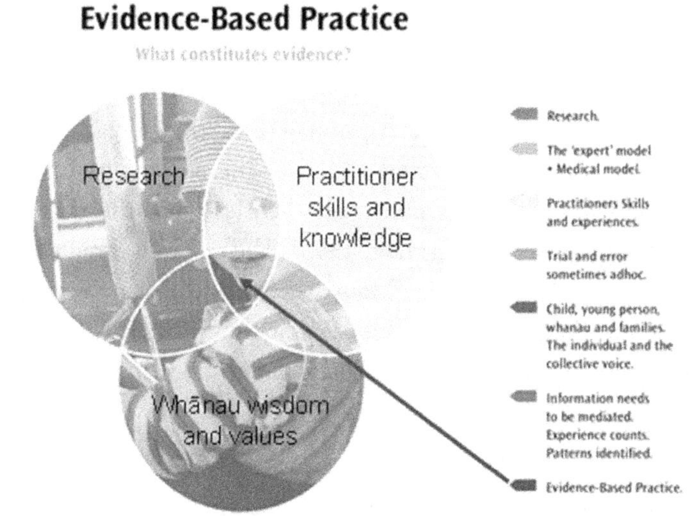

Figure 2.1. Evidence-based practice framework (Bourke et al., 2005)

For each of the three evidence circles, six Māori-affiliated participants were chosen. Of the 18 participants, six were working in senior academic, Māori-focused research positions in universities across Aotearoa / New Zealand. The remaining 12 had amassed a wealth of practical SE experience, having worked within a Māori focus. Of these 12, six had worked in leadership as managers and specialists, and six had worked closely alongside whānau in the areas of advocacy, liaison and brokerage (see Table 2.1).

		Evidence domain																	
		Research						Practice						Whānau					Totals
Method	Questionnaire	✓	✓	✓	✓	✓	✓	✓	✓	✓	✓	✓	✓	✓	✓	✓	✓	✓	✓	18 questionnaires
	Interview	✓	✓	✓	✓			✓	✓	✓	✓			✓	✓	✓	✓			12 interviews
	Focus group					✓	✓					✓	✓					✓	✓	1 focus group discussion
										Participants										

Table 2.1. Data gathering and participant selection

The research design drew on the traditions of qualitative research methodology and utilised a grounded theory inquiry approach (Strauss & Corbin, 1998). This qualitative research methodology aligned with the Johnson and Christensen (2000) description of research, which explores people's experiences, behaviours and feelings. The goal of grounded theory inquiry is to inductively construct theories from the data in order to understand experiences (Haig, 1995). The research design and approach were guided by kaupapa Māori theory and research methodology, which worked from the premise that the values, beliefs and favoured practices of te ao Māori are valid and legitimate (Smith, 1992).

Research, evidence and policy

The overriding intention for the research process was to uphold the integrity of Māori knowledge, language and culture (Durie, 1997) by drawing on the narratives of the research participants. Bevan-Brown (2002, 2006) contends that for SE policies and practices to be more culturally responsive to and for Māori, there is a need to incorporate Māori values and philosophies. Bishop (1996) further asserts that the solutions for Māori are not located within the culture that has traditionally marginalised Māori, but within Māori culture.

Agents of change in special education

Simon and Cistaro (2009) believe that the most important driver of constructive cultural change is *leadership*, and that implementing this within an organisation that has deeply entrenched sub-cultures presents immense challenges that need to be managed and led purposefully. Cultural change is premised on the fundamental cultural values and beliefs that underpin perspectives about relationships, knowledge, ownership, power sharing and leadership. Simon and Cistaro outline four phases of constructive cultural change to shift perspectives that maintain cultural dominance, power and control:

- enlisting and educating *leaders as advocates*
- *assessing the current culture* to identify strengths and opportunities
- driving culture change *from the grassroots*
- generating *culture-based projects* to embed the culture change.

As mentioned above, this study selected 18 Māori-affiliated agents of constructive cultural change, chosen because of their cultural knowledge and expertise, their leadership and status within the Māori community, and their advocacy and passion for Māori advancement over many years. They were all familiar with the tenets of the Māori Education Strategy, *Ka Hikitia* (Ministry of Education, 2008), understood the importance of culturally responsive approaches, and were committed to the principles of Te Tiriti o Waitangi.

What emerged was a recurring pattern of discourse (across all three research groups) which served to connect the two constructs (*culturally responsive practice* and *evidence-based practice*) as mutually interchangeable. They were continually described as synonymous terms that clarified how significant, pervasive and all-encompassing six key cultural concepts were to both (see below).

A synthesis of the key emerging themes

Six key themes emerged from the data:

1. mātauranga Māori—the centrality of Māori knowledge

2. whanaungatanga—the centrality of relationships

3. rangatiratanga: the centrality of self-awareness

4. research in context: the centrality of relevance

5. honouring the Treaty: the centrality of power sharing

6. cultural competency: the centrality of enabling potential.

Theme 1: Mātauranga Māori—the centrality of Māori knowledge

The participants felt strongly that mātauranga Māori was undervalued and marginalised in research, policy and practice. They discussed the concept of 'monocultural' thinking that continually relegates Māori knowledge to the periphery:

> It is actually quite a monocultural environment when it comes down to it. It's bicultural when they need us to run a pōwhiri for someone important, or do a karakia for our team meeting. Apart from that it is white-stream. That's why they need us here.

> Māori values are vital. Māori knowledge is legitimate.

Ermine, Sinclair and Jeffrey (2004) contend that Eurocentric hegemony has promoted the Western body of knowledge as the singular and privileged consciousness. Shiva (1993) discusses the notion of hostility being unleashed on indigenous cultures by the dominant West, whereby indigenous knowledge systems are rendered invisible in research, policy and practice. Shiva believes that this is actually a sinister tactic as it effectively results in indigenous knowledge disappearing over time through being denied the status of a logical knowledge system within literature and research.

Aluli-Meyer (2008) vigorously challenges hegemonic subtleties, believing that the enduring nature of indigenous knowledge, which is regularly passed down, intact, over successive generations through an oral tradition of knowledge transmission, is testimony to its integrity. This resonates with comments previously made by Durie (1997), who describes Māori knowledge as having integrity of its own. How, then, might Māori knowledge claim a more legitimate space in SE?

Many of the core values, beliefs and practices associated with indigenous world views are now being recognised as having an enduring and adaptive integrity that is as valid in the present as it was in the past (Kawagley & Barnhardt, 1997). The risks associated with the rejection of legitimate indigenous knowledge are highlighted by Hardman, Drew and Egan (1999), who declare that it ultimately marginalises those who have the greatest need. As cautioned by Howitt and Owusu-Bempah (1994), a lack of attention to indigenous knowledge will constantly leave professional services impoverished and inadequate.

Theme 2: Whanaungatanga—the centrality of relationships

Whanaungatanga is deemed to be an essential component of culturally responsive, evidence-based practice. The participants described it as a process that requires investment, and that needs to be acknowledged as integral to effective service delivery. They felt strongly that whanaungatanga needs to be premised on a deeper understanding of kaupapa Māori philosophy, specifically the ways in which protocols of engagement are facilitated when bringing people together. This includes being responsive to spiritual dimensions, building trust and maintaining ongoing connections. They talked about the importance of being respectful, showing empathy, not judging, listening more than speaking, avoiding the use of jargon, using appropriate body language, upholding the mana of others, and remaining humble. They also discussed particular cultural obligations, which sometimes extend beyond core work (e.g. attending tangihanga and hui). This reflected the findings of Lipman (1995), who discusses the benefits of educators being visible in community activities that are important to indigenous cultures. Lipman declares that this is likely to have positive spin-offs for the educational engagement and achievement of students, because it indicates to the community that there is interest in them as people.

Durie (1997) asserts that whanaungatanga is fundamental to all professional interactions with Māori, as it engenders collective responsibility for others' wellbeing through a commitment to sharing knowledge and information for a common purpose. The participants described whanaungatanga as being something that needs to precede everything else. Like Durie (1997) and Lipman (1995), they argued strongly for the centrality of relationships in all professional interactions with Māori, and felt that it needed to be accorded a much higher status within SE.

Theme 3: Rangatiratanga—the centrality of self-awareness

The participants discussed the need for SE professionals to know and understand themselves as a precursor to self-empowerment, and the development of the prerequisite competencies for working effectively with Māori. They felt that it was essential for professionals to have a realistic understanding of their own world view and cultural identity. They believed that this required professionals to reflect on any cultural biases, stereotypes or deficit beliefs they may hold about Māori in order to recognise the potential impact of their own culture on their professional interactions. They reiterated the damage that can be done when strongly held negative assumptions about Māori may effectively discount the realities that Māori are dealing with on a daily basis as a result of the historical, environmental, social, political and economic influences of colonisation.

Berryman (2008) and Papps (2005) urge professionals to take cognisance of the impact their own culture may have on practice interactions so as to avoid unsafe practice that may damage the cultural identity and wellbeing of the client. According to Campinha-Bacote (2007), the deliberate and in-depth exploration of one's own cultural biases, stereotypes, prejudices and assumptions is an enabler of 'cultural awareness'; a precursor to the development of cultural competency, which Cross, Bazron, Dennis and Isaacs (1989) assert requires professionals to accept and respect diversity. Zion (2005) believes that a process of self-exploration can alert professionals to the legitimacy of diversity, which manifests as a capacity to honour one's own culture as well as the culture of others.

Theme 4: Research in context—the centrality of relevance

The participants were frustrated that research emanating from other countries is privileged over what they described as "the legitimate and valid evidences" that derive from the lived realities of Māori. They felt that Māori voice is silenced by large-scale domestic studies where Māori are a minority, preferring smaller and replicated studies undertaken within meaningful contexts where Māori are the majority. Like Barkham and Mellor-Clark (2003), they viewed practice-based evidence, or PBE, as a relevant source of information and untapped potential. Several were frustrated at being directed to culturally enhance Western programmes for use with Māori.

A. Macfarlane (2011) asserts that many kaupapa Māori programmes which are not deemed to be "evidence based" from a Western perspective are not funded or mandated, but they may be effective and have the potential to achieve positive outcomes. Conversely, there are Western programmes that are "evidence based" and are mandated for use with Māori, but are not effective and limit the potential for better outcomes. Clearly the terms *evidence based* and *effective* are not necessarily synonymous. For Māori, what is important is that a programme or approach is culturally congruent, premised on, and initiated through, kaupapa Māori philosophy (Macfarlane, Glynn, Grace, Penetito, & Bateman, 2008).

Theme 5: Honouring the Treaty—the centrality of power sharing

The participants viewed the Treaty of Waitangi as a foundational and abiding agreement that must underpin all aspects of SE core business. They felt that a bicultural partnership approach needs to be adhered to at all levels of the organisation, and that a failure to do so is a direct breach of the Treaty principles. Perspectives on inequitable power sharing and power imbalances permeated the other five themes, particularly in the areas of hegemonic practices that questioned the legitimacy of Māori knowledge and programmes, inequitable resourcing to enable the advancement of a more culturally relevant research evidence base, and the marginalisation of Māori in decision making, research, policy development and practice approaches.

The research data indicate that the Treaty retains a great deal of mana for Māori—that it is as meaningful today as it was when signed in 1840. It influences perceptions of fairness, partnership, respect, status and power sharing. One participant stated, "We are definitely the junior partner in this Treaty relationship". Another stated, "Knowledge is power, so when your knowledge is not valued you have no power". Given Glynn's (1998) assertion that Māori language, culture and knowledge all qualify as tāonga, to be protected under principle two of the Treaty, then it is essential that power be equitably distributed at all levels of SE to prevent monocultural hostility being unleashed on Māori (Shiva, 1993).

Culturally responsive policies of inclusion: Notions of power sharing
The participants referred to policy as being akin to tikanga—protocols that should guide culturally responsive services. They felt that SE policy was often foreign to and in conflict with their world view and preferred ways of doing things. They expressed frustration at the ways in which policy continually changed, and how Māori were not consulted in policy development, despite the fact that Māori are a large client group. One participant stated, "Our tikanga stays the same, so we just know how to do things with our whānau".

Solomos (1988) contends that policy development is shaped by the philosophical positioning of those who control competing interests and discourses. Given that Māori discourse is regularly absent in SE policy development, the theoretical stance that underpins many of the policies is bereft of Māori thinking. Larkin (2006) refers to policy needing to actively target ethnicity so as to avoid "hegemonic cultural domination" (p. 23) and to have an impact for minority populations that regularly have the greatest need (Durie, 2004; Sullivan, 2009).

Theme 6: Cultural competency: the centrality of enabling potential
The participants felt that SE professionals need to have a prerequisite level of cultural competency for working with Māori, and believed that the cultural aspects of practice are as important as the clinical aspects but are accorded minority status. They discussed the idea of embedding a cultural competency attestation process within performance

appraisals, whereby salary progression is contingent on achieving and evidencing particular competencies.

A. Macfarlane (2011) argues that for too long now many Māori have not received the benefits of culturally competent SE provision. He believes that ascertaining and addressing cultural competency needs to be a projective rather than a retrospective activity, something that is proactive and planned. Macfarlane believes that professionals need to have achieved a base level of competency prior to being endorsed to practice. He contends that this is not unlike the requirement that a doctor be qualified and competent prior to dispensing medicine or advice on matters to do with people's health and wellbeing.

A pathway forward

The emerging themes have raised questions about how 'evidence' is defined. This created an opportunity to contribute two kaupapa Māori frameworks to support SE practice.

He ritenga whaimōhio: A framework to guide culturally responsive evidence-based practice

The current EBP framework encompasses three worthy kete of evidence, but the parameters of each kete are ultimately defined by a dominant discourse that chooses to include certain evidence and simultaneously exclude other evidence. In its current form, it is 'culture-less', as the *research evidence circle* appears to privilege Western knowledge, literature and research that has been derived from contexts that do not include, or are irrelevant to, Māori. It does not provide Māori rightful access to the richness of mātauranga Māori. The *practitioner evidence circle* privileges the clinical aspects of practice and does little to enforce an expectation that practitioners acquire prerequisite levels of cultural competency. The *family/whānau evidence circle* does not reflect the centrality of paying due regard to whanaungatanga as a core construct of practice.

Figure 2.2 is an EBP framework that reflects three concepts highly regarded by Māori: tika, pono and aroha. It shows how these concepts permeate and broaden the parameters of each of the evidence kete. Te ao Māori and Te Tiriti o Waitangi are acknowledged and surround the three evidence kete.

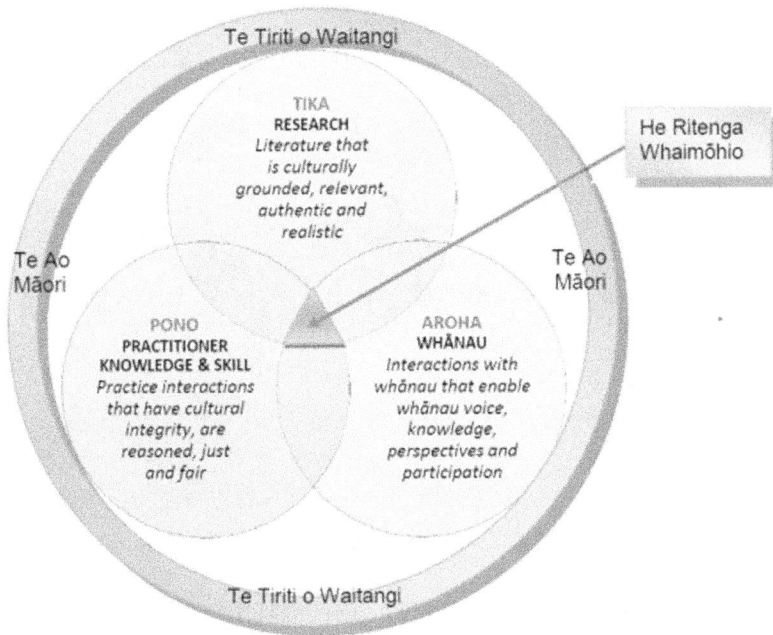

Figure 2.2. He Ritenga Whaimōhio: culturally responsive evidence-based practice
Source: Macfarlane, S., 2011

Te Pikinga ki Runga: Raising possibilities: a Treaty-based framework for special educators

Te Pikinga ki Runga (Macfarlane, 2009) is a framework that supports professionals in their interactions with Māori students at risk of educational failure (see Figure 2.3). It is guided by the three Treaty principles:

- Principle 1: partnership—whānau engagement
- Principle 2: protection—tamaiti wellbeing
- Principle 3: participation—inclusive ecologies.

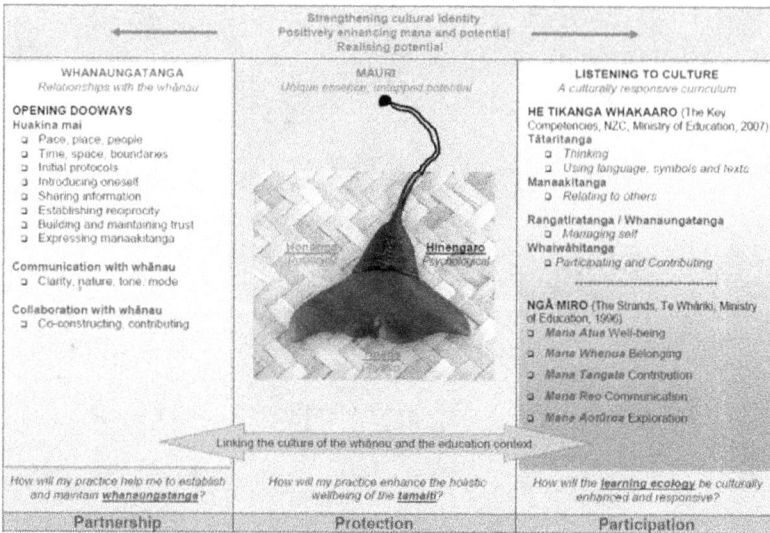

Figure 2.3. Te Pikinga ki Runga: raising possibilities (Macfarlane, 2009)

Holistic frameworks promoted by Durie (1994), Irwin (1984) and Pere (1991) are drawn on (under Principle 2: protection) to identify four domains deemed relevant to an educational approach to wellbeing. Three domains (hononga, hinengaro, tinana) comprise the core configuration, with a pervading and emanating fourth domain (mauri).

These four domains have been broken down further into 12 dimensions, affectionately known as the huia grid: a name gifted by a kuia who felt that the 12 dimensions metaphorically represent the 12 prized tail feathers of the now-extinct huia bird. She stated that if we do not care for the feathers (her metaphor for tamariki), then they are at risk. A set of reflective prompt questions is included to stimulate deeper thinking.

Dimensions	Domains		
	Hinengaro (Psychological aspects)	**Tinana** (Physical aspects)	**MAURI** (Unique essence)
Honanga (Relational aspects)			
Whānau (Interdependency and connectedness)	**Motivation** Inspiration and drive	**Demeanour** Appearance and body language	**Cultural identity** Pride and security
Whenua (Kainga and belonging)	**Emotions** Thoughts and feelings	**Energy levels** Alertness and zeal	**Attitude and spirit** Manner and disposition
Friendships (Cooperation and sociality)	**Cognition** Learning and understanding	**Physical safety** Respect for self and others	**Potential** Courage and confidence

Reflective questions

Domain	Reflective questions
Honanga: Relational aspects .... with and within the whānau... and with others. Consider how planning will strengthen relationships so as to maximise special qualities and potential	☐ How strong are whānau relationships .... connectedness to whānau? ☐ How strong are the student's connections to / relationships with others (whānau whanau, hapū, iwi...)? ☐ How is the student's position in the whānau being acknowledged (ie. the eldest, youngest, only son....)? ☐ How strong are the student's connections to / relationships with places (papa kainga, marae, whenua...)? ☐ Whānau whānui... how might wider whānau contribute or feature? ☐ How strong (positive) are the student's relationships with key others (peers, teachers...)?
Hinengaro: Psychological aspects .... thoughts and feelings, learning. Consider how planning will enhance motivation, thoughts and feelings so as to maximise confidence	☐ What are the things that inspire and motivate the student? ☐ How are the student's emotions (verbally, non-verbally) displayed / expressed? ☐ How respectful is the student of others' thoughts and feelings? ☐ Does the student understand what others are communicating to him / her? ☐ What might be the barrier(s) to the student's engagement and participation in learning activities? ☐ How might this be impacting on enjoyment, learning and achievement - and reaching potential?
Tinana: Physical aspects ....demeanour, physical health and wellbeing. Consider how planning will elevate energy, alertness and vigour so as to maximise wellbeing	☐ How is the student's 'ahua' (demeanour, appearance) – how does the student 'look'? ☐ What messages might the student be expressing by way of body language? ☐ What are the student's energy levels like? ☐ How alert is the student / does the student appear to be? ☐ Are others respecting the student's personal space? ☐ Is the student respecting others' personal space?
Mauri: Unique essence ..... cultural identity, attitude, potential. Consider how planning will maximise the expression of special qualities and potential	☐ How is cultural identity being supported and strengthened by others (education setting, teachers, peers..)? ☐ How is meaning derived from the student's name? ☐ How might self concept be affecting the student's attitude – ie. responses to others, manner, outlook? ☐ How might motivation and mana be enhanced and uplifted? ☐ What opportunities are being provided which enable positive choices to be made? ☐ How can the student be supported to build confidence and strengthen resilience?

Table 2.2: Te Huia: protecting the holistic wellbeing of the tamaiti
Source: Macfarlane, 2009.

Conclusion

When attempting to define the key characteristics of the two research constructs (*culturally responsive practice* and *evidence-based practice*), the participants were more comfortable with the former because it was a term that resonated for them. They described cultural responsiveness as the essence of being Māori; it is what Māori do as a natural part of being Māori, which means thinking and doing things in kaupapa Māori ways (Durie, 1994; Ratima, 2001). They felt that the two research constructs should not be mutually exclusive, alleging that it was important not to differentiate to any degree between them, as both needed to comprise an overall set of six kaupapa Māori characteristics.

Macfarlane (2004) reminds educators to pay attention to alternatives to conventional Western knowledge. This includes having a willingness to embrace new learning and focus on processes (how things are done) as well as outcomes (what needs to be achieved). In 1999 Manuka Henare alerted educators to the importance of valuing and holding on to Māori cultural imperatives. His comments reiterated the words that were spoken by the first Māori woman to ever graduate from an Aotearoa / New Zealand university, Dame Mira Szaszy. Her speech was captured by Rogers and Simpson (1993) when she spoke at the 1993 Māori graduands capping ceremony at Victoria University of Wellington. Dame Mira offered an ethical response to the contemporary world, claiming that the essence of being Māori could be found in ancestral cultural values:

> … what we need in essence is a new Māori humanism, that is, a humanism based on ancient values but versed in contemporary idiom. Our current humanism does not seem to have found its balance— with the rich lurching forward, disposing of their cultural roots and becoming rootless, and the poor, particularly unemployed, becoming poorer without even the sustenance of cultural or spiritual strengths. (Rogers & Simpson, 1993, p. 7)

This challenge is not dissimilar to the one that has emerged out of the rich information gathered in this study. The participants were asked to determine the key characteristics of two SE constructs: *evidence-based practice* and *culturally responsive practice*. They identified six characteristics they perceived to be common to both, and in doing so enabled two functional considerations to be offered. SE services need to be operationalised with thoughtful attention paid to the myriad ways that culture is able to be encoded into the basic structures and ethos of the organisation (Banks, 2004). These considerations require decision makers to stop being dismissive of Māori knowledge and perspectives and enable Māori to lead the responses to their own issues by way of evidence that has meaning and relevance.

To do so reflects a proactive organisation willing to accept liability. The outcome will be proactive SE professionals who are cognisant of real-world problems, and who are hungry to draw on the necessary cultural evidence that is central to making a positive difference for tamariki and whānau.

Many SE professionals may maintain a tidy file, write wonderful case notes and produce impressive reports, but will their professional interactions actually make the positive difference that is needed? Culturally responsive, evidence-based special education services are not only desirable; they are essential.

References

Aluli-Meyer, M. (2008). Indigenous and authentic: Hawaiian epistemology and the triangulation of meaning. In N. K. Denzin, Y. S. Lincoln, & L. T. Smith (Eds.), *Handbook of critical and indigenous methodologies* (pp. 217–232). Los Angeles, CA: Sage Publications.

Banks, J. A. (2004). Multicultural education: Historical development, dimensions, and practice. In J. A. Banks & C. A. McGee-Banks (Eds.), *Handbook of research on multicultural education* (2nd ed., pp. 3–29). New York, NY: Macmillan Publishing Company.

Barkham, M., & Mellor-Clark, J. (2003). Bridging evidence-based practice and practice-based evidence: Developing a rigorous and relevant knowledge for the psychological therapies. *Clinical Psychology and Psychotherapy, 10*(6), 319–327.

Berryman, M. (2008). *Repositioning within indigenous discourses of transformation and self-determination.* Unpublished doctoral thesis, University of Waikato.

Bevan-Brown, J. (2002). *Culturally appropriate, effective provision for Māori learners with special needs: He waka tino whakarawea.* Unpublished doctoral thesis, Massey University [Palmerston North].

Bevan-Brown, J. (2006). Beyond policy and good intentions. *International Journal of Inclusive Education, 10*(2–3), 221–234.

Bishop, R. (1996). *Whakawhanaungatanga: Collaborative research stories.* Palmerston North: Dunmore Press.

Bourke, R., Holden, B., & Curzon, J. (2005). *Using evidence to challenge practice: A discussion paper.* Wellington: Ministry of Education.

Cajete, G. (2000). *Native science: Natural laws of interdependence.* Santa Fe, NM: Clear Light Publishers.

Campinha-Bacote, J. (2007). *The process of cultural competence in the delivery of healthcare services: A culturally competent model of care* (5th ed.). Cincinnati, OH: Transcultural CARE Associates.

Cashmore, J. (2003). Linking research, policy and practice: Including children's input. *Childrenz Issues, 7*(2), 12–17.

Cross, T. L., Bazron, B. J., Dennis, K. W., & Isaacs, M. R. (1989). *Towards a culturally competent system of care: Vol. 1: A monograph on effective services for minority children who are severely emotionally disturbed.* Washington, DC: Georgetown University Child Development Center.

Davies, H. T. O., Nutley, S. M., & Smith, P. C. (2000). *What works?: Evidence-based policy and practice in the public services.* Bristol, UK: Policy Press.

Durie, M. (1994). *Whaiora: Māori health development.* Auckland: Oxford University Press.

Durie, M. H. (1997). Identity, access and Māori advancement. In N. T. Curtis, J. H. Howse, & L. S. McLeod (Eds.), *New directions in educational leadership: The indigenous future: Proceedings of the New Zealand Educational Administration Society Research Conference.* Auckland: Auckland Institute of Technology.

Durie, M. H. (2004, November). *Race and ethnicity in public policy: Does it work?* Paper presented at the Social Policy, Research and Evaluation Conference, What Works?, Wellington.

Eisner, E. (1984). Can educational research inform educational practice? *Phi Delta Kappan, 65*(7), 447–452.

Ermine, W., Sinclair, R., & Jeffrey, B. (2004). *The ethics of research involving indigenous peoples.* Report to the Interagency Advisory Panel on Research Ethics. Vancouver, BC: Indigenous Peoples' Health Research Centre.

Glynn, T. (1998, July). *A collaborative approach to teacher development: New initiatives in special education.* Paper presented at the 28th Annual Conference, Australia Teacher Education, Melbourne, VIC.

Haig, B. (1995). *Grounded theory as scientific method.* Retrieved from http://
www.ed.uiuc.edu/EPS/PES-Yearbook/95_docs

Hammersley, M. (2001, September). *Some questions about evidence-based
practice in education.* Paper presented at the British Educational Research
Association (BERA) annual conference, Evidence-based Practice in
Education, University of Leeds, Leeds, UK.

Hardman, M., Drew, C., & Egan, M. W. (1999). *Human exceptionality, society,
school and family* (6th ed.). Sydney, NSW: Allyn & Bacon.

Hattie, J. (2003, February). *New Zealand education snapshot: With specific
reference to the Yrs 1–13 years.* Paper presented at the Knowledge Wave 2003
Leadership Forum, Auckland.

Henare, M. (1999). Sustainable social policy. In J. Boston, P. Dalziel, & S. St
John (Eds.), *Redesigning the welfare state in New Zealand: Problems, policies,
prospects.* Oxford, UK: Oxford University Press.

Holm, M. B. (2000). Our mandate for the new millennium: Evidence-based
practice. *American Journal of Occupational Therapy, 54*(6), 575–585.

Howitt, D., & Owusu-Bempah, J. (1994). *The racism of psychology.* London,
UK: Routledge.

Irwin, J. (1984). *An introduction to Māori religion.* Adelaide, SA: Australian
Association for the Study of Religions.

Johnson, B., & Christensen, L. (2000). *Educational research.* Boston, MA:
Allyn & Bacon.

Kawagley, A., & Barnhardt, R. (1997). *Education indigenous to place: Western
science meets native reality.* Fairbanks, AK: University of Alaska.

Larkin, S. (2006). Evidence-based policy making in Aboriginal and Torres
Strait Islander health. *Australian Aboriginal Studies, 2,* 17–26.

Lipman, P. (1995). Bringing out the best in them: The contribution of
culturally relevant teachers to educational reform. *Theory into Practice, 34*(3),
202–208.

Macfarlane, A. (2004). *Kia hiwa rā!: Listen to culture: Māori students' plea to
educators.* Wellington: NZCER Press.

Macfarlane, A. (2011, November). *Diversity's challenge to research in psychology:
In pursuit of a balance.* Keynote presentation to the 4th Annual Educational
Psychological Forum, Massey University [Auckland].

Macfarlane, A., Glynn, T., Grace, W., Penetito, W., & Bateman, S. (2008).
Indigenous epistemology in a national curriculum framework? *Ethnicities,
8*(1), 102–127.

Macfarlane, S. (2009). Te Pikinga ki Runga: Raising possibilities. **set:** *Research Information for Teachers, 2,* 42–50.

Macfarlane, S. (2011, October). *In pursuit of culturally responsive pathways: Whaia ki te ara tika.* Keynote presentation to the New Zealand RTLB Annual Conference 2011, Palmerston North.

Marsden, M. (2003). *The woven universe: Selected readings of Reverend Māori Marsden.* Wellington: Te Wananga o Raukawa.

Mayne, J., & Zapico-Goni, E. (1997). *Monitoring performance in the public sector: Future directions from international experience.* New Brunswick, NJ: Transaction Publishers.

Metge, J., & Kinloch, P. (1984). *Talking past each other: Problems of cross-cultural communication.* Wellington: Victoria University Press.

Ministry of Education. (2005). *Springboards to practice: Enhancing effective practice in special education.* Wellington: Ministry of Education.

Ministry of Education. (2008). *Ka hikitia: Managing for success: The Māori education strategy, 2008–2012.* Wellington: Author.

Ministry of Education. (2011). *Ngā haeata mātauranga: Annual report on Māori education.* Wellington: Ministry of Education.

Papps, E. (2005). Cultural safety: Daring to be different. In D. Wepa (Ed.), *Cultural safety in Aotearoa New Zealand* (pp. 20–28). Auckland: Pearson Education.

Pere, R. (1991). *Te wheke: A celebration of ultimate wisdom.* Gisborne: Ao Ako.

Ratima, M. (2001). *Kia uruuru mai a hauora: Being healthy being Māori: Conceptualising Māori health promotion.* Unpublished doctoral thesis, University of Otago.

Rogers, A., & Simpson, M. (Eds.). (1993). *Early stories from founding members of the Māori Women's Welfare League: Te tīmatanga tātau tātau, te rōpū wāhine Māori toko i te ora—as told to Dame Mira Szaszy.* Wellington: Bridget Williams Books.

Salmond, A. (2003). "To the Social Policy Research and Evaluation Conference." *Social Policy Journal of New Zealand, 20,* 1–5.

Shiva, V. (1993). *Monocultures of the mind: Perspectives on biodiversity and biotechnology.* New York, NY: Zed Books.

Simon, S., & Cistaro, P. (2009). Transforming safety culture: Grassroots-led / management-supported change at a major utility. *Professional Safety, 1,* 28–35.

Slee, R. (2001). Driven to the margins: Disabled students, inclusive schooling and the politics of possibility. *Cambridge Journal of Education, 31*(3), 385–397.

Smith, G. H. (1992, July). *Research issues related to Māori education.* Paper presented at the New Zealand Association for Research in Education (NZARE) Special Interest Conference, Massey University, Palmerston North.

Smith, G. H. (1995). Whakaoho whānau: New formations of whānau as an innovative intervention into Māori cultural and educational crises. *He Pūkenga Kōrero, 1*(1), 18–36.

Smith, L. T. (1999). *Decolonising methodologies: Research and indigenous peoples.* Dunedin: University of Otago Press.

Solomos, J. (1988). *Black youth, racism and the state: The politics of ideology and policy.* Cambridge, UK: Cambridge University Press.

Strauss, A., & Corbin, J. (1998). *Basics of qualitative research: Techniques and procedures for developing grounded theory* (2nd ed.). Thousand Oaks, CA: Sage Publications.

Sullivan, A. (2009). Racism and the invisibility of Māori in public policy. *He Pūkenga Kōrero Raumati, 9*(1), 1–10.

Tooley, C. (2000). *Māori education policy in the new millennium: Policy rationality and Government mechanisms.* Unpublished master's thesis, University of Auckland.

Zion, S. (2005). *Understanding culture: On point 1.* National Institute for Urban School Improvement, Arizona University, Tucson.

Chapter 3

Akoranga whakarei: Learning about inclusion from four kura rumaki

Mere Berryman

Waihoa ko ōku whengu,
Mauria mai ko ōku painga.

Heed not my weaknesses,
Nurture my strengths.

Introduction

In 2004 the New Zealand Ministry of Education proposed two research projects to understand how learning, social and cultural outcomes were being promoted for tamariki and rangatahi Māori with special educational needs in both kura auraki (English-medium schools) and kura rumaki (Māori-medium schools). They also wanted to understand how this played out for other whānau members. At the time, a description of the services being promoted for Māori with special education needs acknowledged the philosophy that "tamariki and rangatahi with special needs and their whānau learn effectively through the provision of culturally competent services, which will ensure mana and tikanga are upheld" (Ministry of Education, 2003, p. 56).

This chapter will briefly describe how this research was undertaken in kura rumaki and then discuss the findings that emerged. Perhaps not surprisingly, it will show that the staff from the kura who participated in this study, as with all of their students and whānau, had a very holistic and inclusive view of educating all tamariki and rangatahi, especially those with identified special education needs. The conclusion will consider some of the implications of these findings for others and propose that these research outcomes maintain relevance in 2014, a decade later.

Background

When this research was undertaken in 2004, about 14 percent of school-aged Māori students accessed some form of Māori-medium education, either total Māori immersion or bilingual.[1] Fifty-five percent of these students were in Level 1 immersion programmes. The remaining 45 percent were in Level 3 to 4 bilingual programmes (Ministry of Education, 2005). In 2014 these figures have largely been maintained.

The demand from whānau for access to learning in Māori-medium education is expected to continue, reflecting the increasing population of young Māori students, the desire among Māori to be bilingual, and the increased participation of iwi and Māori organisations in setting priorities for education and delivering education services.

The research

Purpose of the research

The Akoranga Whakarei (Enhancing Effective Practices) research that was contracted by the Ministry of Education aimed to develop understanding of the learning, social and cultural contexts considered important and effective for students with identified special education needs in a number of Māori-language immersion sites. The aim was to develop a clearer picture of how to enhance capability in special education from the perspectives of the students themselves, their parents,

---

1 Full Māori immersion education is defined as Level 1 and reflects learning programmes where between 81 and 100 percent of the learning programme is taught through the medium of the Māori language. Bilingual education includes different levels of Māori immersion, from Level 2 (51–80 percent), to Level 3 (31–50 percent) and Level 4 (12–30 percent). Education settings such as these are more often associated with a growing number of bilingual units within mainstream schools.

caregivers and other whānau members, their kaiako and their tumuaki. In so doing, it was hoped that more effective pathways could be developed for other schools and their Māori communities.

Methodology and methods

This research was undertaken using kaupapa Māori theory and methodology. An essential underpinning of this approach is access to and use of knowledge that stems from a world view that is Māori (Durie, 2012). A kaupapa Māori approach also opens up avenues for critiquing Western approaches by looking at the effects of colonisation, power and social inequalities, and by questioning Western ideas about whose 'knowledge' counts and how this is understood and applied in practice (Smith, 2012). The kaupapa Māori methodology that underpins this type of research allows for the Māori communities, within which the research is situated, to contribute to the research agenda in order to legitimate its procedures and to grow from and with them (Bishop, 2005). Most importantly, the cultural principles, metaphors and practices applied to guide these processes enable the knowledge gained to empower, protect and embrace all that it means to be Māori.

The Poutama Pounamu research whānau

A group of Māori from a number of different iwi, a range of generations and with many different interests and aspirations came together with a Pākehā researcher to combine their skills and expertise in pursuit of the common vision of achieving Māori potential through Māori language and cultural revitalisation. Led by kaumātua from Tauranga Moana, and guided by Māori cultural principles and practices, this group became known as Poutama Pounamu (Berryman, 2008). Constituted as a metaphorical whānau-of-interest (Bishop, 1996), it was this group that undertook this particular research, using the following three main research methods:

1. the close reading, synthesis and review of related literature in terms of its specific applicability to kaupapa Māori, language and cultural contexts, as well as special education

2. field work in four kura rumaki to gather the stories of experience from the people who teach and learn in these spaces

3. collaborative analysis through noho marae with Māori who have

recognised expertise about education and inclusion, together with the participants themselves.

Although these methods may be viewed as quite Western, the ways in which the research procedures were enacted ensured that kaupapa Māori principles were maintained throughout. All ethical requirements were adhered to.

Research procedure

Kura were largely identified by extending invitations where connections already existed. Members of the research whānau then spent some time formally making or renewing connections and developing relationships with the participants in those kura that had agreed to participate. Henceforth staff and community members from these kura will be referred to as kura whānau. The establishment of formal connections involved members of the kura whānau determining, as the host, the forms of mihimihi, whakawhanaungatanga and, in some cases, karakia they would begin these relationships with. After the research whānau had responded to all cultural rituals of encounter, they explained the research project in detail and responded to any research-focused questions. Members of the research whānau then spent at least two consecutive days in each kura with those identified by the kura whānau as their kaikōrero or spokespeople. These sessions involved separate groups of: students identified as having special education needs; members of their family; their teachers; their teacher aides; and the principal, who was also interviewed. In one kura this also involved kaumātua. Kura whānau identified these opportunities as kōrero whakawhitiwhiti: the type of learning conversations at which people are comfortable to exchange and build on the ideas of others and where all can contribute to and through the emergence of spiralling discourses, in which new learning is constructed. Bishop (1996) refers to this type of interview as participatory, in-depth, semi-structured and face-to-face interviews as conversation.

Researchers listened to and audio-taped these kōrero, made careful notes, examined other evidence that was identified as important (such as policies related to special education needs and inclusion), and observed teaching and learning activities using stimulated recall interviews (Bishop, Berryman, & Richardson, 2001). By talking directly with key participants after classroom observations, researchers were facilitating reflections on the relationships and interactions they had observed, what was believed to be most effective for including students, the people who participated, and the outcomes of these processes. This helped to identify the specific elements that kaikōrero in each kura believed contributed to effective inclusion, thus developing a detailed and rich picture of the attitudes, feelings and beliefs of the kaikōrero themselves. In some cases, follow-up interviews further clarified their stories.

Interview transcriptions were returned to the people for their verification and further annotation. The research whānau then edited the verified and annotated transcripts into collaborative stories, each representing the stories they had heard through the kōrero whakawhitiwhiti. In these stories the names of students and whānau members were changed to respect confidentiality, but the names of the specific kura and some staff members remained unchanged by choice.

From these 17 collaborative stories, each containing the metaphors, concepts and social realities of the separate kaikōrero groups, researchers sought to identify answers to the set research questions around what the groups of people themselves believed enhanced effective educational practices in their schools. Supporting evidence from each kura was also analysed and compared with what the national and international literature were saying. Researchers considered the findings from a Western world view and then sought to find out how these findings might be relevant to or best understood from a Māori world view.

The collaborative stories were further drafted into individual case studies for each of the four kura before being presented to an advisory group of Māori and special education needs educators to analyse collectively at a 1-day hui. Shortly thereafter they were shared with members from each of the participating kura whānau at an overnight noho marae. The Ministry of Education managers responsible for this project also attended and contributed at this meeting. By again using the processes of kōrero whakawhitiwhiti, working through the emerging themes with a group of experts and also the participants themselves, the research whānau were able to ensure the messages had greater legitimacy and clarity for all involved.

Overview of the kura

Site one was a decile[2] 2, kura kaupapa Māori in the central North Island with 38 students who came from a community of 20 families. Site two was a decile 1 wharekura in Auckland with 34 students who came from a community of 26 families. Site three was a decile 2 kura reorua (bilingual school) in the Bay of Plenty with 216 students who came from a community of over 150 families. Site four was a decile 1 kura kaupapa Māori in the Eastern Bay of Plenty with 84 students who came from a community of 40 families.

Results: Narratives of experience

Part of a narrative from one of the kura is presented below to exemplify what the practices looked like when there were challenges; for example, challenges with a student's behaviour. This was a common problem that appeared across the kura, but it was often more frequent when new students were transitioning into the kura from other schools, often with the kura seen as their last hope. The principal begins by stating what she believes is important:

> … making mistakes is not an issue, it's waiho oku whenu, mauria mai oku painga—heed not my weaknesses, but heed to my strengths, and together we will learn. Yeah we've made plenty of mistakes. Hell who doesn't? (Principal)

Communication with whānau was understood as essential if a collaborative, potential-focused solution was to emerge.

> We talk to parents about that when we have raruraru [problems]. It's not focussed on the negativity of the issue. The kōrero is focused on what can we do together to help as a whānau to move forward, and we're going through that one right now with a couple of issues and so we're meeting with parents. It's a big people thing, so we're going to be meeting with parents next week and we're going out to the various people in our community, and saying, 'Hey we all got to be on this waka [canoe], or else we're not going to do it together', so we do a lot of talk with our whānau. (Principal)

---

2   In New Zealand, schools are categorised by decile. Deciles are determined by a range of socio-economic factors, with 10 being the most socioeconomically advantaged decile and 1 the lowest.

This type of response was verified by a mother who had enrolled her son in this kura. She talked about the difference this type of response had made for her and for her son. She explained that her son had been going through a whole host of behavioural issues and that she had been looking for a new place to enrol him.

> When both my son and I came in touch with this kura I decided to try and work it out for him. He was working with SES [Specialist Education Services] prior to that, special education, that sort of thing. He had behavioural problems quite bad, dysfunctional, and he just had a whole list of problems that he was going through at the time. (Māmā)

She recalls the differences that were immediately evident.

> From the time that he started here, it's been a hard journey it hasn't been all good, but just to now, his wairua, his spirit, his self-esteem, his confidence and his learning has just lifted. He got stood down for fighting at the last school, and the other boy that was in the fight never got stood down, but my boy got stood down. I didn't think that was fair or that he was dealt with fairly. The kids knew that he was different and he felt he was different, so whenever he got upset or angry, his SES teacher would just jump in and make arrangements for him or movements for him that tended to his needs. He knew that and he would use that to his advantage. I felt he could never just settle in, whereas here, he was given the opportunity to settle in. (Māmā)

She then discusses the changes that the new kura had been able to bring about for her son.

> He believes in himself, he is more confident, he's more responsible and the actions that he takes now, he realises the outcomes can be detrimental to him and to those around him. I believe that this school has encouraged him to, maybe not as far as the system goes with his academic side yet, but more with his spiritual side, and this one on one, which does really nurture him. And I'll say that for all of them. He had one teacher working with him when he started at this school, he just fell in love with her, so there was a connection with him straight away. (Māmā)

She reflected on how this school had responded to her son.

> Ooh he never had this at any other kura that he's been enrolled in. This is how I feel personally in this town. He's been to three other mainstream schools and then here. I just believe they gave him love, they gave him a side that the other schools were too set in their mainstream systems ways to see that there were reasons why this boy was doing what he was doing, and they were willing to dig that bit harder to find the good in him. I believe that they dealt to a side that my boy hasn't felt since we lived up North, and we came from a small place up North, and the teaching up there is done on a one to one. He pretty well much found it here, you know, they took him and realised that he was quarrelsome and they pretty much took him on as being part of their own, not just as a child they were going to isolate him from the rest of the school. (Māmā)

She also recalls what it had been like at some of the other schools.

> It just felt like a job interview going into a mainstream kura. It didn't feel real, it felt like he was just a number. There was no personal touch, yeah just put in the paper work and filed away. They didn't do that here. They went the extra mile to make sure that his needs were dealt to in every way that they possibly could address and that was a big difference. Very informal, very much tikanga Māori, yeah, the comparison between us and mainstream. The interest and the love that they give out is just part of their kaupapa.

> You don't get that in the mainstream, you just don't. They can be just as loving and kind, and I'm not radical, I'm just saying it for what it is, but at the end of the day I felt that you were just part of the system, you were just a number and you were filed away like anything else. This is why a lot of our Māori people get upset, because my partner is a Mob member. This is why he wanted to go down and kill the principal in those other schools, yeah do a spinout. But in here, it's completely different. Here they feel you before they see you, you are part of them, and that makes a big difference for your child. You know that your child's wairua is going to be dealt to on a daily basis, and that's what he needs to grow, yeah, and that's him.

What they have done for him here at school hasn't just affected him at school, but he's brought that behaviour home. They just love and care for him and listen to him. Gee if you'd seen him two years ago, you wouldn't have thought he was the same kid. Honestly, he never lasted at school until lunch time without getting into a fight or without giving a couple of kids a hiding, or without getting into some sort of trouble or putting a hole in the wall. He's just not the same child at all, at all. If somebody had said this to me a year and half ago, I would have thought I had faith, but I don't know whether you could work miracles that fast with him. But he was just adamant that this is the way that I am, handle it or get out of my face, this is how I'm going to be.

They've dealt to him in a way that—you can't put it down on a piece of paper in a mainstream school and file it away, because it's not something that can be done just like that, they've just turned him right around. I mean, but my son has just floated through it all. Because it's completely different here, they feel you before they see you, you are part of them and that makes a big difference for your child. You know that your child's wairua is going to be dealt to on a daily basis and that's what he needs to grow. The love and spiritual healing that they've given to him. You can't put that down on a piece of paper. It's been an awesome, enriching loving and fulfilling journey that will give him tools for the rest of his life I suppose. (Māmā)

The son adds his thoughts to these experiences and explains why he thinks the changes have come about.

Student: They understand me and they just understand me better than all the other schools … all the teachers listen to what you have to say. Yeah. Māori helped me.

Researcher: So you're not naughty anymore?

Student: Nah, I just changed when I came here in the last year.

Researcher: Oh yeah, why?

Student: Big change! Because of the teachers, they listen. The other school they just used to ring up my mum and just send me home, because I hit people but they didn't listen to my reasons why I hit them, but not here.

Findings

A shared understanding of the outcomes from this research saw support for an existing model and the emergence of a new model. Durie's (1985) Whare Tapa Whā model was supported by stories across the kura validating the importance of each dimension.

Te taha wairua

Parents spoke of the spiritual dimension as contributing to the holistic stability and development of their children. While the spiritual dimension relates to the spiritual inner presence of a person, they also identified within this element attributes such as heightened self-esteem and confidence. They conceded that while the spiritual dimension came in many forms, all of these forms had positive effects on the attitude and confidence of tamariki (*tama*, child/children, of the *ariki*, gods) to attend and engage. For example, the mother from the story above talked about the sense of love and support these teachers shared with and for her son and how this had promoted inclusiveness and a sense of belonging for him. This parent had witnessed the ability of this kura to engage at different levels with her child, thus developing in him a sense of value towards his own spirituality. This parent understood that until her son's wairua was intact, his learning would continue to be jeopardised.

All kura were building strong relationships among their students and whānau, recognising the importance of acknowledgement and encouragement to one's personal development. Encouragement was carried through to the homes, thus ensuring whānau were involved as well. Establishing grounds for personal growth and spirituality also came with leadership roles and responsibilities, such as when the older students within the kura were expected to be good role models and act as tuakana for the younger students. Parents were assured that their child's strengths and qualities were being supported and reinforced, and in turn their sense of spiritual wellbeing.

Te taha whānau

The whānau or social dimension within these kura could be seen in the strong relationships that were established, some of which were strengthened through whakapapa, others by parents who had attended the same kura as the students themselves. Some even saw their children's attendance at the school as fulfilling a family tradition. An extension of this relationship was the links that had been forged in the previous century by their hapū and iwi ancestors, leaving the responsibilities, as mana whenua or guardians of the land, over the school for future generations. Parents were quick to identify the genealogical ties to both the kura and the land upon which these were located.

Whanaungatanga was identified as the driving force behind establishing effective sustainable relationships among the kura, the students and their whānau. Lines of communication were kept open and clear so that whānau members were always consulted and their contributions always respected. Whānau endorsed efforts to involve them with the education of their children over everyday things as well as important issues and at times of trauma. The ability of kura to engage openly and honestly with whānau when circumstances and events become challenging was of great importance, along with taking affirmative action towards finding effective, culturally appropriate solutions to problems that arose.

Te taha hinengaro

By focusing on the strengths of every pupil, rather than on weaknesses, each kura was able to fully stimulate and connect to their students' intellectual wellbeing. Whānau held the intellectual and mental wellbeing of their children in the highest regard. They spoke about how the curriculum and the pedagogical practices that were currently being used by the teachers in each kura were grounded in the culture of their children, thus building on their children's prior knowledge and experiences. All emphasised the importance of the Māori language and associated traditions as foundational, even in the kura that were required to teach the curriculum through both the Māori and English languages. Teachers provided cultural contexts for learning that had a positive effect on the students' willingness to learn and resulted in parents understanding that their children felt valued.

Te taha tinana

Parents associated physical wellbeing directly with how their child felt and how they behaved within the school grounds and in the wider community. Parents spoke honestly and frankly about their children. They explained that their children's behaviour affected how they were perceived by others. Most family members interviewed talked about how when their children experienced problems with their learning, they had been able to work with the school to improve their child's learning. A grandfather who had taken custody of his two mokopuna when their own parents found this too challenging, talked frankly about how working with this kura had been for him and for his mokopuna. While some of his ideas may have implied a harsh parenting style, many of his contributions were perceptive and deep. He believed that behaviour should not just be extrinsically rewarded, and that some jobs were done as part of fulfilling one's basic requirements for food and shelter. He spoke of being called in to school to deal with the physical confrontations when his mokopuna got into arguments and fights with other students. Together, he and the kura had found their own way of maintaining the physical and intellectual dimensions, and the wairua, of all students.

Te Mataora: An emerging model

The emerging model was named Te Mataora, which literally means the living face. Te Mataora was the name of the first Māori human to receive the moko. This full facial adornment traditionally marked the time when an individual had attained the utmost in personal identity and integrity and was seen by others to have reached, or be reaching, their potential. Thus in naming it Te Mataora it was understood that this model would provide an interactive way of instilling the tamariki with cultural identity and integrity through experiences unique to a Māori world view, which would then equip them to participate more effectively in education and within the global community.

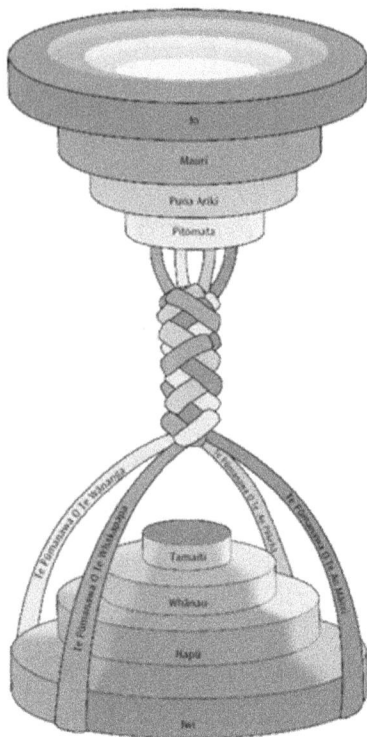

Figure 3.1. Te Mataora

These components are now described using some of the particular theorising and metaphors that emerged at the noho marae with kura whānau as the discussions went on long into the night.

The lower view

From the lower view, the tamaiti, supported by his or her whānau, hapū and iwi, is central to this model (see Figure 3.1). *Tamaiti* is the Māori word for child. Composed from two words (tama and iti), *tama* stands for Tama-Nui-Te-Ra, the Sun, while *iti* means small. Given that the Sun is positioned at the centre of the solar system, the child can also be seen as occupying this position (Pere, 1982), thereby, from a Māori perspective, demonstrating the central importance of the child.

All aspects of the development of the tamaiti—the cultural, spiritual, intellectual, emotional and social needs—are strongly influenced by the tamaiti's whānau. In these kura, whānau were understood to be not only their parents, caregivers and extended families but also their teachers and other kura members. Similarly, whānau were understood to be influenced by their relationships and interactions with their hapū, and the hapū in turn were influenced by their relationships and interactions with their iwi.

The upper view

Directly above these four elements, and joined to the base by four interconnected strands, is another set of four elements: pitomata, puna ariki, mauri and Io (see Figure 3.1). Milroy (2004) explains pitomata as relating to the face of the unborn child, for it is at this stage of life, before birth, that our potential is hidden and untapped. Next, puna ariki are the springs used by the gods for cleansing and purification. Spiritually and metaphorically, puna ariki are available still when tested or faced with challenges. Mauri is the life force sourced from and placed by Io within all living and non-living things. Thus, mauri is the energy that binds a person's spirit to their mind and body, allowing all things to flourish within the confines of their own being. The uppermost element is Io, representative of ngā atua (the gods), both the origin and originator of all things.

Shirres (2000) contends that the world of the gods is not separated from the world of humanity, while Marsden (1977) suggests "a two-world system in which the material proceeds from the spiritual, and the spiritual (which is the higher order) interpenetrates the material physical world of Te Ao Mārama" (p. 160). Within this world, all things possess a mauri or life essence, and because the physical state is complemented by a spiritual state, any distinctions between inanimate and animate objects are blurred (Durie, 2001). Just as the guardians of old had a role to protect and care for their own domains, human beings are now a part of this interacting network of inter-related elements that must be maintained in balance for future generations (Durie, 2001).

Ngā pūmanawa: Connecting the two

Within this context, the emphasis and priorities in education were activated by four pūmanawa that provide essential life-links from the past to the present, from the spiritual world to the world of people. These pūmanawa provide the ongoing inextricable links for each tamaiti— from their spirituality, through their many different whānau/educators, to the development of their learning pathway and thus to their potential for achievement. These pūmanawa are:

- te pūmanawa o te ao Māori (the Māori world)
- te pūmanawa o te whakapapa (genealogy and other connections)
- te pūmanawa o te wānanga (teaching and learning)
- te pūmanawa o te ao Pākehā (the Pākehā world).

All things within a Māori world view (te pūmanawa o te ao Māori) are understood to have spiritual origins and direct connections to Io, from whence all things were created and have since been developed.

Whakapapa (te pūmanawa o te whakapapa) represents the genealogical descent of Māori from the divine sources of creation. Whakapapa establishes whānau and personal identity, status and connectedness. It also provides permission to access certain ancestral knowledge and to participate fully in cultural activities.

Wānanga (te pūmanawa o te wānanga), according to its most traditional definition, represents all knowledge and the means of preserving, building upon and sharing knowledge. The Pākehā world (te pumanawa o te ao Pākehā) is the world view outside te ao Māori and is often referred to as Western society in the widest sense.

It was the interconnection of the spiritual world with the world of people via these four pūmanawa, and their integration in theory and in practice by the whānau in each kura, that resulted in the effective educational practices and outcomes for all concerned, but especially for each tamaiti and their whānau.

Discussion

It was clear that across the four kura a number of essential understandings from within a Māori world view, and embedded in te reo Māori and the metaphors and understandings of Māori, had emerged (Berryman, Glynn, Togo, & McDonald, 2004). Many parents talked about the challenges they had faced with their children at other schools, and how their children's standing in education had been given a new lease of life in these kura. Students with special education needs were perceived as being able to be supported, not only by the kura but also by their whānau and wider communities. These students were perceived as able to be included. At each kura, all members took collective, whānau-like responsibility for initiating collaborative actions to support all students. Education and special education were viewed in a holistic manner that was grounded upon Māori beliefs and principles. When it was deemed necessary, these practices also incorporated a Western, Pākehā perspective. These practices were found to be inclusive of all students in the kura, no matter what the circumstances were, as well as students who were yet to arrive from kōhanga reo or from mainstream primary schools. Inclusive practices also included providing ongoing support for students after they had left the kura to attend wharekura or any other secondary schools.

The students themselves, their whānau and their educators all brought their own expertise, both in defining the problem and also in developing solutions. Problems therefore generated collaborative, culturally appropriate and interdependent responses. Although people from these kura faced many different challenges, their collective approach to problem solving led to more innovative and effective outcomes.

Implications for working with Māori

There are four important trends internationally in the context of special education.

1. Schools are having to respond to challenges from students of increasing diversity.

2. Inclusive education practices are requiring an increasing proportion of these students to be educated in regular education settings.

3. There is a major shift in locating the causes of (and therefore the responses to) students' learning and behavioural difficulties away from the students themselves, their families and their communities, and towards the day-to-day relationships and interactions they experience in the learning contexts in which they find themselves.

4. However, while inclusive education approaches avoid characterising and labelling students on the basis of deficits and difficulties, governments and school systems still make funding and support available under these types of criteria. The rhetoric leans towards inclusion, but the resourcing remains tied to labelled categories.

In addition, the research literature on special education is strangely silent on the issue of culture and its impact on inclusion. Māori traditionally have a culture that is based on inclusion, and a collective approach to learning and teaching that values the contribution of all. In this way collective responsibility can be taken for meeting intellectual, physical and spiritual needs and the need to be connected and included within whānau. This research strongly suggests that many Māori communities already have effective solutions for assessing and meeting the needs of their own children, and that they also have the capacity to find new solutions as required. Within a model of relational care and connectedness, power sharing and collaboration in these kura were largely able to determine who would participate and how.

This research suggests that these practices for Māori are more likely to result in the goals Durie (2001, 2004) defined for success in education for Māori: all Māori students are able to live as Māori, to participate actively as citizens of the world, and to have good levels of health and a high standard of living. By listening to these communities rather than telling, we may all stand to benefit more.

Study questions

1. How might understandings from a Māori world view both support yet also confuse some educators? What advice would you give? What questions would you pose?

2. These kura, their whānau members and communities were seen as inextricably inter-related. What have you learnt from this theorising? What do you still want to know?

3. Why do you think one of the implications of this chapter is to listen to these communities rather than tell? What might lie behind this?

References

Berryman, M. (2008). *Repositioning within indigenous discourses of transformation and self-determination.* Unpublished doctoral thesis, University of Waikato.

Berryman, M., Glynn, T., Togo, T., & McDonald, S. (2004). *Akoranga whakarei: Enhancing effective practices in special education: Findings from four kura rumaki.* Report to Ministry of Education, Group Special Education. Wellington: Ministry of Education.

Bishop, R. (1996). *Whakawhanaungatanga: Collaborative research stories.* Palmerston North: Dunmore Press.

Bishop, R. (2005). Freeing ourselves from neo-colonial domination in research: A kaupapa Māori approach to creating knowledge. In N. Denzin & Y. Lincoln (Eds.), *Handbook of qualitative research* (3rd ed., pp. 109–138). Thousand Oaks, CA: Sage Publications.

Bishop, R., Berryman, M., & Richardson, C. (2001). *Te toi huarewa: Effective teaching and learning strategies, and effective teaching materials for improving the reading and writing in te reo Māori of students aged five to nine in Māori-medium education.* Wellington: Ministry of Education.Durie, M. H. (1985). A Māori perspective of health. *Social Science Medical, 20*(5), 483–486.

Durie, M. H. (2001). *A framework for considering Māori educational advancement.* Opening address at the Hui Taumata Mātauranga, Taupo.

Durie, M. H. (2004). *Māori achievement: Anticipating the learning environment.* Paper presented at the Hui Taumata Mātauranga IV, Taupo.

Durie, M. (2012). Kaupapa Māori: Shifting the social [interview]. *New Zealand Journal of Educational Studies, 47*(2), 21–29.

Marsden, M. (1977). God, man and universe: A Māori view. In M. King (Ed.), *Te ao hurihuri: The world moves on* (pp. 143–163). Wellington: Methuen Publications.

Milroy, W. (2004). He momo whakapuakitanga. In J. C. Moorfield (Ed.), *Te Whanake 4: Te Kōhure* (2nd ed.). Auckland: Longman / Pearson Education.

Ministry of Education. (2003). *Nga haeata mātauranga: Annual report on Māori education 2001/2002 and direction for 2003.* Wellington: Ministry of Education, Group Māori.

Ministry of Education. (2005). *2004 ngā haeata mātauranga: Annual report on Māori education.* Wellington: Author.

Pere, R. (1982). *Ako: Concepts and learning in the Māori tradition.* Working paper No.17. Hamilton: University of Waikato.

Shirres, M. P. (2000). *Te tangata: The human person.* Auckland: Accent Publications.

Smith, L. T. (2012). *Decolonizing methodologies research and indigenous peoples* (2nd ed.). London & New York: Zed Books.

Chapter 4

Tātau tātau: Engaging with whānau hauā from within a cultural framework

Huhana Hickey

He waka eke noa.

A canoe which we are all in with no exception.

Introduction

The history of disability discourse has not included diversity of identity, including indigenous people's identity, hence the focus of this chapter. Law, policy and practice on disability have always been developed from within a homogeneous framework and constructed with a focus on the individual rather than the family. This approach does not easily incorporate identities that come from collective non-Westernised frameworks, such as indigenous and some other minority identities. The Māori disability identity paradigm in relation to non-disabled Māori needs exploring. This chapter introduces the term *whānau hauā*, which better reflects Māori disability identity in te reo.

This chapter discusses Māori disability identity and looks at eight specific disability models. It then examines a number of Māori models of wellbeing and discusses their suitability as models of wellbeing for whānau hauā. Finally, the tātau tātau framework is examined as a means of incorporating the needs of whānau hauā when working with them. The tātau tātau framework recognises te ao Māori (the Māori world view) as the foundation for whānau hauā identity.

Māori disability identity

Defining whānau hauā

Whānau hauā, as a term unique to Māori, was given by a Tūhoe kaumātua to Tania Kingi, the kaiwhakahaere of Te Rōpū Waiora, to explain Māori with disabilities from a Māori world view. The phrase whānau hauā provides Māori with disabilities with a non-Westernised umbrella term that does not incorporate the negative connotations of the word *disability*. Whānau hauā is also a term that implies a collective identity rather than the Western individualised terms used to describe disability.

The term *whānau hauā* derives from the word *hau*, or wind. The wind can be a breeze, a gale or a cyclone. Depending on the mood of Tāwhiri-mātea (god of wind), the wind can change the environment and make it unstable. Whānau often struggle to bring the balance back to the environment and to their lives. The balance is dependent on the efforts of the whānau collectively, and not on the individual alone.

The whānau hauā concept is similar to the Western social model of disabilities, whereby the barriers are caused by society and not the individual with disabilities. The term whānau hauā, however, includes the additional dimension of whānau working together to restore the balance.

The difference between disability and whānau hauā identity

While whānau hauā and the social model concept of disability are similar, as noted above, whānau hauā differs in that it highlights the role whānau play in the lives of Māori with disabilities rather than the preferred individual concept adopted by non-indigenous people with disabilities. This is consistent with Māori concepts of a collective identity rather than individual identity. Māori have a place of belonging through whakapapa within their iwi, hapū and whānau, and it is within these three identities that whānau hauā also have a role. Since colonisation these roles appear to have diminished. Whānau hauā also differs in that it gives a specific indigenous identity to the term 'disability', thereby giving a non-Western identity that does not come from a paradigm of discrimination.

The disability models

To understand the importance of this new identity given by Māori for Māori, we need to explore the disability models as they currently exist in policy and practice in Aotearoa / New Zealand. The question that remains is whether they adequately meet the needs of whānau hauā and their wellbeing within their whānau, hapū and iwi.

There are eight distinct disability models, which reflect changing societal attitudes.

- The tragic/pity/charity model sees people with disabilities as tragic victims. We often see this model portrayed in fundraising advertising for disability organisations, where a child with disabilities is used to induce people to give to the charity. People with disabilities are not seen as valued individuals but as something to pity, to be afraid of, or even to shun (Shakespeare, Mercer, & Barnes, 1999; Wendell, 1996).

- The religious/moral model views disability as a punishment or infliction on the individual and/or family from an external force. Sometimes the disability inflicts a lower status on the whole family, affecting their standing in their community. Psychosocial conditions may be seen as being the result of 'evil spirits'. The disability is inevitably seen as the result of a sin or indiscretion caused by the individual and/or their family, hence the rationale for punishing, isolating or even excluding the individual and their family from their community (Clapton & Fitzgerald, 1997).

- The medical model argues that disability results from an individual's physical or mental limitations. The disability is largely unconnected to the social or geographical environments. It is sometimes referred to as the biological-inferiority or functional-limitation model (Campbell & Oliver, 1996; Clapton & Fitzgerald, 1997).

- The expert/professional and rehabilitation model is an arm of the medical model, which views the impairment as the identifying factor, with the provider being the fixer of the situation and the fixee being passive and accepting the paternalism imposed on them (Clapton & Fitzgerald, 1997). The disability is seen as a deficiency, with the only way of fixing the problem being the engagement of a professional (Campbell & Oliver, 1996; Clapton & Fitzgerald, 1997).

- The economic model is based on the level or lack of productivity of people with disabilities in the workforce. This is primarily exemplified by policy framed around economic development and the limited role of people with disabilities (Charlton, 2000).

- The social model identifies disability as a consequence of environmental, societal and attitudinal factors (Campbell & Oliver, 1996; Corker & Shakespeare, 2002; Oliver, 1990; Shakespeare, 1998; Shakespeare et al., 1999).

- The customer/empowering model is the opposite of the professional/expert model, with the professional working alongside the client and not making the decisions for the client (Corker & Shakespeare, 2002; Oliver, 1996).

- The rights-based model conceptualises disability as a socio-political construct within a rights-based discourse. It is based on the social model of disability. The focus shifts from dependence to independence and bases itself within a political civil rights framework challenging ableism, racism and sexism (Breslin & Lee, 2002; Lawson & Gooding, 2005; Oliver, 1990, 1996; Shakespeare, 1998; Shakespeare et al., 1999).

There are clear themes running through these models, which show an evolution from the paternalistic, deficit and blaming approaches to disability, to a civil rights, empowerment approach which challenges attitudes and involves including people with disabilities into society (Clapton & Fitzgerald, 1997; Corker & Shakespeare, 2002; Oliver, 1990, 1996). The approach of the rights-based model, while focusing on inclusion, is individualistic, favouring independence over dependence without the acknowledgement of interdependence. Conversely, indigenous identity emphasises the central role through interdependence and empowering the role that whānau relationships play in the individual's wellbeing (Lapsley, Nikora, & Black, 2002).

In Aotearoa / New Zealand a mixture of models is used. For example, while the social model of disability is widely advocated by government agencies, service providers such as Support Link NZ still utilise the medical/rehabilitation/professional models when providing services to clients with disabilities, and the rights-based model when advocating for individuals with disabilities. The issue of collective identity, as applicable to indigenous people with disabilities, is seldom addressed, if at all, in any of these models.

The question can also be asked about whether the prevalent social model of disability is suitable for looking at certain groups within the community given their existing marginalised status and lack of identity within society. While the social model does recognise society's attitudinal barriers towards disability, it does not address cultural specificity in relation to impairment, and without this it is difficult for whānau hauā to achieve full inclusion in their own community and society in general. Despite the social model being promoted in policy development relating to disability, the issues for whānau hauā and the growing gaps they experience remain unresolved.

Māori health models: Are they inclusive of whānau hauā?

There are no disability models for whānau hauā identity. There are, however, several Māori health and wellbeing models (Nikora, Karapu, Hickey, & Te Awekotuku, 2004). The three most commonly known and utilised Māori health models are Whare Tapa Whā, Te Wheke and Ngā Pou Mana. Other models used in developing the framework for promoting and monitoring Māori health are Te Pae Mahutonga and Te Rōpū Awhina o Tokanui.

Te Pae Mahutonga (the Southern Cross) was developed by Durie (ALAC, 2003) to provide a framework for Māori health promotion. The four components of this model are:

- te ao Māori—the Māori world (Mauri Ora—Breath of Life)
- environmental protection (Waiora—Healthy Water)
- healthy lifestyle (Toiora)
- participation in society (Te Oranga) (ALAC, 2003).

These four elements provide significant steps towards good Māori health (ALAC, 2003). This model is utilised in providing psychosocial services, particularly in the field of alcohol and drug services.

Te Rōpū Awhina o Tokanui was developed at Tokanui Hospital (which closed in the 1990s) in 1986 by a group of Māori health professionals. This model was aimed, in particular, at providing good psychiatric nursing care to Māori mental health patients. The elements contained in this model derive from the four elements of Durie's Whare Tapa Whā model. The remaining elements are:

- taha whenua (environment)
- taha tikanga (compliance)
- Māoritanga (old world)
- Pākehātanga (new world)
- taha tangata (self) (Durie, 1994).

Although these two models are designed for psychosocial, drug and alcohol services, they each have elements of the three more commonly used Māori health models.

It becomes clear that a problem exists in disability policy for Māori when trying to define concepts within a Pākehā/Westernised disability framework. A framework for monitoring and measuring whānau hauā wellbeing within a Māori conceptual paradigm could address this.

The problem in relation to whānau, disability and wellbeing concepts is the lack of work undertaken so far that incorporates the construct of disability from within a Māori identity framework. While Māori health models are appropriate for measuring Māori wellbeing, they lack the inclusion factor when addressing the issues for whānau hauā. It is one thing to have the right terminologies and theories when trying to implement policy, but the reality of that implementation and the results appear to be very different, thus demanding an investigation into why whānau hauā are not achieving equity of health with non-Māori with disabilities. As identified earlier, and discussed below, there are three main Māori health models utilised in services providing health and disability supports to whānau hauā.

Te Whare Tapa Whā

Te Whare Tapa Whā, designed and outlined by Professor Mason Durie, is the most commonly cited model in Māori health and development policies. At a health hui in Palmerston North in 1982 Durie presented the Whare Tapa Whā model as a four-part framework resembling the four walls of a whare (house). This analogy was made to ensure strength and symmetry, thereby giving balance in the wellbeing of the individual and the community. The four dimensions are:

- taha wairua (the spiritual side)
- taha hinengaro (thoughts and feelings)
- taha tinana (the physical side)
- taha whānau (family) (Durie, 1994, p.70).

Integration is another theme Durie identified in the Whare Tapa Whā model, in that individual health is dependent on the ability of the whānau to be well. This concept is not always clearly outlined in policy and is not clearly identified within disability policy. Although whānau are mentioned in policy, it is not as integrative or inclusive as would be considered by Māori for the wellbeing of the whānau hauā member.

Te Wheke

Another model of Māori health is Te Wheke, which was discussed by Rangimarie Rose Pere at the Hui Whakaoranga in 1984. Te Wheke (the octopus) looks at Māori health mainly from a Māori whānau perspective. Although this model relates to wellbeing within education, it is relevant to health and possibly disability wellbeing for Māori in that it is easily adaptable to the subject matter at hand. Each of the eight tentacles of the octopus contains a symbol of a particular dimension of health, with the body and head of the octopus symbolising the family unit. The tentacles attached to the head and body symbolise the inter-connection of each dimension as it relates to the family.

The different dimensions of wellbeing are:

- wairuatanga (spirituality)
- tinana (body)
- hinengaro (mind)
- whānaungatanga (family relationships)
- mana atua ake (ancestral link)
- mauri (life force)

- whatumanawa (seat of emotions, heart, mind)
- hā a koro mā a kui mā (breath of life from forebears).

Each dimension or tentacle is important in considering the wellbeing of the individual. The eyes of the octopus represent the waiora or wellbeing of the person: it is this that can identify the state of the individual (Pere, 1985). Each tentacle has its own function or role and, while each is independent, it is important to note the interdependence again with this model, as with Te Whare Tapa Whā, in that each has an independent, yet connected, role to the whānau and to the individual.

A review of Pere's model shows how the eight tentacles all have a role to play in relation to the wellness of whānau hauā, and it is apparent that these tentacles are often severed by non-Māori with disabilities and non-Māori generally, who deny aspects of wellbeing for whānau hauā simply through denying them access to their whānau, whenua, reo and other elements that make up their identity as Māori. Both Te Wheke and Te Whare Tapa Whā contain elements of whānau and environment that are also key parts of whānau hauā wellbeing.

Ngā Pou Mana

In 1988 the Royal Commission on Social Policy described another set of values and beliefs—four supports, Ngā Pou Mana—as prerequisites for health and wellbeing. Ngā Pou Mana is another model that has interacting dimensions as the key to wellbeing. This model concentrates on the dimensions of mana, cultural integrity, a sound economic base, and a sense of confidence and continuity. This model has a greater emphasis on the external environment and the significance of oral tradition as the stabilising influence. Originally Ngā Pou Mana was developed to examine the foundations for social policies and social wellbeing, but it still has significance for health because it outlines four supports for social wellbeing:

- family (whanaungatanga)
- cultural heritage (taonga tuku iho)
- the physical presence (te ao turoa)
- an indisputable land base (tūrangawaewae).

The emphasis on environment is thought to have been influenced by the Waitangi Tribunal's decisions regarding claims relating to the pollution of tribal waterways. These claims recognised that a clean environment is important for wellbeing (Royal Commission on Social Policy, 1988). There appear to be few studies looking at whether introduced chemicals have affected Māori physiology in any way. Human waste put into the moana (ocean) and awa (river) is also an issue for many Māori, and though this practice has reduced, it has not been stopped completely around the country and is still polluting and affecting the environment where Māori get their food. The Waikato River is an example of a polluted river (often from fall-out from farms and factories adjacent to the river) and of a river that is also central to an iwi (Tainui). If the river is unhealthy, then it makes sense that the people who have a close affinity to that river are also likely to be unhealthy.[1]

Comparing the Māori models

The easiest way to compare Te Whare Tapa Whā, Te Wheke and Ngā Pou Mana is through Table 4.1 (based on Durie, 1994, p. 77).

	Whare Tapa Whā	Te Wheke	Ngā Pou Mana
Components	Wairua Hinengaro Tinana Whānau	Wairuatanga Hinengaro Tinana Whanaungatanga Mana ake Mauri Hā a koro mā a kui mā	Whanaungatanga Taonga tuku iho Te ao tūroa Tūrangawaewae
Features	Spirituality Mental health Physical health Family	Spirituality Mental health Physical health Family Uniqueness Vitality Cultural heritage Emotions	Family Cultural heritage Environment Land base
Symbolism	A strong house	The octopus	Supporting structures

Table 4.1. Māori health perspectives— the three models

---

1 Landcare research (http://landcareresearch.co.nz) has submitted various reports on the state of the waterways in New Zealand, with Waikato being one of those waterways. In December 2006 Raglan experienced a broken sewerage pipe, which caused sewage to flow into the sea, affecting the shellfish. Other reports can be found at http//:www.nzherald.co.nz

As previously stated, none of the models specifically address the wellbeing of whānau hauā. Although the existing models can be fitted into a disability framework, some of their structures could clash with the social model of disability preferred by the current government in developing policy for people with disabilities in New Zealand. To understand these possible clashes, it is worth noting that there appears to be a monocultural approach to disability in policy, and this further compounds the issues for whānau hauā.

Towards a whānau hauā model of wellbeing—tātau tātau

In developing a whānau hauā model of wellbeing, it is important to consider the models of Māori wellbeing discussed previously and to take into account other models and frameworks that outline kaupapa Māori principles. One promising approach is the Tātau Tātau framework, developed by Māori and used by Collins and Hickey (2006). Tātau Tātau includes a set of core Māori values for explaining how whānau hauā is placed within a Māori world view rather than a Pākehā world view. The Tātau Tātau framework has two dimensions. The first dimension focuses on the person with a disability and his or her relationship with the whānau. It includes the components of: whanaungatanga, mana, te oranga hinengaro and taha tinana. This dimension places the individual at the centre, looking outward towards the whānau and beyond.

The second dimension places the whānau at the centre and looks at how it maintains its wellbeing. The components within this dimension are: manaakitanga; tātau, tātau; wairuatanga; mana tiaki; and ngā taonga tuku iho (Collins & Hickey, 2006, p. 12).

It is clear that Māori values form the basis for explaining a Māori world view. They provide the concepts, principles and lore Māori use in everyday life to varying degrees, affecting their interaction with others and governing responsibilities and the relationship with both the natural and supernatural world. Metge (1995) outlines in more depth some of these essential Māori values that help strengthen whānau, however it is defined. These values, which are integral to the Tātau Tātau framework, are explained below.

- *Aroha*—love (in all its permutations), longing, closely associated with kinship ties and the caring acts expected to be performed towards kinsfolk, especially in times of sickness, need or trouble (Metge, 1995, p. 11).

- *Whanaungatanga*—kinship in its widest sense. The value of whanaungatanga reinforces the commitment members of a whānau have to each other, but also reminds them of their responsibilities to all their other relatives. This imperative of extending aroha to all whanaunga ensures that every whānau is embedded in a web of cross-cutting kinship ties (ibid., p. 82).

- *Taha wairua, taha tinana*—the spiritual and physical dimensions complete and enrich each other. What is most valued is the connection and appropriate balance between them (ibid., p. 82).

- *Tapu and noa*—*tapu* often attracts public attention and respect but is closely associated with danger, anxiety and restrictions on freedom of action, within the limits of tikanga. *Noa* is the opposite of tapu in that it is the opposite of sacred. Noa, once tapu is lifted now is the state that takes over which is free from the limitation and extensions of tapu (ibid, p. 85).

- *Ora*—life of a special quality (i.e., energised life). It is life in all its fullness (ibid., p. 86).

- *Tika, tikanga, pono and te tika*— these terms refer to what is right. *Tikanga* refers to doing the right thing in a given situation. *Pono* relates to being true, genuine and loyal in relations to others. This latter quality is reserved for those in leadership positions within the whānau. *Tika* means to be fair, upright and honest. *Te tika* means the fairness, the honesty, the uprightness (ibid., p. 87).

- *Mana*—this word has various meanings. It is "divine power made manifest in the world of human experience. Individuals and groups have mana. This is a combination of mana acquired by inheritance from ancestors (mana tūpuna), by direct contact with the supernatural (mana atua) and as a result of human achievement (mana tangata). The store of mana is not fixed but it is … affected by the holder's behaviour, by the actions of others and by the vicissitudes of life" (ibid., p. 88).

- *Mahi a-ngakau*—work done from the heart (ibid., p. 98).

- *Utu*—the principle that anything received should be requited appropriately. It is essential to the management of internal relations. Recipients of affection, approval, support, care, protection and respect from other whānau members are under an obligation to reciprocate in kind and to do so generously, without counting the cost. The returns made are widely distributed to the giver's close kin and descendants, to those in need, and to whānau members as a group (ibid., p. 101).

- *Kotahitanga*—oneness or unity that is achieved when whānau members invest time and energy into getting to know one another in order to work through differences. It also means accepting responsibility for each other's actions (ibid., p. 102).

- *Relations with outsiders*—whānau members recognise a collective responsibility to reciprocate the help received from other groups. They also recognise a collective responsibility to their own group, to secure compensation for insult or injury by others (ibid., p. 102).

There are also a number of duties that are part of the Tātau Tātau framework. There is the duty to:

- support one another in good times and bad
- care for one another, which includes meeting the physical needs of others as well as the need to be nurtured mentally and spiritually
- protect one another against physical and spiritual attack
- work together for the common good
- value and cherish those of the most senior generation (ibid., p. 100).

These principles provide a framework within which whānau hauā can develop an indigenous-specific model that fits perfectly within both an individualistic identity construct and a collective identity that meets the needs of whānau hauā and does not have the negative connotations attached to the word 'disability' that mainstream Westernised models all have—whether they are based on the medical model, social model or human-rights empowerment model. The term 'disability' cannot escape its negative meanings, and even claiming the word in a positive sense still lends its negative identity to all things to do with disability.

Whānau hauā claim their whakapapa as the centre of their identity.

Non-Māori with disabilities don't frame their identity in the same way, and therefore will always struggle with an identity that is a socially constructed political one. Whānau hauā, however, have the comfort of knowing they belong within their whānau identity and that their impairment is simply a natural part of who they are—nothing more and nothing less. Non-Māori often don't have that same support from whānau or even consider whānau a relevant part of their disability identity. This is the key difference between Māori and non-Māori, where priorities differ in relation to how they see the role of whānau in their lives. Tātau tātau is not a new concept, yet it is one that can give a clear framework to an identity largely hidden within Māori society. The disability community talks of rights and responsibilities; tātau tātau provides a framework within which to work to provide an inclusive environment for whānau hauā.

Conclusion

No whānau hauā model has been developed, and Māori models of wellbeing have not developed in over 10 years. This provides Aotearoa / New Zealand with the opportunity to lead the world in developing indigenous disability identity. Tātau tātau concepts do not exist in any policy for whānau hauā. Although elements of tātau tātau exist in Māori models of wellbeing, they do not include the needs or specific issues for whānau hauā. Without including whānau hauā, we will continue to see this group suffer the consequences of their invisibility. Statistics NZ (2014) state that one in three Māori have a disability, whereas non-Māori make up one in four with a disability. Although whānau hauā make up a proportionately higher demographic number than non-Māori with disabilities, they are almost absent from policy, almost non-existent in the representation of Māori (other than Ngāti Kāpō) at the local and national levels, and non-existent internationally at the United Nations level. How can they have a presence, how can they have a voice, if they are not present? Tātau tātau is a concept of placing whānau hauā in the centre of any decision, identity and policy. Until that occurs, until whānau hauā begin to count as an identity, they will remain hidden from society with only a few speaking for them. There is a need for whānau hauā to work together to speak to their issues within Māori society and within society as a whole.

For those working with whānau hauā, it is important not to take over the decision making for the individual and their whānau. By developing the empowerment and leadership of the individual and their whānau, we have the opportunity to develop the ability for whānau hauā to be independent representatives, domestically and internationally, and to live their lives to the fullest extent. In doing these things, tātau tātau becomes a foundation from which to build a whānau hauā model.

Study questions

1. Whānau hauā are not well represented at the local, national and international level. Why might this be? What are the implications of this lack of representation?

2. What are the eight models of disability, and why don't whānau hauā fit well into these models?

3. What are the principles of the tātau tātau framework, and how are they relevant to whānau hauā?

4. What is the difference between disability and whānau hauā identity?

References

ALAC. (2003). Māori matters: Manaaki tangata: Promoting safe alcohol use. *Newsletter, 4*(1).

Breslin, M. L., & Lee, S. (Eds.). (2002). *Disability rights law and policy: International and national perspectives.* Ardsley, NY: Transnational Publishers.

Campbell, J., & Oliver, M. (1996). *Disability politics: Understanding our past, changing our future.* London, UK: Routledge.

Charlton, J. I. (2000). *Nothing about us without us: Disability oppression and empowerment.* Oakland, CA: University of California Press.

Clapton J., & Fitzgerald, J. (1997). The history of disability: A history of 'otherness'. *New Renaissance magazine, 7*(1).

Collins, A., & Hickey, H. (2006). *The role of whānau in the lives of Māori with physical disabilities.* Blue Skies Report no. 12/06. Wellington: Families Commission.

Corker, M., & Shakespeare, T. (Eds.). (2002). *Disability/postmodernity embodying disability theory*. London, UK: Continuum.

Durie, M. (1994). *Whaiora: Māori health development*. Auckland: Oxford University Press.

Lapsley, H., Nikora, L. W., & Black, R. (2002). *Kia mauri tau!: Narratives of recovery from disabling mental health problems*. Report of the University of Waikato Mental Health Narratives Project. Wellington: Mental Health Commission.

Lawson, A., & Gooding, C. (Eds.). (2005). *Disability rights in Europe from theory to practice: Essays in European law*. Portland, OR: Hart Publishing.

Metge, J. (1995). *New growth from old: The whānau in the modern world*. Wellington: Victoria University Press.

Ministry of Health. (2001). *The New Zealand disability strategy: Making a world of difference: Whakanui oranga*. Wellington: Author.

Nikora, L., Karapu, R., Hickey, H., & Te Awekotuku, N. (2004). *Disabled Māori and disability support options: A report prepared for the Ministry of Health*. Hamilton: Māori & Psychology Research Unit.

Oliver, M. (1990) *The politics of disablement*. Basingstoke, UK: MacMillan.

Oliver, M. (1996). *Understanding disability: From theory to practice*. New York, NY: St Martins Press.

Pere, R. (1985). *Te Wheke whaia te maramatanga me te aroha*. Gisborne: Gisborne Education Centre.

Royal Commission on Social Policy. (1988). *The April report*. Vols I–IV. Wellington: Government Printer.

Shakespeare, T. (Ed.). (1998). *The disability reader: Social science perspectives*. London, UK: Continuum.

Shakespeare, T., Mercer, G., & Barnes, C. (1999). *Exploring disability: A sociological introduction*. Cambridge, UK: Polity Press.

Wendell, S. (1996). *The rejected body: Feminist philosophical reflections on disability*. New York, NY: Routledge.

PART II
Disabilities Categories

Chapter 5

Refocusing lenses on Māori deaf children and their whānau

Kirsten Smiler

Kua takoto te mānuka.

The leaves of the mānuka tree have been laid.

Introduction

During pōwhiri, the laying down of mānuka leaves (or a weapon or feather in some regions) on the ground indicates the initiation of a formal wero. This action represents a test to clarify the intentions of the manuhiri. The manner in which the item that has been laid down is received and/or picked up is closely observed by the tangata whenua, who will assess the nature of the responses to form an understanding of the visitor's intentions. The primary assessments made are to answer the question 'Do you come in the spirit of warfare, control, and conflict, or in peace, collaboration and connectednesses?' In the context of this chapter, the whakataukī and its explanation above must be viewed from the perspective of two parties—the tangata whenua (Māori deaf people and their whānau) and the manuhiri (professionals)—coming together for a common reason, as is the case with professionals and deaf people and their whānau in the process of early intervention (EI).

Professionals working with Māori deaf people and their whānau (across the life span) often operationalise their work within discourse and narrative silos. They often lack, or have had limited exposure to, the social and linguistic experiences of Māori deaf people and their whānau, and there is an absence of a cultural lens to contextualise their specialist skill set. This chapter presents findings from a kaupapa Māori research project, *Ka Puāwai ngā Kōhungahunga Turi: A Study of the Nature and Impacts of Early Intervention for Māori Deaf Children and Their Whānau* (Smiler, 2014) undertaken by me as a part of a doctorate. Kete mātauranga case studies were co-constructed by the researcher, deaf people (young and old) and their whānau with the idea that these insights would inform and strengthen service provision. Specifically, the research questions were as follows.

- What shapes whānau perceptions of deafness?
- What are the early intervention experiences of whānau of deaf children?
- How do the design and delivery of early intervention services and supports for deaf children need to be adapted to be more effective for Māori?

This chapter synthesises the main findings from this study and acts as an offering of mānuka leaves: a challenge or invitation to revisit and review the meaning of old and new narratives and discourses about deaf and Māori people and how these inform the nature of service provision for Māori deaf children. The chapter explores the question 'Do we need to refocus our lenses in order to reach better outcomes for Māori deaf people and their whānau?' This research suggests that we do indeed. Kua takoto te mānuka!

The effect of deafness on pathways to language and social experiences within whānau contexts

Early life experiences play a formative role in determining how the social and linguistic identity of Māori deaf people is perceived and expressed (Smiler, 2004). Participation in the daily routines of whānau life, and developing healthy relationships with other members within the whānau, hinge on positive social and linguistic experiences during the synchronous process of socialisation and language acquisition occurring in early childhood (Clarke & Siraj-Blatchford, 2000; Erting 2003; Marschark, Lang, & Albertini, 2002; Rose, McAnally, & Quigley, 1987; Spencer & Marschark, 2006).

In a delicate process of reciprocal interaction between older whānau members and the child, older whānau members typically engage, scaffold and facilitate language development and communication by employing skills subconsciously acquired through their own child-hoods (Papoušek & Papoušek, 1987). However, the spoken mode of language and communication is naturally inaccessible to the 96 per-cent of deaf children who are born to hearing parents (Mitchell & Karchmer, 2004) thus rendering the approaches that hearing whānau members employ to facilitate this language learning process largely inaccessible and ineffective.

Consequently, deafness is often described in terms of language deprivation and social and linguistic isolation, leading to further devel-opmental delays and negative long-term life outcomes (Meadow, 1980). Therefore, providing a deaf child and their whānau with EI supports during the early years is linked with improved long-term outcomes for the deaf child and whānau (Meadow-Orlans, Mertens, & Sass-Lehrer, 2003). This specifically includes the need to support the child's lan-guage development during what is described as the "critical-period"—a period during which a child is naturally primed for rapid language acquisition and learning (Dettman & Dowell, 2010; Mayberry, 2010; Mayberry, Lock, & Kazmi, 2002).

There are various ways in which a child can understand, process and express language through the senses, the primary ones being visual, auditory and tactile.[1] Spoken and sign language are natural examples of languages processed in these modalities. The introduction of sophis-ticated hearing aid technology and cochlear implantation now means that many deaf children are able to access language via either mode (Paludneviciene & Leigh, 2011). This is the reason why deaf children follow a differing pathway to language and communication. Marschark and Spencer (2006) note a difference between language development

---

1   The tactile approach is mainly used by deaf people with vision loss; they have not been a focus of this research.

and language learning, describing language *development* as a naturally occurring process and language *learning* as the result of an intentional and structured activity of language teaching and learning from an intervening source, as is the case with EI supports for deaf children.

Supporting whānau with Māori deaf children

The introduction of early supports is important for ensuring developmental delays are minimised or avoided (Mayberry et al., 2002) and to help foster confidence and a sense of competence within older family members to take lead roles in facilitating language development and learning. The efficacy of these supports, however, hinges on the nature of the partnerships between supports and families (Brown & Nott, 2006; Sass-Lehrer & Bodner-Johnson, 2003). A shift from the professional–parent dichotomy to one that emphasises the significance of families—known as family-centred early intervention—is becoming acknowledged as best practice (Sass-Lehrer & Bodner-Johnson, 2003). It is claimed that within this model families are recognised as the primary unit of socialisation and are thus encouraged to take the roles of goal setters, enhancers and facilitators of the learning, development and wellbeing of their child.

An international consensus statement, *Best Practices in Family-Centered Early Intervention for Children Who Are Deaf or Hard of Hearing: An International Consensus Statement* (Moeller, Carr, Seaver, Stredler-Brown, & Holzinger, 2013) presents a set of agreed-upon guidelines, evidence-based principles and associated provider/programme behaviours to promote the wider implementation of validated, evidence-based principles for family-centred early intervention. The authors of the consensus statement advocate the international adoption of these principles to ensure that services are consistently employing evidence-based approaches. However, their significance has yet to be examined within the context of Aotearoa / New Zealand, especially in relation to Māori.

The signing of the Treaty of Waitangi between Māori and the British Crown on 6 February 1840 provides the macro-context for service provision and social outcomes for Māori, and also provides guiding principles for the partnership between Māori peoples and the state. This is a consideration with regard to the applicability of the consensus statement. Macfarlane (2012) investigates two critical special education constructs—culturally responsive practice and evidence-based practice—in relation to Māori. She argues that special education (of which deaf education is one specialist area) derives much of its philosophy and content from Western philosophy and psychology, and it is within these traditions that specialists are trained. Macfarlane argues that inequities in outcomes have long characterised the experiences of Māori within special education, and thus evidence-based practice in relation to Māori should be based on localised evidence, solutions and perceptions (mātauranga Māori).

Ngā kete mātauranga: Theorising from whānau case studies

This research was conceptualised and framed within the tradition and practice of raranga (Māori weaving). Writing on the transformative potential that indigenous-led research can have, Smith (2008) reminds indigenous peoples that our stories are rich with metaphors, which can act as motivational drivers that "inspire a transformative praxis that many indigenous researchers identify as a powerful agent for resistance and change" (p. 119). At the outset the research was framed as case study research, with five whānau of deaf children participating as case studies, but after initial engagement with whānau the research was reframed within the tradition of raranga, with the cases being described as kete mātauranga.

Individual whānau stories (kete mātauranga) were co-constructed between whānau participants, EI professionals and the researcher using Māori methods of qualitative data collection:

- kōrero ā-tinana (observations of action and behaviour)
- kōrero ā-waha (spoken language)
- kōrero ā-ringaringa (signed language)
- kōrero ā-tuhituhi (written language).

This data collection took place over a period of 3 years. Towards the end of this intensive data collection process 36 whānau participants (and 15 support people) were able to attend a hui whakawhanaungatanga, which was held to support whānau to develop relationships with one another and undertake wānanga: collective reflection of and debate on the themes arising from individual experiences in relation to others.

The final kete mātauranga presented in the thesis were written and structured by me in collaboration with the whānau participants.

To provide a service context to the kete mātauranga, interviews were also undertaken with 29 professionals who were either working directly with a whānau involved in the research or who were involved in leading or designing the implementation of services and supports delivered within the Universal Newborn Hearing Screening and Early Intervention Programme (UNHSEIP). UNHSEIP is an initiative that evolved parallel to this research, and so these latter informants provided commentary on how the different supports were intended to support Māori whānau during the early years of the child's development.

The early intervention experiences of Māori deaf children and their whānau

This chapter presents a series of rich, contextually situated kete mātauranga to outline the early intervention experiences of five whānau. They stand as contextual items to be examined from the researcher's lens. However, for the purposes of this chapter, a number of key themes have been identified for consideration by professionals working with deaf children and their whānau.

Pathways to language

Prompt identification, diagnosis and commencement of supports are critical to ensuring prompt access to language and reducing the negative impacts of language delay. The experiences of whānau participants in this research affirm these assumptions, but also highlight the fact that professionals' ability to understand and respond to the social context of the whānau is equally important. Such understanding supports the pathway to language, in particular the professionals' ability to:

- develop respectful and meaningful relationships with the wider whānau membership (not just those who can be present at appointments), and to include other children

- develop an understanding of the hierarchy of the membership, the nature of hierarchy and the differing roles that individuals play

- respect the fact that the pathway to language learning is not a linear journey experienced by a deaf child alone, but rather by the whānau as a whole

- understand that decisions around language use are made by both the child and the whānau in a given context: the child will have his or her own preferences and responses, which must be recognised by both the professionals and the whānau, and the whānau will have language aspirations that will reflect their desire to have their child socialised in cultures and communities of significance to them.

The experiences of whānau and children in this research emphasise that the pathway to language for the deaf child is one that is travelled by both the child and those supporting them. This was recognised by one kindergarten teacher, who highlighted the need to surround a whānau and child with a transdisciplinary community of support in order to foster language:

> It's about language, building on language, but also too it's about us all working together as a whole whānau. So it's a whole village that we need on board for [this child's] education. No one person can do it. (Kindergarten teacher of a Māori deaf child)

Experiences of identification, diagnosis and commencement of EI supports for language learning

All the children involved in the research experienced delayed access to language due to untimely access to language supports. Early identification and diagnosis have been touted as important contributors to decreasing the impact of deafness. The experiences of whānau affirm this relationship and indicate that developing relationships with whānau and managing the transition between diagnostic services to language supports is also critical. There are two very differing types of supports: one is situated in a clinical setting, where routine procedures are undertaken; the other requires an ongoing relationship, which responds to the developing child in the fluid context of the whānau.

Two children (child A and child B) in this study were identified and diagnosed shortly after birth, and three (C, D and E) were diagnosed after 6 months (the age at which UNHSEIP aims to have undertaken a diagnosis and to have begun EI supports).

Child A was identified and diagnosed as a part of a newborn hearing-screening initiative, and child B was identified shortly after deafness was suspected as a complication arising from her premature birth.

Child A was identified as having a bilateral severe hearing loss and fitted with hearing aids to support access to spoken language. However, these were often ineffective during prolonged periods of otitis media, and so basic New Zealand Sign Language (NZSL) was used as an interim communication strategy. Once the otitis media cleared, the child's receptiveness to spoken language improved. Towards the end of the research the child was developing a capacity in spoken English and te reo Māori, and maintaining use of his basic NZSL repertoire.

Child B was identified with bilateral severe-to-profound hearing loss and fitted with hearing aids a year following her birth (this child was born prematurely, at 27 weeks). These were not tolerated well by the child and a cochlear implant was undertaken when she was 18 months old. Basic NZSL was used (with support from professionals) in the home as an interim communication strategy. Once the implant was switched on, EI supports worked intensively to support this child to learn spoken English. Towards the end of the research the child had developed what was described by her mother as "roughly age-appropriate language", yet she still required ongoing intensive supports for educational settings.

For child A and child B the timeliness of diagnosis meant they were able to begin engagement with professionals and access technological supports such as cochlear implants and hearing aids, although this engagement was strained by domestic circumstances, which offset the child's access to supports. Sadly, the mother of the first child passed away shortly after his birth and diagnosis, and he was whāngai (adopted) by a relative. This relative then had to begin the process of engaging with professionals and constructing an understanding of the implications of deafness and the ways she might be able to support the child's language development. In the case of child B, her mother ended her relationship with the child's father, became a sole parent and moved away from the child's paternal whānau (and EI supports that had just begun engaging with the mother and child) in order to live in proximity to the child's maternal family. The mother then had to begin new relationships with various EI professionals in this new location.

Children C, D and E were all late identifications and had late access to language due to complex contextual reasons. Child D and child E experienced progressive hearing loss, which was detected by whānau, who had to actively pursue a diagnosis despite professionals' discouragement. These experiences illustrate that attention is required to ensure that those who are categorised by UNHSEIP as being 'at-risk' are diagnosed and engaged with early supports sooner.

Child C had a severe-to-profound bilateral hearing loss, which was identified after she contracted meningitis at 16 months. A bilateral cochlear implant was undertaken 2 months later and EI supports helped the development of spoken English. The child was unresponsive to her implant and was diagnosed with having an additional disability which influenced her language development. Towards the end of the research professionals were exploring differing pedagogies to support the child's language development.

Child D was whāngai to his grandparents at birth and was one of three deaf children being raised by grandparents. This child was diagnosed as a toddler, fitted with hearing aids and accessed spoken English in his household and te reo Māori at kōhanga reo. Towards the end of the research this child started attending a mainstream school where spoken English was used.

After numerous attempts to address ongoing bouts of otitis media (from the age of one), child E was diagnosed with a severe-to-profound hearing loss at three and a half. This child was promptly given cochlear implants, and EI professionals worked intensively to support spoken English. Up until her diagnosis, however, this child's parents used the visual communication efforts of the child and a number of idiosyncratic home signs as a platform for language and communication. These were still used by the child as part of her language and communication repertoire towards the end of the research, despite her accessing spoken language and an emerging competence in spoken English.

Which language? When? How?

Tensions over which language the child would use, when she would be introduced to this language, and how, were evident throughout the research. Professional supporters were only well equipped to support spoken English (with support from a hearing aid and cochlear implant). Consequently, spoken te reo Māori and NZSL were poorly supported. Spoken English was the language of all households (with some using te reo Māori on occasions), and so it was pragmatic that the child develop capacity in this language, but there were instances where supporting other language options (alongside spoken English) was in the interests of the child and whānau. What was not apparent to whānau was that the route to language learning can take multiple paths, and that aspirations for bilingualism, while poorly supported, are achievable if creative solutions and commitment are applied to reach this goal. Although all whānau involved in this research indicated a desire to support multilingualism, they had a limited understanding of how to facilitate this.

Choices, opportunities and decisions

> If I gave advice to other parents I'd say 'It's not a big deal. There are still lots of opportunities and there's going to be challenges—but there are still opportunities for them.' (Father of a Māori deaf child)

> I'd say, 'Get informed,' but you know, there's the question of 'How do you get informed?' (Mother of a deaf child)

Developing a schema of what deafness means was an iterative process in which whānau drew on various sources of information: specialist information from professionals, personal experience of raising children in whānau contexts, exposure to other deaf people and their whānau, views from wider society, and observations and reflections of their child in the whānau context. During initial encounters with professionals, the focus was placed on the medical perspectives of hearing loss, framing deafness as a medical concern remedied through routine technical and medical interventions. However, as the child entered developmental stages where language acquisition and the social acculturation process began, whānau started to relate to their deaf child in more social terms and sought information about the 'lived experience of deafness' and tried to construct an understanding of what it meant to be a deaf person in real-world contexts. This schema was important because it provided a primary platform from which information was contextualised, choices were reviewed and decisions eventually made.

Whānau respected professionals' expertise and knowledge about how to best support their child, and they also valued the position of experience. The view that raising a deaf child would require support from both professionals and those who could and would provide natural forms of support was accepted as inevitable, and to some degree expected, as one mother of a deaf child explained:

> [My child] is my wee village child. From 'day-dot' there have always been heaps and heaps of people caring for her. That's why I think she copes really well with lots of people because it's always been like that. And I like that. I like that she can experience everything if she can. Why not? Because I don't know everything [implies she has no experience from which to inform her decision making]. (Mother of a deaf child)

Interestingly, four whānau had intergenerational experiences of deafness within their membership. Knowledge of how these people fared (both positive and negative experiences) in whānau and real-world contexts was often used as a basis for developing aspirations for their child, contextualising and evaluating information from professionals, and providing a platform on which the deaf child was raised. As one grandparent of a deaf child explained, "He's the baby ... after all we've been through with the others; we just copy on."

The lived experiences of a single deaf person presented a contextual case however. So, while barriers of language and communication for deaf people in hearing society were evident to hearing whānau members, the historical context of how these arose were not. Hearing whānau often did not have a contextual understanding of how the education system had contributed to these challenges through their discriminatory pedagogies and policies towards deaf and Māori children. As a consequence, hearing whānau members admired the resilience demonstrated by these deaf adults, yet were fearful that their children would also experience similar struggles and discrimination. This fear was eased by the knowledge that the dominant language of wider society (spoken English) would be more readily accessible with the support of cochlear implants and improved hearing aid technology. This was in juxtaposition to a reverence for te reo Māori (since this was seen as providing social and linguistic access to differing Māori-specific domains) and a curiosity about their child's gravitation towards visual language (NZSL). All whānau wanted to address their need to foster strong language competence in at least one language, as well as diversifying their children's social and linguistic experiences, enabling them to take a participatory role in multiple social and cultural domains.

Constructing a meaning of deafness

> I hate that people struggle with words whenever they talk about deaf people. (Mother of a Māori deaf child)

> I'm still struggling with calling her 'special needs' … they're just different. (Mother of a Māori deaf child)

Constructing a meaning of deafness was an iterative process for all whānau participants. Perceptions of the deaf child evolved as the child moved through developmental stages and as members encountered different sources of information and experiences relating to deafness. The apt description of "a life-long journey" given by one child's mother astutely encompasses this experience, whereby whānau members developed an understanding of deafness as it related to the individual child's development, but also the implications of having a deaf person within a whānau. Each whānau raised their deaf child within an intergenerational unit, each with its own whakapapa (histories) of residence in and relationships with locations and landscapes (and the meaning constructed from these), structure of membership, hierarchies (and how these were decided upon), daily-life routines, lifestyle preferences and priorities. These were all factors that influenced the way individual deaf children were placed.

In most whānau the social division between younger and older generations was marked, and each cohort had its own hierarchy (constructed and influenced by contextual and cultural factors). The deaf child's positioning within the hierarchy of both cohorts was significant. It was, however, within the younger cohort of children that they developed relationships with siblings, cousins (and in some cases the general peer group at kōhanga reo), as one grandparent highlighted:

> We talked about kōhanga reo or kindergarten. I say why not put him with all the rest of the Māori kids at kōhanga reo, they'll all learn together. At this kōhanga reo everybody is related—everybody, even the teachers were related or a friend!

The birth order of the deaf child within the whānau also played an important role in determining the nature of the interactions within this group. Constructing deafness was thus an activity that occurred at the individual level (depending on the nature of the relationship of individual members and the deaf child) and at a collective level (the influence of the deaf child on the whānau as a whole).

At a very basic level, deafness was framed as a sensory experience—a natural aspect of the deaf child's body and being, and the lens through which their environment was perceived. Deafness was not framed as the absence of a sense; rather, the visual orientation of engaging with the environment (including people) was recognised. This was a strengths-based view of the child, one that did not leave whānau members, and was based on ongoing observations of and interactions with the child in daily routines, play and social interactions. Identified by many whānau members as idiosyncratic peculiarities, or, as one mother described, 'quirky' preferences and behaviours, this visual orientation was not always understood in relation to a developmental trajectory, but was accepted as an innate 'setting' within the child.

The onset of language learning and development—or lack of it, in some cases—prompted whānau members to re-create a perspective of deafness as a 'social disability'. Through the experience of isolation from social and linguistic experiences in hearing families, their child's development would be inhibited. Full participation in the life of the whānau, which hinged on the synchronous process of language learning and socialisation, was a critical aspiration held by whānau members, who recognised that participation cemented a sense of belonging and identity to the whānau unit. It was for these reasons that all whānau wanted their child to access and acquire at least one spoken language, typically English and/or te reo Māori. Visual language (NZSL) and communication strategies were recognised by whānau as being a natural approach to language learning for a deaf child, as they engage the innate visual orientation of the child. However, there were numerous challenges to facilitating this, specifically the dearth of support for NZSL for the deaf child and wider whānau. Sadly for three whānau, diagnosis and EI supports had yet to begin by the time their child had reached the stage where one would expect the onset of language, emphasising the view of deafness as a social disability. Once identified, the delayed access to supports created a sense of urgency around the need for intense intervention, reinforcing a negative perspective of the child as developmentally delayed and socially disabled.

The desire to socialise a child within the language and culture of hearing families provides a key impetus for the decision to pursue cochlear implants and hearing aid technology. Gaining access to such interventions began within medical settings, where whānau engaged with clinically trained professionals who undertook medical procedures, and measurements of deafness were described in terms of degrees of deafness. The physiological aspects of deafness provide the key platform for responses in these settings, and since these interventions led to the desired outcome of spoken language, they were one of the primary reference points for whānau members when discussing deafness with professionals during the early years of deaf children's lives. In juxtaposition to the physical reference point for deafness, whānau members held on to specific knowledge of 'their child' and their idiosyncrasies, almost as if it was in their 'back pocket', often privately theorising among themselves about the relevance of this knowledge to information provided by professionals.

Interestingly, what was often omitted (or not received by whānau members) from much information shared by professionals with whānau members was that the physiological state of deafness does not typically reduce the capacity for language (unless an additional disability influences this), and while the child may have had delayed access to language and communication (which will have some implications on the child's development), it is not the physical experience of deafness that disables language development; rather, it is how people respond. This was a confusing factor for whānau members. Instinctively they recognised the innate intelligence in their children and were frustrated that they were constrained in facilitating the synchronous process of language acquisition and socialisation effectively, and so requested support on this basis. However, the support they received from professionals through UNHSEIP was premised on the medical model of deafness as opposed to using knowledge and descriptions of the cognitive capacities of, and expected developmental trajectories for, deaf children.

One of the benefits of raising a deaf child within an intergenerational unit was the potential depth and richness of experience, and the insights and mentoring offered by more experienced members. Older and more experienced whānau members (often grandparents) were recognised for their status. They played various critical roles in raising children, ranging from occupying primary care roles, to providing encouragement and practical support to main carers. Members of the parents' generation tended to offer similar forms of support and also provided a peer group where parents could share experiences. The youngest cohort of the whānau, the 'child group', offered a context for play and learning.

Four out of five cases presented in this research had known intergenerational experiences of deaf people within the whānau context. Observations of a deaf person within a hearing whānau provided a single trajectory, which also influenced decision making during the EI period. Social disadvantages resulting from poor educational experiences and limited social participation in whānau settings fuelled whānau insistence on improved educational experiences and socialisation experiences in the whānau. Professionals' opinions and perspectives were respected as 'specialist views' on deafness, but these were always mediated by personal knowledge of the deaf child, which whānau members had gained through experience.

Whānau members were very interested in this 'voice of experience': the insights, histories and wisdom of deaf people and their families (Māori whānau in particular) across the generations and along the developmental trajectory. Developing relationships with others who had experience of deafness in the 'real world' was important. These voices were viewed as authentic and placed within context; they provided insights into how to navigate a majority culture as a minority identity. In some cases, deafness was role modelled as a positive social identity, and those 'quirky' idiosyncrasies observed during early childhood, present in many individuals, were reframed as 'deaf culture'.

Refocusing lenses: The need for a new programme philosophy

In 2007 a programme of universal newborn hearing screening, whereby all families of newborn infants are offered the option of screening for hearing loss at birth, was introduced within the public health system in Aotearoa / New Zealand (Ministry of Health, 2013). A number of existing supports for deaf children and their families (provided by the Ministry of Education and the Ministry of Health) were then placed under the umbrella of a new configuration: the Universal Newborn Hearing Screening and Early Intervention Programme (UNHSEIP).

The core goals of UNHSEIP emphasise the need for timely intervention, and are geared towards ensuring infants with congenital hearing loss receive intervention supports by the age of 6 months. Framed as the '1-3-6 rule', the programme aims to:

• have babies screened by 1 month
• undertake an audiology assessment to ascertain a diagnosis by 3 months
• initiate appropriate medical, audiological and EI services by the age of 6 months.

EI services and supports involve a tailored programme of support which aims to facilitate language learning and early development for the deaf child. This approach is consistent with recent international approaches that aim to pull disparate services closer together to promote seamless access to and between medical and educationally based services and to ensure timely diagnosis and access to EI supports (Yoshinaga-Itano, 2003).

The experiences of whānau in this research reveal that the wider, long-term aspirations of Māori deaf children and their whānau will not be supported within the current UNHSEIP as it is currently structured. The UNHSEIP appears to support a very narrow purpose: engaging families promptly to ensure deaf children and their families are able to access supports within the critical period in which a deaf child is most receptive to language supports. Underscoring this premise is that if a deaf child's language skills develop along an age-appropriate trajectory, this minimises the potential negative impact of deafness. The vision expressed by whanau, however, mirrors Māori models of holistic well-being and healthy development outlined by Māori academics (Durie 1985; Pere 1991), whereby deafness is acknowledged as a life-long state that will characterise life experiences beyond the early years of a child's early experiences. Embedded in this vision is the assumption that the experience of deafness (as a sensory experience and as a social identity) is inseparable from an identity as Māori (or any ethnic identity for that matter). Through linguistic and social experience they are fused within the individual. The identity of individual whānau members is also shaped by the experience of deafness; they, too, live with the holistic implications of deafness, and the experience has a life-long bearing on how they express their identity as individuals and as a whānau collective. Therefore this research proposes an alternative programme philosophy (kaupapa), one that was co-constructed by the researcher, whānau research participants and the kaumātua and kuia who guided the research.

Ka puāwai ngā kōhungahunga turi: A kaupapa Māori programme philosophy

In keeping with the metaphor adopted for the research approach, this research extends from the metaphor of raranga and proposes that the wider metaphor of the harakeke (flax plant) and pā harakeke (the flax plantation from which leaves are used to weave in the tradition of raranga) offers a conceptual basis for a kaupapa Māori programme philosophy for Māori deaf children and their whānau. These are key metaphors used in traditional oratory to discuss and theorise about the social organisation of people, particularly the family unit, or in the case of Māori, the whānau (Walker, 2013). They offer a Māori way of conceptualising and framing the experience of deafness and a system of supports for Māori deaf children and their whānau.

The harakeke plant grows in a fan-like formation, and te rito (the central shoot of the flax plant) is likened to the child; the central position elevates the status of the child, and both the present and future life of the plant rest on the wellbeing of te rito. The responsibility for te rito care is borne by the outer rau (leaves), representing parental and outer generations, yet the wellbeing of the outer rau are equally dependent on the life of te rito. This illustrates that while all generations must fulfil roles and responsibilities, the wellbeing of everyone rests on healthy intergenerational interdependence. Pā harakeke refers to a collection of harakeke plants growing in proximity to one another, and is often used to refer to a wider social unit of interconnected people connected through whakapapa or kaupapa. Kōhungahunga are the fine silky fibres found within harakeke leaves; the metaphorical use of the term by Māori orators to refer to young children offers a paradox: the vulnerable silky threads (the kōhungahunga) of the harakeke plant (metaphorical whānau) are the internal substance which provides strength and resilience.

Te puāwaitanga o ngā kōhungahunga turi (the wellbeing and

healthy development of the deaf child) encompasses a holistic kaupapa to inform the nature of supports for Māori deaf children and their whānau. This kaupapa emphasises the healthy holistic development of the Māori deaf child (based on Māori and deaf perspectives of healthy development) within the interdependent context of whānau. There is a transformative synergy inherent in the concept of pā harakeke as it promotes the competence of whānau to raise a child while simultaneously acknowledging the need to create a specialised community of support to do so—a transdisciplinary community with wide expertise to co-construct an approach to raising their child with a focus on supporting whānau to provide the optimal ecological environments to facilitate healthy development.

This broad focus allows for the inclusion of professionals (groups already employed within the health and education sectors) to work with deaf children and provide supports that address healthy whānau function, and those with language and socialisation expertise of relevant language communities. The potential contribution of members from these communities is two-fold: support with contextualising and naturalising language, and mentoring support (to child and adult whānau members) to enhance the mana of the child through modelling deaf and/or Māori-centred communicative and social resiliency strategies. Multiple intergenerational experiences and knowledge of these experiences provide whānau with longitudinal insights into the child's development and potential life trajectory. This, alongside contributions from professionals who facilitate the navigation of services and specialist forms of support, provides whānau with a sound base for decision making, and a base from which decisions can regularly be evaluated by whānau and professionals.

Study questions

1. Reflecting on your own experiences and perspectives of Māori deaf children and their whānau, what are the key assumptions you have, and how do these influence the way you might interact with Māori deaf children and their whānau?

2. The pathway to language learning for Māori deaf children and their whānau is complex. Decisions and choices on language (and

the approaches to support this) tend to evolve as a child develops and whānau members process and make sense of information. What sorts of considerations would whānau of Māori deaf children have to make when considering supporting a child's learning of English, te reo Māori and New Zealand Sign Language?

3. Given that deafness can be constructed in multiple ways, what are the practical implications of these various views?

4. What are the potential implications of the kaupapa Māori programme philosophy of pā harakeke in your practice?

References

Brown, P., & Nott, P. (2006). Family-centred practice in early intervention for oral language development: Philosophy, methods and results. In P. E. Spencer & M. Marschark (Eds.), *Advances in the spoken-language development of deaf and hard-of-hearing children*. Oxford, UK: Oxford University Press.

Clarke, P., & Siraj-Blatchford, I. (2000). *Supporting identity, diversity and language in the early years*. Maidenhead, UK: Open University Press.

Dettman, S., & Dowell, R. (2010). Language acquisition and critical periods for children using cochlear implants. In M. Marschark and P. E. Spencer (Eds.), *The Oxford handbook of deaf studies, language and education* (pp. 331–342). Oxford, UK: Oxford University Press.

Durie, M. (1985). A Māori perspective of health. *Social Science & Medicine, 20*(5), 483–486.

Erting, C. J. (2003). Language and literacy development in deaf children: Implications of a sociocultural perspective. In B. Bodner-Johnson & M. Sass-Lehrer (Eds.), *The young deaf or hard of hearing child: A family-centered approach to early education* (pp. 373–398). Baltimore, MD: Brookes Publishing. Retrieved from http://products.brookespublishing.com/The-Young-Deaf-or-Hard-of-Hearing-Child-P48.aspx

Macfarlane, S. (2012). *In pursuit of culturally responsive, evidence based special education pathways in Aotearoa New Zealand: Whaia ki te ara tika*. Christchurch: University of Canterbury.

Marschark, M., Lang, H. G., & Albertini, J. A. (2002). *Educating deaf students: From research to practice*. Oxford, UK: Oxford University Press.

Marschark, M., & Spencer, P. E. (2006). Understanding sign language development in deaf children. In B. Schick, M. Marschark, & P. E. Spencer

(Eds.), *Advances in sign language development of deaf children*. Oxford, UK: Oxford University Press.

Mayberry, R. (2010). Early language acquisition and adult language ability: What sign language reveals about the critical period for language. In M. Marschark & P. E. Spencer (Eds.), *The Oxford handbook of deaf studies, language and education* (pp. 281–291). Oxford, UK: Oxford University Press.

Mayberry, R., Lock, E., & Kazmi, H. (2002). Development: Linguistic ability and early language exposure. *Nature, 417*(38), 38.

Meadow, K. P. (1980). *Deafness and child development*. Berkeley, CA: University of California Press.

Meadow-Orlans, K. P., Mertens, D. M., & Sass-Lehrer, M. A. (2003). *Parents and their deaf children: The early years*. Washington, DC: Gallaudet University Press.

Ministry of Health. (2013). *Universal Newborn Hearing Screening and Early Intervention Programme: National policy and quality standards*. Wellington: Author.

Mitchell, R. E., & Karchmer, M. A. (2004). Chasing the mythical ten percent: Parental hearing status of deaf and hard of hearing students in the United States. *Sign Language Studies, 4*(2), 138–163.

Moeller, M. P., Carr, G., Seaver, L., Stredler-Brown, A., & Holzinger, D. (2013). Best practices in family-centered early intervention for children who are deaf or hard of hearing: An international consensus statement. *Journal of Deaf Studies and Deaf Education, Theory/Review, 18*(4), 429–445.

Paludneviciene, R., & Leigh, I. (2011). *Cochlear implants: Evolving perspectives*. Washington, DC: Gallaudet University Press.

Papoušek, H., & Papoušek, M. (1987). Intuitive parenting: A dialectic counterpart to the infant's integrative competence. In J. D. Osofksy (Ed.), *Handbook of infant development* (2nd ed., pp. 669–720). New York, NY: Wiley.

Pere, R. (1991). *Te Wheke: A celebration of infinite wisdom*. Gisborne: Ao Ako Global Learning New Zealand.

Rose, S., McAnally, P. L., & Quigley, S. P. (1987). *Language learning practices with deaf children*. Boston, MA: College-Hill Press.

Sass-Lehrer, M., & Bodner-Johnson, B. (2003). Early intervention: Current approaches to family-centred programming. In M. Marschark & P. E. Spencer (Eds.), *Oxford handbook of deaf studies, language, and education* (pp. 65–81). Oxford, UK: Oxford University Press.

Smiler, K. (2004). *Māori deaf: Perceptions of cultural and linguistic identity of Māori deaf members of the New Zealand deaf community.* Wellington: Victoria University of Wellington.

Smiler, K. (2014). *Ka puāwai ngā kōhungahunga turi: A study of the nature and impacts of early intervention for Māori deaf children and their whānau.* Wellington: Victoria University of Wellington.

Smith, L. T. (2008). On tricky ground: Researching the native in the age of uncertainty. In N. K. Denzin & Y. S. Lincoln (Eds.), *The landscape of qualitative research.* Los Angeles, CA: Sage Publications.

Spencer, P., & Marschark M. (2006). *Advances in the spoken-language development of deaf and hard of hearing children.* Oxford, UK: Oxford University Press.

Walker, T. W. (2013). *Ngā pā harakeke o Ngati Porou: A lived experience of whānau.* Wellington: Victoria University of Wellington.

Yoshinaga-Itano, C. (2003). From screening to early identification and intervention: Discovering predictors to successful outcomes for children with significant hearing loss. *Journal of Deaf Studies and Deaf Education, 8*(1), 11–30.

Chapter 6

Kāpō Māori: Overcoming barriers

Jill Bevan-Brown and Tai Walker

E kore taku moe e riro i a koe.

My dream cannot be taken by you.

Introduction

After setting the scene with respect to the prevalence of blindness and vision impairment (BVI) among Māori in pre-European times and today, this chapter reports on a small study of Māori blindness and vision impairment conducted by the authors.[1] General, educational and cultural barriers identified by participants are outlined, as are their suggestions for how these barriers can be overcome. Findings from this study are discussed in tandem with three other research projects that have investigated kāpō Māori. Common themes are identified and their implications discussed.

The prevalence of blindness and vision impairment

Kāpō is a widely used Māori word for BVI. However, a variety of terms

---

1   This chapter draws substantially on unpublished research data, and Bevan-Brown and Walker, 2013.

and tribal variations of the same words exist. Higgins, Phillips, Cowan, Wakefield and Tikao (2010, p. 7), for example, identified 10 different te reo Māori words for blind/blindness. This suggests that, despite minimal information about BVI in pre-European times, its occurrence was reasonably prevalent. This hypothesis is further supported by the existence of Māori atua and prominent tūpuna who are recorded as being blind. These include Māui's whanaunga, Muri-ranga-whenua and Mahuika, and Tawhaki's grandmother, Whaitiri, who were all powerful, respected elders.[2]

> Being kāpō was their source of power because they were not reliant on all of their senses and had high levels of ability, which were displayed in their use of the senses that they did possess. (Higgins et al., 2010, p. 8)

Other well-known blind tūpuna include Waikato chief, Horomona Maruhau, and Hongi Hika's wife, Turi-ketuha, who were both highly respected and knowledgeable members of their iwi. It appears that in all cases it was the tūpuna's whakapapa, abilities and blindness that together contributed to their mana.

The prevalence of BVI in pre-European times is attributed to constant working over fires, living in smoky dwellings, and injuries sustained in tribal combat (Beattie, 1990, 1994). Higgins et al. (2010) maintain that in those days Māori who had a vision impairment

> were known for the talents that they possessed, not for what they didn't have. They also held great knowledge and shared that knowledge with others. As time has progressed, though, this notion appears to have changed. (p. 14)

The exact current number of Māori who are blind and vision impaired is unknown. This is because there is no nationally agreed definition of what constitutes BVI. Relevant organisations such as Statistics New Zealand, the Royal New Zealand Foundation of the Blind (RNZFB)[3] and the Blind and Low Vision Education Network of New Zealand (BLENNZ) use different criteria. However, an indication of the size of the BVI Māori population can be gleaned from Statistics New

---

2   See Higgins et al., 2010, pages 8–10, for a description of the feats of these tūpuna.

3   In 2013 the RNZFB changed its name to the Blind Foundation.

Zealand's 2001 and 2008 estimates of 12,225 and 12,300, respectively. The RNZFB 2012/13 annual report noted that 856 (7 percent) of their 11,680 members were Māori

Despite these prevalence figures, there is a dearth of research focusing on kāpō Māori. This situation, together with research findings showing that Māori with a range of disabilities often do not receive culturally appropriate services (Bevan-Brown, 2002; Massey University, 2002), were the motivating factors behind the study presented in this chapter.

The research

The aim of the research was to gain an understanding of the life experiences of kāpō Māori, with a particular focus on the cultural appropriateness of the education and services they had received and were still receiving, and the impact of their vision impairment on their cultural development. It was hoped that, ultimately, the knowledge gained would contribute to improvement in the education and services provided to kāpō Māori. The research was conducted by Jill Bevan-Brown from Massey University and Tai Walker, a colleague from Victoria University who is vision impaired.[4]

Methodology

Ethical approval

Ethical approval was gained from the Massey University Human Ethics Committee. The researchers also attended a Ngāti Kāpō o Aotearoa meeting to explain the research and gain approval and assistance from executive committee members. Ngāti Kāpō is a national Māori health and disability service provider run by and for Māori who are vision impaired. Founded in 1983, Ngāti Kāpō's vision is one of self-determination and improving the quality of life of kāpō Māori and their whānau.[5]

Participants

After giving approval, Ngāti Kāpō provided a list of members in the Wellington, Horowhenua and Manawatu regions. Purposive sampling

---

4   Since this chapter was written, Tai Walker has passed away.

5   For information about this organisation, its aims, services and history, see http://www.kapoMāori.com

was used to select potential participants across a wide age range. After having the research explained to them, all 10 people contacted agreed to participate. This sample consisted of eight males and two females. Two young men were attending secondary school, three men were in the 20–60 years age bracket and three were over 60. One woman was in her 50s and the other 76. While all participants met the RNZFB's criteria for registration, their degree of vision impairment varied considerably: from the two adolescents, who had self-reported functional vision, to one participant who was "totally blind". Only one participant was born with a vision impairment; three had accidents in their teens or early twenties, while the others' loss of sight was caused by brain tumours, medical misadventure and a variety of degenerative eye disorders, two occurring in childhood and the rest in adulthood.[6]

Data collection and analysis

Face-to-face interviews were conducted with all participants. Although a formal questionnaire was used, the interviews were more in the nature of informal chats covering a wide range of topics introduced by the interviewer and the participants themselves. They were about 2 hours long and were conducted in the homes of nine participants and in the workplace and home of the other participant. Five of the ten interviews also included family members who contributed information.

Questions focused on barriers that participants had faced, services and strategies they had found helpful, and their suggestions for improving education and services to Māori who are vision impaired. Emphasis was placed on the cultural appropriateness of the education and services participants had received.

Interviews were taped and transcribed, and a thematic approach was used to analyse the data gathered. Barriers experienced and suggestions for overcoming them were sorted into three areas: general, educational and cultural. A CD of the results was sent to each participant to provide them with a record of the research and the opportunity to give feedback on findings if they wished.

---

6   Given such a small sample, no conclusions can be drawn about the causes of BVI. However, of interest is a finding from Higgins et al.'s (2012) research, which included 150 kāpō Māori: "the leading causes of childhood blindness in Māori children in NZ was [*sic*] similar to the causes of childhood blindness in the rest of the Western World" (p. 7).

Results

General barriers

Nine general barriers were identified. They are listed below, with example quotes.

1. Adjusting to becoming blind—this included both psychological and practical adjustments.

    I tried for two years to learn Braille and I couldn't pick up a lot of it. It seems the feeling in my fingers has gone because of working with concrete and labouring.

2. Difficulty in maintaining relationships and forming new ones.

    I lost a lot of friends who were too whakamā [shy and embarrassed] to come and say hello—too uncomfortable. They thought they couldn't treat me the same as they used to—I haven't changed, just my situation has.

3. Negative attitudes, perceptions and lack of understanding.

    The greatest barrier is probably stereotypes—you're blind so you're deaf as well ... Blind people can instantly read Braille, but they can't find their way around the place, they bump into things, they can't use phones, they can't, can't, can't! People place restrictions on you. They don't ask me, just decide themselves I can't do things. You'd be surprised what we can do!

4. Problems associated with restricted mobility, such as inaccessible and costly public transport; unhelpful bus drivers; uneven, cracked footpaths and steps; bad road layouts; and having to depend on unreliable people for transport.

    Your greatest risk is on the footpath ... people walking down the street don't know you are visually impaired so bash into you—maybe they are expecting you to move and you don't.

5. Difficulty accessing needed resources and services because of the bureaucracy and 'red tape' involved.

6. Challenges in performing daily living tasks, such as shopping for groceries, getting things from the freezer and handling money.

7. Environmental issues such as poor lighting, reflection from highly polished surfaces, buildings with a lot of glass, shiny floors, glass doors, loud music causing sensory overload and confusion, door bells placed too high, students' bags obstructing bus stop areas, sandwich boards, sidewalk cafes and displays.

    I have been known to talk to a mannequin thinking it was my wife!

8. Reading difficulties, mainly associated with small print (e.g. website addresses).

9. Financial costs, including the expense of equipment, such as white canes and talking clocks, the cost of attending rehabilitation and skill courses, and the extra costs employers incur when hiring people who are vision impaired—costs that can discourage them from doing so.

Educational barriers

Two participants were still at school and five had studied or were still studying at tertiary level. Two of these participants studied at wānanga and the other three attended mainstream universities.

Primary education

No barriers were mentioned in relation to primary school, possibly because most participants became blind later in life. The two participants who talked about their primary schooling in respect to being vision impaired were very positive about the experience. They mentioned assistance given both by teachers and by their peers.

Secondary education

Both secondary school pupils had functional vision but had opposite experiences of how their impairment was accommodated. One reported that he had no problems and participated actively in all facets of school life. Unfortunately, this was not the case for the other participant. He could not read the whiteboard, and although he had part-time teacher aide assistance, when s/he was not present this pupil struggled to cope. He reported getting extremely frustrated with some teachers who ignored his needs: "I feel like whacking them!" The woodwork teacher was a case in point. He believed teacher aide assistance was not needed in the woodwork class because he could provide any help required. However, the participant reported that this teacher was "often away with other students when I need help. I keep whacking my fingers with the hammer."

A major complaint was that the resources and help promised at IEP meetings were not forthcoming: a computer was an example given. Other difficulties experienced were restricted course selection, difficulty making friends, and problems with "unhelpful" teacher aides. The participant's mother explained that her son could have up to six different aides working with him in one week. When she requested that he have just one teacher aide, she was told that this was not the school policy as they did not want students to become "too attached and dependent" on particular teacher aides.

Tertiary education

Participants attending tertiary institutions mentioned difficulties they had in common with all students and difficulties that were directly related to their vision impairment. The former included the high cost of course fees, course material, computers and travel to wānanga and university, and not being informed of changes in timetabling and programmes. The latter included having to rely on taped material to write assignments and join in discussions, the extra time needed to complete work, the cost of specialised equipment and note takers, unreliable note takers, and not being permitted to submit assignments on CD or tape.

The two participants who had attended wānanga identified many barriers specific to studying in these Māori institutions. Some barriers were related to studying Māori subjects, while others were more general. Barriers mentioned included:

- a lack of Māori-related and te reo Māori resources in accessible formats, both at the wānanga and at local libraries

- no Māori-speaking computer dictionary or spell check being available

- additional costs relating to studying Māori (e.g. getting material transcribed by someone who is proficient in te reo Māori costs twice as much as transcriptions in English)

- a government funding model that disadvantages wānanga where PhD students are not enrolled, which in turn results in less money being available for disability support and equipment

- limited disability support services, equipment, and teacher knowledge about vision impairment
- tutors' reliance on visual prompts to teach te reo.

One wānanga participant reported having to give up his studies because of the difficulties encountered in completing assignments and the extra costs involved.

Barriers relating to culture

The barriers mentioned were environmental, personal, organisational and those associated with Māori tikanga and reo.

Environmental barriers

A major environmental barrier related to marae layout. Marae are often large, spread out, badly designed, unsafe, unmarked complexes, sometimes in inaccessible locations prone to flooding. The following quotes are just two examples of the many given:

> You can't shoreline[7] on some marae because there is no physical or natural thing in between buildings.

> Finding the wharepaku in the middle of the night is impossible and asking someone to take you is so degrading.

Barriers associated with tikanga Māori and te reo Māori

A variety of marae protocol were reported as creating barriers for vision-impaired people. For example, removing shoes before entering the meeting house presented problems for kāpō Māori, who had difficulty locating their shoes when leaving. The practice of hongi, handshake or kiss following a whaikōrero is another potentially problematic practice, as this quote illustrates:

> If they stuck to the one protocol it would be OK, but sometimes I have gone to kiss a man because they have long hair and I think it is a woman.

Taking guide dogs on to the marae was a problem for another participant:

> Dogs are not accepted on some marae because of tapu. A dog is just a dog not an aid ... Cultural principles can go against the vision

---

7   Shorelining is using a cane to tap along a wall, or the edge of a footpath.

impairment principles and sometimes it's vice versa so you are getting a double whammy. Some people can only handle one or another not both.

Participating in whaikōrero was mentioned by a number of participants.

It is one of the most difficult ones of the whole lot because you know that 85 percent of your learning comes through the eyes. I find it very difficult to speak on a marae ... I can't see who's there. I don't know who I'm talking to.

At the other end of the spectrum was a participant who longed to whaikōrero, but despite being a fluent speaker was never asked to do so. He believed that he was not taken seriously and was overlooked because he was blind.

A further language-related barrier related to learning whakapapa. Whakapapa is most often represented and shared visually. One participant noted that he found whakapapa difficult to understand and learn because he could not remember the connecting lines.

Personal barriers

Negative personal attitudes were linked with some cultural practices. For example, one participant reported patronising and dismissive behaviours masquerading as manaakitanga. Other barriers were: unhelpful whānau; being "talked past"; and a general lack of awareness and understanding of vision impairment in the Māori community, coupled with limiting attitudes and lowered expectations of people who are vision impaired.

Organisational barriers

A number of organisations were criticised for being unresponsive to Māori needs. They did not take whānau into account in the services they provided and consulted with Māori in general rather than Māori with "the lived experience of disability." A further criticism was levelled at particular funding organisations:

They know that Māori can get grants so instead of considering requests for assistance they say, 'Why don't you go back to your hapū and get a grant from them?' Not all hapū have money available. They expect me to get help elsewhere because I'm a Māori.

Suggestions for improvement

Raising people's awareness and understanding of vision impairment was a major theme to emerge across all areas (general, educational and cultural). Many previously mentioned barriers were created because of this lack of awareness and understanding. To improve this situation, participants suggested that decision makers in top organisational positions should "get out into the community to meet people who are vision impaired and see what it is really like for them—reading about it is not enough!" Similarly, there was a strong push for vision-impaired Māori to have greater visibility in the community:

> Probably one of the most influential ways of informing and educating our community is by people being visible in the community ... warts and all. Because there are some perceptions that people have of blind people ... 'They can sing, very good at playing music.' Well I've got the news for them, I'm neither of those and yet I'm a blind man! 'They're very good because they're very even tempered, they don't get upset.' Well that's because they're not so visible out in the community. If you're visible in the community then you can display whatever emotions that anybody else displays as part of the community, so when you're closed away, some of those perceptions develop and grow.

With greater awareness, understanding and visibility, it was hoped that attitudes towards people who are vision impaired would change to become more realistic, accepting, inclusive, responsive and helpful. One participant also mentioned a need to change the charity paradigm to an investment one:

> I think the people who got all this fisheries money can do well to invest in blind children. So we'll do well and make a huge contribution to disabled people ... we need to try to get rid of that 'charitability' notion, and talk about investing in people.

A variety of ways organisations could improve their services were discussed. These included: the provision of practical help and emotional support for the partners and whānau of vision impaired people; increased face-to-face consultation with kāpō Māori to ascertain and target services to needs identified by them; and disability-friendly venues and processes. A further suggestion was governmental price regulation to cut prices on vision impairment equipment and resources to make them more affordable.

Educational suggestions

Suggestions for improving educational provisions included the following.

1. Introduce 'key elements' at an early age. One participant gave his definition of 'key elements':

   Simply the tools of reading and writing and that is Braille, typing and access to computers. Also orientation and mobility. Those are the key elements to the ability of our kids to function well.

Another participant was an advocate for coping strategies:

   Challenges come up all the time—you have to develop strategies to overcome these. Teach kids to try out different things, find out what works for them and they are comfortable with and then practise with it.

2. Increase the use of available services, such as those offered by Homai,[8] itinerant teachers, the Blind Foundation and Ngāti Kāpō by advertising them extensively and making them easily accessible to kāpō Māori

3. Include the skills needed to teach vision-impaired students in all pre-service and in-service teacher education. As one participant explained:

   Teachers need to learn not to be so visual—not to rely on visual prompts—break down and explain it without having to rely on the visuals to help students understand.

4. Increase opportunities for teachers to get to know their students and build relationships with them and their whānau:

   Teachers need to take more time just to observe kids and get to know them—accommodate to what they find out. They need to build up their awareness, learn to become 'peaceful'. If they are up-tight, the kids will react. If they do become peaceful they will see what is required … It comes back to the individual, to the teacher.

---

8   Homai is a specialist early childhood centre and school for children who are blind and vision impaired.

5. Raise awareness, understanding and positive attitudes towards vision impairment among peers. A variety of teaching activities were mentioned, including teachers and/or vision-impaired children talking to class members about the challenges faced; peers learning how to guide correctly; and experiential exercises, such as 'being blind for the morning' and discussing what it felt like with class members.

6. Provide study material in accessible forms, necessary aides and resources, and adapt programmes, routines and requirements to accommodate the needs of vision-impaired students; for example: provide lessons on CD, allow taped assignments, install Māori spell check, and offer extra computer assistance:

> They have to be equipped and exposed to those things. Even if it means that they are singled out in the classroom as being seemingly favoured, that's the cost of blindness we're talking about.

7. Increase ancillary assistance where needed. Seek extra funding to enable additional note-taker and teacher aide time.

8. Provide extra assistance for total immersion education.

One participant who was very involved with kura kaupapa Māori noted:

> The whole Māori education system needs to be revamped because we are so far behind in resources—there's no resources for blind kids in total immersion situations, no backup for kaiako … knowledge and resources are not there… we are the minority of the minority so there's nothing.

Cultural suggestions

Participants believed that kāpō Māori children from kōhanga reo level upwards should have opportunities to be fully involved in cultural activities such as kapa haka and learning te reo if they so choose. They should also be given opportunities to experience noho marae and learn about tikanga and kawa.

Cultural input should be provided from an early age, and may need to involve adaptations and accommodations to ensure accessibility, involvement and enjoyment. For example, on a noho marae time should be spent orienting vision-impaired children around the marae. They should sleep near the door, and their shoes should be brought inside the meeting house and placed in a plastic bag along with their clothes. They could also be provided with a buddy, who would explain such things as the placement of food on their plate.

> If you don't explain these things to them they'll become afraid of the place because they're always getting told off.

In discussing marae layout, participants suggested that upgrading should be done to provide interconnecting buildings, clearly marked footpaths, additional lighting, raised seating and bedding. Such renovations would not only assist kāpō Māori, but also elderly people who stay on marae.

> We need to write about these things in Māori magazines, local Māori radio, and target Māori media to raise awareness.

Discussion

The following discussion presents points of commonality and convergence between the research described above and three other studies of kāpō Māori. As far as I (Jill Bevan-Brown) am aware, these four studies represent the only published/available research specifically focusing on kāpō Māori.[9]

A research team led by Nancy Higgins and supported by Ngāti Kāpō conducted two significant research projects. The first (Higgins et al., 2010) examined how health and education services affect the identity, cultural wellbeing and health of kāpō Māori and their families. Information was gained from interviews with 43 key informants and case studies of 10 kāpō Māori, ranging in age from pre-schoolers to kaumātua. The second study focused on the general demographics and causes of vision impairment in kāpō Māori children and on barriers to accessing ophthalmological services and a visual diagnosis (Higgins et al., 2012). In this study the whānau of 150 kāpō Māori children and youth were interviewed in order to complete a demographic questionnaire, the vision records of the children concerned were reviewed, and

---

9   However, it is acknowledged that there are other studies that include kāpō Māori among the participants (e.g. Higgins's 2001 PhD thesis) or have a different focus (e.g. Tibble's 1992 comparison of services provided to kāpō Māori and indigenous North Americans with vision impairment).

follow-up interviews with 37 whānau members were conducted.

The third study is a master's thesis conducted by Ivan Te Momo, who is, himself, vision impaired (Te Momo, 2007). Prompted by his own experience and struggle to learn te reo Māori, Te Momo's research investigated the issues kāpō Māori face when learning their language. He interviewed eight participants to answer his research questions: "What does te reo Māori mean for kāpō Māori? What strategies do they use to learn te reo Māori? What battles have kāpō Māori engaged in?" (p. 9).

Complementary aspects

While all four studies focused on differing experiences of kāpō Māori, there were specific areas of interest and emphasis that were complementary. The Higgins et al. studies provided extensive information about the cultural unresponsiveness of Pākehā systems and providers. Te Momo focused on the barriers participants faced in learning te reo, while a significant component of the Bevan-Brown and Walker research was the impact of participants' vision impairment on their cultural development. All four studies reported a variation in the life experiences and quality of education and services received by kāpō Māori. However, there were also striking similarities within and between studies, especially in relation to the barriers experienced. These are outlined below.

1. Deficit thinking and lowered expectations

In the Bevan-Brown and Walker study, the majority of barriers participants experienced related to the accommodation and acceptance of vision impairment in general, although some barriers were Māori-specific. A major barrier experienced and discussed by most participants was the underestimation of their ability to perform tasks in both general and cultural situations. As one participant stated, "They are handicapping me. I am not the problem—they are."

Because the main focus of Te Momo's study was on learning te reo, most of the barriers discussed related to that kaupapa. However, the researcher noted an "ever-present sense of struggle through all the themes" (p. 75) that extended beyond participants' experiences with the Māori language. Stories of discrimination, humiliation, exploitation and embarrassment were frequent, and were often underpinned by deficit thinking and lowered expectations. A typical example was the shopkeeper who looked straight past the participant and asked her companion, "What would your friend like?" (p. 77).

The Higgins et al. studies also reported lowered expectations and discriminatory practice, both in respect to vision impairment and as a result of negative cultural stereotyping—a double whammy. Whether it be in everyday living, education or cultural activities, lowered expectations of what kāpō Māori are able to achieve were reported in all four research studies. This deficit thinking often limited the support provided by whānau and the advice and services offered by professionals.

2. Socioeconomic status and financial issues

Phillips and Higgins (in press) reported that in their study of 150 kāpō Māori:

> the average number of people living in a household was 4.7 people compared to 2.6 people in the 2006 general population ... $40,690 was the participants' average household income compared with $79,300 in the general population ... the average decile rating of schools that participants attended was '4' with the median being '3'. (n.p.)

Twenty-five percent reported experiencing discrimination because of their financial status.

Of Te Momo's (2007) eight adult participants, only three were employed; the rest were on benefits. One participant explained:

> the benefit's only allowing you to survive, so you're on a haere to nothing ... for blind people, access to radio, television, talking books, computer access, all that stuff which is very, very expensive, and so for Māori those mediums become inaccessible. Just cost too much and a lot of us are unemployed ... I know for a lot of our kāpō people it's just unaffordable. They ... haven't got a shit show in getting into this technology. It's one of the issues that comes back to the cost of blindness. (p. 86)

While socioeconomic data were not collected for participants in the Bevan-Brown and Walker study, the high cost of equipment, resources, courses and services was a major issue. One participant reported financial hardship as a factor contributing to his withdrawal from wānanga studies. Of particular note was the additional cost of te reo transcriptions, coupled with a funding model that disadvantages wānanga that do not offer PhD qualifications. Given this, it can be argued that kāpō Māori are being triply disadvantaged: despite being over-represented in New Zealand's lower socioeconomic group (as indicated by the Higgins et al. data), they are having to pay more to gain a Māori qualification in an underfunded Māori tertiary institution

3. Availability and accessibility of services, courses and resources

In all four studies, participants reported difficulties accessing various services, courses and resources in both the health and education domains. It can be argued that this situation exists for all people who are vision impaired regardless of their ethnicity. However, data suggest that this problem is exacerbated for Māori.

In the health domain, for example, Higgins et al. (2010, p. 223) found "fewer kāpō Māori access services: and were less likely to have a diagnosis or be assessed for vision loss and have treatment for their condition." Similarly, the Higgins et al. (2012) study reported that:

> the average age of receiving the first vision service for the kāpō child was 43 months and thus, almost two years from the average age of when vision impairment was first noticed. (p. 5)

Factors identified as contributing to these statistics included the rural location of many Māori families, lack of information about and availability of services to/in Māori communities, and Māori-specific funding issues.

In the education domain, Te Momo and Bevan-Brown and Walker identified issues around accessing Māori-language courses and associated resources. Participants in both studies recognised the importance of te reo Māori me ōna tikanga, but there were also consistent stories about the barriers they faced in learning their language, gaining Māori knowledge and participating in cultural activities. The reasons previously cited by Bevan-Brown and Walker's participants were echoed by those in Te Momo's research: costly courses and resources; visual teaching approaches; unhelpful disability co-ordinators; no enlarged Māori dictionaries or computer programmes; shortage of Māori-language resources in Braille; noisy classrooms; and so forth.

4. Culturally appropriate services and resources

One prominent theme across the Higgins et al. and Bevan-Brown and Walker studies was the need for, but shortage of, culturally appropriate services and resources. The discussion of cultural issues in the Bevan-Brown and Walker study showed that participants identified with their Māori heritage and felt strongly that culture needed to be taken into consideration in the education and services provided. Participants were adamant that being vision impaired should not mean they must also be culturally impaired.

Both studies led by Higgins (2010, 2012) identified a similar need:

> Māori do not just want access to appropriate and skilled services, they also want culturally appropriate ones. Services tend to be monocultural and monolingual in their provision. (Higgins, 2010, p. 227)

The 2012 study noted a need for services that better reflect kāpō Māori realities and aspirations. Of the 150 participants in this research, only 22 percent were receiving services from Ngāti Kāpō but 60 percent expressed a wish for referral to this organisation. At the time of the research, 35 percent were not aware of Ngāti Kāpō services. It was believed that accessing such services would contribute to maintaining a strong Māori identity. Participants also noted a desire and right to be self-determining. Reflecting on this, Higgins et al. (2010) note:

> Despite a higher rate of disability compared with non-Māori (Ministry of Health, 2004) Māori participation and representation in the disability sector is low… Not participating in such [disability] forums means that decisions are being made for Māori rather than by Māori. This represents a challenge. On the one hand participation is low because services do not reflect Māori aspirations, values and practices, yet on the other hand it is not the responsibility of Māori to change services through their participation. Rather it is up to the Crown as partner to the Treaty of Waitangi to ensure that services are accessible and outcomes are equitable. (p. 228)

While Te Momo's participants felt strongly about the importance of their cultural identity, they did not mention the shortage of culturally appropriate services as an issue. On the contrary, they commented on the helpfulness of support personnel from RNZFB and other service organisations. We speculate that because the main focus of the Te Momo research was on learning te reo Māori, participants limited their consideration of cultural issues to that kaupapa.

The implications of research findings for people who work with kāpō Māori

Many strategies to remove barriers experienced by kāpō Māori have been reported in the earlier description of the Bevan-Brown and Walker study. We suggest that because of the similar themes in Higgins et al.'s and Te Momo's research, these strategies would also be supported by their participants. Based on these themes, we recommend a three-step approach to improving the quality of life of kāpō Māori and their whānau.

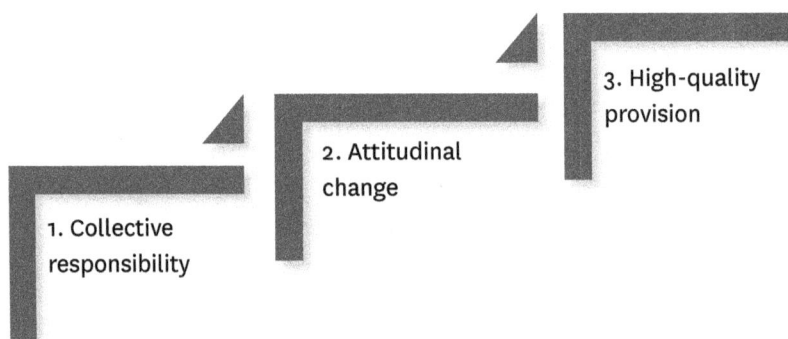

3. High-quality provision

2. Attitudinal change

1. Collective responsibility

Figure 6.1. Steps to overcoming barriers

Step 1: Collective responsibility

Responsibility for improving provision for kāpō Māori should not be restricted to their friends, whānau and relevant organisations and pro-fessionals, but rather shared by all New Zealanders, especially those in positions of power. While many people would support this statement in relation to removing general and educational barriers, removing cul-tural barriers might be considered a Māori responsibility. Improving the services available to kāpō Māori studying at wānanga or making marae more accessible are cases in point. *Wānanga* are relatively new educational institutions, with limited funding for and experience in providing disability services. Similarly, the renovations required to improve marae accessibility are well beyond the means of many, if not most, marae committees. Treaty of Waitangi obligations require the New Zealand Government and people to work in partnership with Māori to ensure their culture is actively protected. This translates to helping to remove any cultural barriers that exist.

Step 2: Attitudinal change

Research has shown that negative attitudes in general, and deficit thinking and lowered expectations in particular, are having a detrimental effect on the lives of kāpō Māori and their whānau. A concerted, multi-level campaign to change these limiting attitudes is needed. For example, at a societal level the welcoming and inclusion of people with BVI in the workplace, at all educational institutions, on marae and so forth will contribute to raising awareness, increasing understanding and developing more positive attitudes.

Improved attitudes at an organisational level would be evidenced in a commitment to improve services to kāpō Māori and their whānau. One easily achievable place to start is the collection and use of demographic data. This would address Higgins et al.'s (2010) finding that both health and education organisations lack knowledge about the demographics of kāpō Māori, which has negative implications for diagnosis, treatment and access to services.

At a professional level, improved attitudes will come with increased interaction with kāpō Māori and greater understanding of the barriers they face. This can be achieved by including relevant information and experiences in pre-service and in-service training. With respect to the former, this should be a course requirement for all students. For the latter, there must be a commitment to identify knowledge gaps among qualified professionals and introduce compulsory training to address these gaps.

Step 3: High-quality provision

Collective responsibility and positive attitudinal change should, in turn, lead to increased, improved services and resources for kāpō Māori and their whānau. Research clearly identifies the changes that need to be made, with cultural appropriateness, availability and accessibility being at the top of the list. The professional training mentioned above, along with:

- targeted hiring and empowerment of skilled Māori staff
- the establishment of Māori-run services
- the development of holistic, whānau-focused programmes
- the greater inclusion and empowerment of kāpō Māori and their whānau
- explicit policy commitment to the provision of culturally appropriate services and resources

will all contribute to addressing the shortages identified in the research. Ngāti Kāpō are well positioned to play a leadership role in all these initiatives.

Measures to increase availability and accessibility would include: targeted advertising in popular Māori media and at Māori events; locating services in areas with significant Māori populations; and enlisting the assistance of Māori organisations to advertise and deliver programmes and services, and to develop and distribute resources. Given the financial issues identified in the research, in order for services and resources to be available and accessed in a timely way, they will need to be affordably priced or, better still, freely available to those with limited financial means—both Māori and Pākehā. This will necessitate considerable financial input and commitment from the Government, organisations and personnel involved.

Conclusion

In conclusion, this chapter challenges professionals and organisations to examine their policy, programmes and practices to see whether or not the content, resources, delivery and assessment are culturally appropriate, readily accessible, affordable and relevant to kāpō Māori and their whānau. Similarly, whānau and community members should ask themselves, 'Do kāpō Māori have limited access to cultural and community activities and experiences because of their vision impairment, and if so, what needs to be done to change this situation?'

As the following whakatauākī reminds us, while the task may be a challenging one, working together has its rewards:

He kino tokomaha ki tae kainga a kai, tēnā kia tū ki te mahi, ka aha hoki.

Study questions

1. Higgins et al. (2010, p. 14) maintain that in pre-European times kāpō Māori were known for the talents they possessed, not for what they didn't have, but that this notion appears to have changed over time. Do the findings described in the Bevan-Brown and Walker study support this observation? Justify your answer.

2. The need to raise people's awareness and understanding of vision impairment was a major theme that emerged in all areas in the Bevan-Brown and Walker study. What suggestions were made to meet this need? What additional suggestions can you make?

3. This chapter discusses common barriers identified in the Higgins et al. (2010, 2012), Te Momo (2007) and Bevan-Brown and Walker (2013) studies and outlines three steps to address them. Given limited time and financial resources, how would you prioritise these barriers and the interventions to address them? What specific interventions would receive top priority? Why?

References

Beattie, H. (1990). *Tikao talks*. Auckland: Penguin Books.

Beattie, H. (1994). *Pre-European lifeways of the southern Māori*. Dunedin: University of Otago Press.

Bevan-Brown, J. (2002). *Culturally appropriate, effective provision for Māori learners with special needs: He waka tino whakarawea*. Unpublished doctoral thesis, Massey University [Palmerston North].

Bevan-Brown, J., & Walker, T. (2013). Taking culture into account: A Māori perspective on visual impairment. *Journal of Visual Impairment and Blindness, 107(*5): 388–392.

Higgins, N. (2001). *Blind people: A social constructivist analysis of New Zealand education policy and practice*. Unpublished doctoral thesis, University of Otago.

Higgins, N., Phillips, H., Cowan, C., Wakefield, B., & Tikao, K. (2010). *Growing up kāpō Māori: Whānau, identity, cultural well-being and health / E tipu kāpō nei: whanaungatanga, māramatanga, Māoritanga, hauoratanga*. Dunedin: Donald Beasley Institute, & Hastings: Ngāti Kāpō o Aotearoa.

Higgins, N., Phillips, H., Stobbs, K., Wilson, G., & Pascoe, H. (2012). *Summary of the findings—Growing up kāpō Māori: Accessing paediatric ophthalmology services*. Hastings: Ngāti Kāpō o Aotearoa.

Massey University. (2002). *Special Education 2000: Monitoring and evaluation of the policy*. Final report to the Ministry of Education. Palmerston North: Institute for Professional Development and Educational Research, Massey University.

Phillips, H., & Higgins, N. (in press). Growing up Māori and disabled in Aotearoa New Zealand. In C. Freeman & N. Higgins (Eds.), *Childhoods: Growing up in Aotearoa New Zealand*. Dunedin: Otago University Press.

Royal New Zealand Foundation of the Blind. *RNZFB annual report 2012–2013*. Retrieved from http://blindfoundation.org.nz/about/our-organisation/our-performance/annual-report-2012-2013

Te Momo, I. P. (2007). *From darkness to dawn?: A forum for kāpō Māori*. Unpublished master's thesis, University of Waikato.

Tibble, M. (1992). *Kia teitei te piki: Climb high: A fellowship report to the Sir Winston Churchill Memorial Trust Board*. Auckland: Māori Services Department, Royal New Zealand Foundation of the Blind.

Chapter 7

Living with physical disability: A Māori woman's perspective

Huhana Hickey and Jill Bevan-Brown

Kei tēnā, kei tēnā, kei tēnā anō.
Tōna ake āhua, tōna ake mauri, tōna ake mana.

Each and every one has their own uniqueness,
life essence and presence. (Fred Kana)

Introduction

This chapter consists of an interview with Huhana Hickey (affectionately known as 'Dr Hu'). In it she discusses her physical disability, the barriers she has faced in childhood and as an adult, what she has found helpful and unhelpful, her future dreams, and her advice to professionals who work with Māori children who have physical disabilities.

At the time of writing this chapter, disability statistics from the 2013 Aotearoa / New Zealand census were not available. However, in the 2006 census there were an estimated 96,600 Māori with a disability. Physical disability was the largest disability category among Māori adults; in fact 12 percent of all Māori aged 15 years and over were reported as having a physical disability. The number of Māori children with a physical disability was not given.

Despite the large number of Māori with a physical disability, research in this area is relatively scarce. One study of note was conducted by Huhana, along with a colleague, Adelaide Collins (Collins & Hickey, 2006). This research focused on the role whānau plays in the lives of Māori with physical disabilities. While the 13 informants reported a diverse range of experiences, many of the common themes that emerged are also reflected in the interview reported below.

Huhana and her physical disability

Huhana: Kia ora. My name is Dr Hu, Huhana. I'm from Waikato iwi. I'm Ngāti Tahinga, from Pukerewa Marae. My maunga is Karioi and my moana is Whāingaroa. My main physical disability is primary progressive multiple sclerosis [PPMS], but added to that I also have COP, which is chronic obstructive pulmonary disease, and gastro reflux, and a whole range of other little things that have happened that are part of the process really, that have come in over the years with age, arthritis, and all those bits and pieces, but the main one is PPMS.

Jill: And when did this start? Is this something from childhood?

Huhana: We don't know how it began. I lived in Taranaki, right by Paritutu, which is where the producers of dioxin had their factory. My nana used to live on Paritutu Road, which is just down from the factory. My mother worked there. We used to play around the drums as kids. They used to spray it over the farm lands in Taranaki and Waikato up until 1965, and I lived on a farm in Taranaki until 1965. I was a toddler then. They sprayed, so we don't know if it's a result of dioxin or poisoning, or whether it's something that's been there, because, it's one that is very rare. It is not one that is easily detectable. It took the doctors 11 years to diagnose and even then it's a preliminary diagnosis.

Jill: Right … so they haven't made up their minds yet?

Huhana: Well they can only treat the symptoms. There is absolutely no treatment that can really help it, whereas with other forms of MS [multiple sclerosis] you can get some kind of treatment. This one you can't. So they can only treat the symptoms, but they can't treat the cause and so, in other words, I'm in flare up all the time. I don't go into remission at all but it is a very slow progressive type of MS. I detect the symptoms of something happening way before it shows up in any tests.

They also cannot test for PPMS. It's very difficult, not like other forms of MS, because the scarring sits in my spine, up in the neck area, in the cervical area, but normally scarring for MS, it's in the brain. So cognitively I'm fine but physically my spinal column and all of that is quite damaged from it. That's why I struggle to walk. I may fall without reason, whereas with other forms of MS, because it hits the brain you can actually end up with a cognitive impairment as a result.

In 1996 Huhana acquired a brain injury and began using a wheelchair, although she could still walk short distances and stand. That all changed in 2011 when she acquired an infection, that weakened her further and has led her to constant use of a wheelchair.

Huhana: I used to walk around the house, but a couple of years ago I got very, very sick with an infection and I collapsed. My legs became a lot weaker from that point. I can still get from A to B, short distances, but I can't stand for any long period of time, so I need the wheelchair in case I fall.

Jill: So as a child you weren't in a wheelchair?

Huhana: No, as a child I had a lot of respiratory problems. Both my mothers smoked—my birth mother smoked when she was pregnant with me and my adoptive mother smoked. I've always had a respiratory problem from birth. I used to cough up blood as a kid. They put it down to bronchitis. At the age of 18 they said I had asthma, which is not something that apparently they liked to diagnose people with back then, they were reluctant, so they thought bronchitis was a better diagnosis but, I don't know. The mind set of people in the 60s and 70s was weird, but I've always had problems. I was quite attention deficit, all of those things, but they were never diagnosed. There were other things—depression from the age of 11—never diagnosed, but I lived with it. When I look back now I know exactly what was going on, but as a child I didn't know what was happening and people didn't know what was happening, couldn't understand things. They all thought it was all made up. When I had my appendix out, they didn't believe me and the pain was so severe that it burst just as I was going in to hospital. I am very lucky to be alive today, because no one believed me, you know, the pain was severe. I was screaming in pain, nobody believed that it was real.

Jill: Was this because you had a number of things wrong?

Huhana: Yes. Just a number of things, so they couldn't pinpoint anything.

Jill: So when did they start believing you?

Huhana: Well, asthma at 18 was the beginning. I mean every time I got chronic bronchitis and was coughing up blood, I would be treated but no one ever thought anything of it. They just thought they were different incidents.

Jill: Right, they didn't link them?

Huhana: No. So I guess you can say that I was lucky in a way that I didn't get diagnosed with a physical disability label as a kid. The label 'disability' frightened my parents. They saw it negatively in a bad way and any labelling may well have restricted my opportunities, whereas by not being labelled Mum and Dad let me try things out and didn't stop me when I began running for marathons etc. By the time I was diagnosed with asthma, I never told my family, because they saw any diagnosis as a bad thing. So it was their attitude that would have limited me, not so much the impairment itself but their reaction to it. But my birth papers said I was 'an imbecile and an idiot' on my adoption papers, and so my adoptive parents didn't think I could actually achieve much at school. I actually saw them. I was working at my father's work, he was a social worker. I worked at DSW [Department of Social Welfare] back then and the old paper work trail, I was doing the filing and I found my adoption papers. I didn't copy them because they didn't have photocopiers back then, that's how long ago, but I wish I had stolen them! I didn't. I was too much of a goody two-shoes back then, but I read them and I was quite shocked then myself, but that's what it said.

Jill: What age had they diagnosed you as an imbecile and an idiot?

Huhana: At birth, because I was adopted at birth. I was born a month premature. My mother was Māori, Aboriginal and Scots, my father was Sami and Yugoslav. They actually falsified my mother's ethnicity and said she was a Pākehā so they could put down on mine that I was a Pākehā. There was a lot of things that they did that were quite unethical at that time, whether it was to enhance an adoption or put me into foster care, but I happened to get adopted. We don't know. They told my birth mother that I was dying and to forget about me and they would put me with somebody. They told my adoptive parents that my mother was a Pākehā, that they were a young couple and that they didn't want me, so there were all sorts of stories. We don't really know what the truth is because both my mums have passed on and my adoptive father has passed on. I met with my birth father but he doesn't really know the stories either, although they married and I've got five siblings, but yeah it was a bit of a story! It wasn't uncommon. The thing that you'll find with a lot of adoptees of that time—cause I knew a lot of them, I went to school with a lot of them—is that they were often given false information. It wasn't uncommon that there was unethical stuff going down, and it was doctors, nurses, social workers.

Jill: Probably in their eyes it was in the best interests of the child?

Huhana: It was in the best interest of the child, yeah, in their eyes it was!

Jill: But to write 'imbecile and idiot' is obviously not in the best interest of the child!

Huhana: Well I must have had delayed development, a bit like my son did, my baby, and he was born seven and a half weeks early. Back then of course their lungs didn't develop.[1] A month premature baby now was like being 7 and a half weeks, 8 weeks premature back in those days. I

---

1   Drugs used now to speed up lung development in premature babies were not available then.

was very lucky that I made it through, but I guess they put it down as an assumption. Today you would say as a doctor that that is unethical, but back then they thought it was natural and normal. It just shows you how much though, we need to open the documents, and open up the information because they still don't give you the truth. They gave me a little booklet when I made inquiries and said, 'Here, this is all the information we have,' and I think it's just absolute rubbish. It was all set to be a nice little story. It was a nice story but it wasn't mine, not according to my adoptive parents, or my birth parents either.

I think it's actionable behaviour even from the doctors of that time. They often did things that were in the good interest, but it wasn't always true or legal, hence the Treaty claim that has gone in on behalf of a whole bunch of us who were adopted and fostered. For Māori babies, it's the denial of our Treaty rights, basically, you know, to have whānau adoption, to be adopted within the whānau. They would falsify your ethnicity so that you didn't go through the Ministry of Māori Affairs. So that is the whole reason behind it!

Jill: And there's a whole group of you?

Huhana: Yep! There's a heap, there are a few of us that have put in a claim, but there is a whole lot more than a few of us that have been affected! And they are often disabled or they were fostered or they were Māori babies that the doctors believed shouldn't be with their mothers.

Jill: Like in Australia?

Huhana: Yes, it's a form of stolen generation, but people don't want to recognise it in New Zealand. We call it 'the lost tribe'. None of us are lost—we are right here, but we had our information stolen from us. For some people it's irretrievable cause they have gotten rid of the files or the documents.

Jill: When did that Treaty claim go in?

Huhana: A few years ago now, but it is still going through the motions 'cause it's going to be a while, whether it's heard in my life time, I don't know. They are doing all the land claims first, so it may not be.

Major barriers faced as a disabled Māori woman

A literature search can identify a wide range of barriers experienced by people with disabilities, but little has been written about barriers particular to Māori women with physical disabilities. The following section outlines some of the general and cultural barriers Huhana has faced in the past and is still experiencing.

> **Huhana:** Major barriers are people's attitudes, people being raised with their own set of belief systems, I guess you could call them, their own fears, their own issues, and sometimes you become the brunt of those issues. It's not who you are, it's what you represent that frightens them, and some people are frightened. You hear people say, 'Oh, I could never be blind', or 'I don't know what it would be like to be deaf', yet my deaf friends are fine, my blind friends are fine, those of us in wheelchairs, waka tūru mates, are all fine, but society is frightened of us because they see things, weaknesses I think, weaknesses in us that they don't want to see in themselves. I'd argue that they are not weaknesses so to speak, they are strengths, but they don't see that, so they become frightened of us and we become an issue for them and it's sad, but attitudes is the main one.

Huhana went on to note that in her childhood disabled people were seldom seen in schools or the community. They were put into institutions, which was seen as

> normal … you weren't supposed to look after them because it was too much of a burden—according to the doctors. So it was an invisible world. If you had a visual disability, one that was diagnosable, they would put you into an institution. I guess in some ways I was lucky that my disabilities were not diagnosable at that time. Otherwise I would have been institutionalised, I'm sure!

With the late 1970s and early 1980s came deinstitutionalisation, which Huhana believed was introduced to save money, but she added that not enough funding has been allocated to enable quality community care.

Cultural issues

> **Huhana:** You go onto the marae and they won't allow my mobility dog because of some fear they have, or whatever, or it might be very

valid, it may be a historical thing. In the old days perhaps some of their tūpuna were captured by the enemy and fed to the dogs, so they don't want a dog there because it's seen as a threat to their history, to their meanings, but they don't provide an alternative. It's very difficult to go to hui knowing that you have to accommodate your dog somewhere else because they are not welcome on the marae.

Jill: So have they actually given those reasons?

Huhana: Yeah, those reasons were given at one marae, and yet it's ironic because their own dogs were running around outside. I don't know, it's just, you go to a marae and it's not accessible and they don't make any effort to make it accessible. Probably the best marae I could say that I have been to is my in-laws' marae at Motatau, up north. It is beautifully accessible, it is probably one of the best ones I have ever come across, to the point that they actually have a couple of little hospital beds and we were able to use them recently at a tangi, and one of my sisters-in-law who has got emphysema, [and] myself, we were able to grab the beds and sleep on those beds because we can't sleep on the floor. But you know, I have good sleeps except for the bugs, and the heat, but the marae itself, the bathroom was accessible, they had a shower there that was accessible, going in to eat was accessible and getting into the marae was accessible, in and out.

Jill: Is that a new marae or one that has been renovated?

Huhana: No, not one of the new ones, but they have accommodated this over time because of whānau with needs. They also, sometimes, host the turi whānau, the deaf whānau, because one of their own is deaf and the deaf whānau go there and find it really beautifully accommodating because they meet their needs with lighting and all of that. It's all done just right for them. They find it really nice to go to because of the aroha of that marae, the manaakitanga is just beautiful, and it's like we will treat you as we would like to be treated. They have no fear of us and they accommodate us and meet our needs, and it was all of that. It was Tau Henare's marae, the first MP Tau Henare, not the current one.

Jill: Right. So why is that marae doing it and others aren't?

Huhana: I think Ngāti Hine Health Trust is actually a really good health trust around hauā or disability issues, they work with rather than work at us. They work with us, they work with the whānau. That marae for some reason is the best one that I've come across. And it's inclusive, and it accommodates the needs of the whānau and it's not a big issue to have a hauā member there. You're accepted as part of the whānau and they just embrace you.

Jill: I wish other marae would take their lesson on board.

Huhana: Well they could follow their lead, that's for sure. There's bigger iwi and more financially capable iwi, and they can certainly make all their marae accessible and accommodating, but a lot of them have the attitude that they don't want us around, we're invisible to them. They'd rather that we stayed in the background and didn't come into the foreground. You know, stay at home, stay hidden and keep away. They really don't want to know us. Well they don't have to confront with us if we don't get involved. The problem is, we are getting involved and they're finding it quite difficult. You can feel it with the attitudes on some marae, or with some of the whānau members. It's the fear that they have about us.

Jill: Is it the fear of the unknown or fear of you?

Huhana: Fear of the unknown, I think. It's not actually a personal thing. It's an issue that goes beyond personal. It's an issue that goes to their own past issues. And it might be that in the whānau maybe they've got a history of things like strokes and stuff or they see it as a spiritual thing. You know, I have had a couple of people accuse me of having a mākutu, and I look at them and say, 'Well how would you know unless you placed it on me?' It comes from the Old Testament of the Bible and it comes from the Christianisation of our people that we carry the many sins of our ancestors, so therefore we have a mākutu or a hara, so they see that as us representing that, but if they don't make the effort to try and understand then, in their minds we have a mākutu and they stay away from us or they see us as something of a threat, spiritually.

Jill: So accessibility and attitude are the two things that you've been talking about here as barriers.

Huhana: Yes, and ignorance too, ignorance based on the Old Testament, ignorance based on the old version that was taught to them throughout the history of colonisation. Prior to colonisation there were varying attitudes, but it was far more inclusive of multiple disabilities, far more inclusive. It's post-colonisation that this has happened, because we used to see it as being a very natural process. It was a natural thing as you aged, you become more disabled, and if you survived a war battle and you're injured, you become a war hero in the whānau. If you're born blind or deaf, there's something you can offer to the marae and they teach you. For the blind, they might be real tohunga in mirimiri in the old days or of the spiritual world. The deaf they have their own roles, the learning disabled. We didn't label them. We just found what they could do and we accommodated them within the cultural concepts that we had back then, and I think the only ones that they probably got rid of were the ones that were so severely deformed so were not going to survive that they euthanised. But that would have been at birth, but they didn't euthanise every one. They didn't euthanise you as, the blind, the deaf, we're going to top you off! They didn't see it like that. Even those with whaiora, with mental health issues, they saw them as having a role, probably a more spiritual role, but they saw them as having a place. So it wasn't unusual for Māori to embrace disabled before colonisation.

Jill: I've looked into that issue, that debate, that there were children killed at birth, and I haven't actually found any evidence that they were.

Huhana: No, no, well mum, my birth mum, the first thing she said to me was, 'Had I had you in the old days you would have been knocked on the head,' and it was reference to the fact that I wasn't going to survive anyway.

Jill: I just wonder whether that has grown as a myth?

Huhana: I don't know. I don't know that they did euthanise, but the assumption is that they did.

Jill: Yes, that's what I queried because, who knows? It's difficult to ascertain.

Huhana: The difficulty is that we've lost that knowledge of the old people.

Jill: Have you looked back into history? This is what makes me think that it is a myth that has built up, because there were physically disabled kaumātua, tūpuna, and if that was the case, they wouldn't have been around.

Huhana: Exactly! And also the other thing, there is a lot about atua—Muriranga-whenua, gave the magic jawbone, she was blind, she was deaf, she was crippled as they put it. There was Mahuika, goddess of fire, she was blind. You know, they had Māui, who had club feet and was a runt, which means he was a premmy and possibly ADHD, as they would have diagnosed him today. So a lot of our atua also had impairments. So it wasn't seen as a bad thing in the old days. But the ignorance today around it is that the Bible influenced the thinking and changed the thinking of our people to believing that we have a mākutu and a hara, that we carried those. And that's what some believe. Some are very adamant about it so we have a lot of educating to do around people.

Main sources of support

Negative and restrictive attitudes and actions create barriers that Huhana and other disabled people face on an ongoing basis, but research reported throughout this book also shows that particular people are major sources of support. In this section Huhana talks about what has been most helpful to her.

Huhana: What helps in managing is actually my partner, who is fantastic. Having the support around me that I need to be able to do the work that I do, without her, without my support person, I wouldn't be functioning as well as I do. Also my dog, my kurī is just brilliant, he gets things for me. I miss him when I go to hospital. I hate being in hospital! My son, my boy is fantastic. It's support and having whānau around you. It's your whānau, they help. I mean, my partner's whānau are brilliant to us, they look after me and they look after her. They make sure that we are okay, and the nieces are really awesome in that way. They also give us our mokopuna to look after.

We had one on Friday night and he was awesome! You can't be whole without a whānau. I think if I was to manage myself on my own I would be struggling.

The delight Huhana shared in looking after her mokopuna was palpable. She is a proud nanny who plays an important nurturing role within her whānau. This not only helps at a practical level but also provides her mokopuna with positive experiences of disability that they will carry into the future. Nurturing within the whānau is reciprocated: Huhana went on to give a recent example of how her 27-year-old son had helped when she was sick. He lives nearby. She also has a 33-year-old son who lives in Sydney.

Jill: So, have the most helpful people been your whānau?

Huhana: Yes, 'he tāngata, he tāngata, he tāngata',[2] you know, they can either make you or break you. If they get together with you and they don't have an issue, then whānau are fantastic. If the whānau have issues around your disability and abuse you or create difficulties for you, then you have got a problem. And you really need to look at the attitude, and why. There are some out there that do abuse the hauā whānau, but then there are some out there that are absolutely brilliant towards them! And I'm very lucky!

Problems experienced

Despite strong whānau support, Huhana's daily life is peppered with a variety of ongoing frustrations that research shows are common to many people with disabilities.

Huhana: Oh well, service providers, funding, trying to get what you need, the equipment you need, get the support that you need in place. Trying to get anything is like pulling a needle out of a hay stack with the Government, and yet if I was an ACC client I would have far less barriers than what I do have with the Ministry of Health. Ministry of Health disability really are the poor cousins. Why do we have these disparities? We shouldn't be having them, because we are supposed

---

2   The full whakataukī from which this originates is: "Hutia te rito o te harakeke, / Kei whea te kōmako e kō? / Kī mai ki ahau; / He aha te mea nui o te ao? / Māku e kī atu, / He tāngata, he tāngata, he tāngata." (*If the heart of the harakeke was removed, where will the bellbird sing? / If I was asked what was the most important thing in this world; / I would reply, it is people, it is people, it is people!*)

to be in a no-fault system where the Government pays but we pay through taxes. We also pay taxes around medical disabilities but we don't see any benefits of it because it's always around, 'Oh we don't have enough money.' But you know, ACC has made a massive profit. Why don't we amalgamate and utilise that and just up the fees slightly more and then just have it all under one roof and stop the differences. It would make life a whole lot easier!

Jill: So is the problem actually accessing the resources that you need?

Huhana: Yes, accessing resources, for whatever you need, for whatever your needs are you have got to justify that every single step of the way. You have got to write up a 50 page dialogue in order to get a pen half the time, to get special equipment or whatever you need, so most of the time I don't bother. I just fundraise myself through work and try and find the funding some other way where I can. But where wheelchairs and vehicles are concerned, you know, if you're not working or studying you are pretty much screwed! The benefit doesn't cover what you need. The difference for the blind people is if they do work they can actually keep the benefit whereas other disabilities you have to fight for it, under section 66 of the Social Security Act. Whereas if you're blind, it's an automatic right.

Jill: So why are they different?

Huhana: Because they fought for it during the First World War, and it has happened to have stayed, but other disabilities didn't have the same powerful lobbying that ex-war veterans from the mustard gas had, so they got the support that other disabilities never had. While many of them may not work, those that do work can work and keep their benefit. But people with other disabilities have to apply for a section 66.

Jill: What's a section 66?

Huhana: A section 66 provides for people with disabilities to have the right to continue being paid their disability benefit whilst working. Secondary tax is still paid and there is loads of red tape involved but there is not a lot that can be done about the red tape.

Future dreams

Huhana then expanded on how red tape and other restrictive practices adversely affected her ability to achieve her future dreams.

> **Huhana:** I'd like to own a house by the ocean, write poetry and write a book.

> **Jill:** Can I come and live with you please?

> **Huhana:** Oh, and I would like a place to be able to do my art work. I'm a painter and a cartoonist. I would like to have a place where I can create. But I will never own a house. Having a disability costs so much to live and there are no motivational incentives for anyone to go out and work anyway, but I do.

Huhana went on to discuss cheap loans and other potential means of buying a house. She noted that disabled people are less likely to get loans because they have less security and can't afford the massive deposits required. She also described the extra financial costs of having a disability, including high medical and transport costs.

> **Jill:** What about health insurance?

> **Huhana:** They won't give it to me because I'm already too disabled, it costs them too much. They would charge me a fortune in health insurance in order to cover me, so it's not worth it. So the cost of medication, cost of living, things like power, all of that. I have air conditioning running because I can't cope with the heat—common issue with MS is heat, and people don't cope with the heat.

> **Jill:** Those are costs that people are not aware of.

> **Huhana:** No! No, those are all of the hidden costs that come with working. I mean I can't catch a train and a bus, if I could I would, but I can't do that in the time frame I need to get to and from work.

Advice for professionals who work with Māori children with physical disabilities

In the last interview section Huhana was asked about what teachers and other professionals can do to help Māori children with physical disabilities.

Huhana: What could teachers do? When you are dealing with Māori children with physical disabilities, first of all you need to treat them the same as you would treat your non-disabled kids. The only difference is, is that they might not be able to get around the same way. I think first of all, what you do is you make sure the classroom is set up properly so the child can get around the same way all the other kids can get around the classroom, access everything, make it open plan, don't put all the desks in the way, put them in a big square or whatever, and make sure there is room for the child to get around to access everything. So you accommodate the space, make it accessible.

You make sure the child's needs are meet, that if they have got a poo bag on the side, or a catheter in place, that there is a place of privacy for the child to be able to be changed, and if the child has to do it themselves then you may ask them and learn a little bit on what to do or make sure that they have their dignity intact if they have an accident and all of a sudden it smells, 'cause it is quite a smell, that the kids start teasing. The worst thing was my baby got teased for his epilepsy a lot at primary school, and so it's protect the child from that teasing. Maybe even get the child to introduce themselves, and what their disability is. Teach the kids what they can do, what they don't need to do in order to help him or her out. An example of that was with a deaf child in my son's class, when he was five they actually brought a sign-language interpreter in and all the kids learnt sign language. So they could all speak at the same level as the student, and as they go through school they would all go through the same classrooms together.

So there are all those kinds of things. It's also, if you have an issue with the particular disability, deal with it. Deal with your own issues first, don't transfer it onto the child. So if you have got a fear or you have a worry about things, ask the parents and ask the child what they need in order to accommodate that child's inclusion. Don't spoil the child, don't make the child out to be so special that they think of themselves as being in some kind of position that they are not. Give them a reality check, make them as special as all the other kids are in that classroom, but also don't go to the other extreme where the child is so different that the kids end up thinking that difference is a bad thing.

So accommodate. Accommodate your attitude, too. Deal with your own attitudes first—deal with your own fears and then get on with it. We are no different. That child's need is going to be no different than any other kid's. The child will want to play sport. Sport Waikato has a person that comes around and helps teach how to include the child in sports. So in Auckland, wherever around the country, get the council sports people to come out and teach how to include that child in sports. Because there are ways of including them that means they don't have to sit on the side lines while everyone else is doing it. I mean, particularly for cross country, it's actually good if the kids in a wheelchair do cross country, it's a good sport for them. They might even be able to accommodate a special chair, or a walker. You might be able to do a mini cross country with them. There are ways of doing it that make it work for the child. So there are all different ways. If you are going to do school trips, include the child. Make sure you get their wheelchair out, however it is. Make sure that there is a way of including the child on the trip. Doesn't matter how disabled. If the child is non-verbal, it doesn't matter, give them the experiences of life that the other kids are having. Yes, include them, even if they have a special needs teacher, that'll help with the teaching, but the social aspects are all part of what the teacher needs to help to include them, especially the young kids at primary school. Very much so. It's very important to be as inclusive as possible.

Jill: And if they are a Māori child?

Huhana: Don't stop the Māori kids from engaging in kapa haka or any of those things. I've seen kids in wheelchairs doing kapa haka. There are ways of doing it, ways of including them, even if they are deaf, blind, whatever, the disability does not stop them from being Māori. So give them the Māori experience. I think kura kaupapa, kōhanga reo—they really have a lot to learn around including disabled Māori children in their classrooms.

Huhana has an autistic nephew who is fluent in te reo and English. She explains that in her experience she has found kura kaupapa and kōhanga not to be very inclusive despite their inclusive philosophy. For example, many of their buildings have no ramps, which means disabled children and their parents receive a strong message about who can participate in these spaces.

Jill: What about the argument that if a child enrols or a parent comes in that needs a ramp, they build it at that stage?

Huhana: No, I think it shouldn't be like that. It should be that you pre-empt the need because you're actually telling them, then 'Oh we have to find the funding,' 'Oh, it's going to be a cost.' Why should you lay that kind of guilt on the parent? It needs to be that you build for what you're expecting. There might never be a disabled child. But you never know, a parent might be disabled and they might want to participate, why not build the environment for all the whānau? All the nannies who are in their walkers or whatever, or the parents with prams, it all accommodates the needs of that whānau. We always just think of the child, but no, you shouldn't have to build it in, it should be built in from the beginning.

Jill: Right, right! Everyone can use a ramp, but steps exclude some people from accessing buildings. Can you think of other Māori-specific examples?

Huhana: Not really. For a Māori child the only difference around them in being Māori is getting to know who they are as Māori, and that is something that these schools need to be doing, but that is something also that parents need to be doing. That's an ongoing thing for all Māori children, really, and the disabled Māori child should not be exempted from that, it's that simple really. If you are going to do haka, that's okay, position them on the side and let them do what they are capable of, let them learn what they are capable of. I have seen some real passionate haka from kids in wheelchairs. In fact our wheelblacks do a really amazing haka. I used to play wheelchair rugby and I used to do the haka with them, 'cause it was an inclusive female, male haka and it was an awesome one to do. Your legs may not work but your bloody arms do, and the passion on your face is just the same. Kids show the same kinds of passion—include them! It's inclusion, inclusion, inclusion.

We have got to get back to our basic roots of what we were before colonisation and it's simple. We were a natural part of the whānau so bring us back to be a natural part of the whānau. We had our roles in the past and we can have our roles again. But we won't have them if we don't learn our place from the beginning. If you have no expectation of that child, they will have no expectation of themselves and it will end up on barriers and having to fight like I had to do and you shouldn't have to. I am not saying that you put the things on a plate, but I am saying that you have the opportunities there. Don't put the barriers there.

Concluding comments

Jill: You having to fight, is that because of expectations?

Huhana: I think it was because nobody expected anything of me. It was a pity that both of my mums weren't around when I got my PhD because that was the reason that I got it, to prove that I wasn't the idiot and the imbecile that everyone said I was, that I wasn't dumb. My mate chastises me because I still say I am dumb at times when I get down on myself, that the PhD is not good enough, but that is my own demons that come from a lifetime of abuse—very hard to get rid of!

I think we need to learn about the history of all things Māori, and that includes hauā, what that means in our community. We have to embrace it and we have to accommodate naturally, as the old people did. As the nannies said to me when I got my PhD, 'We didn't think anything of it, you were part of our whānau,' even if they didn't physically accommodate like the marae having steps. One politician gave me the story of her brother who is a tetraplegic. Until she became a minister she didn't think anything of the fact that they carried him in and out of the marae, until she realised that they had removed his dignity as a human being, because the dignity of being able to wheel yourself in means mountains to a physically disabled Māori; being carried in is humiliating. It demeans your mana as a person, so if you don't want to demean my mana, let me wheel myself in, accommodate in that way and my mana is intact. But if you are going to lift me and carry me in, I am embarrassed, humiliated. I get whakamā and I don't want to be there. It's as simple as that— physical disability has so many physical barriers—remove them! Put ramps in the place. Don't make it difficult. Make a bathroom wide enough.

Jill: They are not biggies, are they?

Huhana: No, but they make them biggies, they make them into big deals, but there are examples of good marae dotted around the country—not many of them, but the others need to start copying. As for the rich iwi, they need to start leading by example. Provide a fund that can go out annually to each marae so that they can make adaptations, accommodations. Don't go by minimum standards, go by the best standards. For some, they need the privacy for an adult to change their catheter. For children you can lift them up and put them somewhere private. People don't think of it, but you can't change an adult on a marae, in the wharenui. They need a private space to be able to lay down and to be able to be changed. Nobody thinks of that anywhere. It would mean just so much to the individual to have somewhere private where they can have their adult ablutions met. It's not always just about a shower and a toilet … one day.

Jill: We have to believe that it is possible and keep striving towards it.

Huhana: Yes, we do. We can't give up. They have come a long way now, they will come a long way again. There are some days I wonder why I am doing more than others with the same disability are doing, [they may be just] sitting at home. I think, 'Oh God, why don't I just give up,' but then I think, 'No, I don't want that kind of life. I have got too much I want to do before I can rest.'

Jill: My hat's off to you Huhana. You are an inspiration to us all and a model for us to follow. You certainly deserve that little house by the beach and I hope that one day soon you get it. Thank you for sharing some of your incredible life with us—we are privileged.

As Fred Kana[3] said in the whakataukī that began this chapter, "Kei tēnā, kei tēnā, kei tēnā anō, tōna ake āhua, tōna ake mauri, tōna ake

---

3   Fred Kana (1947–2008), of Taharoa and Ngāti Mahuta descent, was a senior lecturer, kaiurungi and mātua at the Faculty of Education, University of Waikato, at the time of his untimely death. The Fred Kana Fellowship was set up by the Faculty of Education to encourage and mentor future Māori leaders in education. See https://education.waikato.ac.nz/qualifications/fees-financial-support/fred-kana-fellowship/

mana." (Each and every one has their own uniqueness, life essence and presence.) This interview has provided a glimpse into the uniqueness, life essence and massive presence of Huhana Hickey—a glimpse that provides many valuable lessons for us all.

Study questions

1. Why was Huhana's particular disability so hard to diagnose? Would children with primary progressive multiple sclerosis receive an earlier diagnosis today, and if so, why?

2. What are the major general and cultural barriers Huhana has faced? Which do you consider the greatest single barrier? Brainstorm strategies for overcoming it.

3. "It's inclusion, inclusion, inclusion." List the strategies Huhana suggests for enabling the inclusion of Māori children with physical disabilities.

References

Collins, A., & Hickey, H. (2006). *The role of whānau in the lives of Māori with physical disabilities.* Wellington: The Families Commission. Retrieved from: http://www.familiescommission.org.nz/publications/research-reports/the-role-of-wh%C4%81nau-in-the-lives-of-m%C4%81ori-with-physical-disabilities

Chapter 8

Intellectual disability: Looking through a Māori lens

Jill Bevan-Brown

E kore e hekeheke, he kākano rangatira.

I will never be lost for I am the product of chiefs.

Introduction

This chapter reports the findings of a small study that investigated pre-European and contemporary Māori concepts of intellectual disability and opinions about the care and education of intellectually disabled Māori children.[1] Subsequent research in the health and education sectors is considered, and the implications of the findings for people who work with intellectually disabled Māori and their whānau are outlined.

What is intellectual disability?

What is intellectual disability (ID)? This would seem to be a simple question, but the answer is highly controversial. Whole books and

---

1   This chapter draws substantially from my unpublished master's research report (Bevan-Brown, 1989) and from Bevan-Brown, 1994.

research reports have been written on the topic.[2] At the root of the problem is the fact that ID is a concept, not a tangible entity. Consequently, what is perceived as ID depends on contexts of place, purpose, beliefs and values, all of which differ between people and across time. I became interested in Māori concepts of ID many years ago as a special education teacher. Despite Māori children being over-represented in special classes and special schools at the time (Kaa, 1987; Wylie, 1988), information about ID from a Māori perspective appeared to be non-existent. If differences in concepts, needs, attitudes, parental and whānau expectations and preferences did exist, were these being taken into account in the education and services provided for intellectually disabled Māori children? What cultural accommodations and adaptations were needed? These questions prompted the study reported below.

The research

From a Māori perspective, the past and present are inextricably linked. Tūpuna are not distant names in a genealogy, but rather people whose influence is still felt within whānau and acknowledged on marae across the country. A true understanding of where Māori are today cannot be gained without reference to the past (Reid, 1986). Consequently, the first research aim was to investigate traditional and contemporary Māori concepts of and attitudes towards ID.

Further aims were to investigate contemporary Māori opinions about the care and education of intellectually disabled Māori, with specific reference to the inclusion of Māori concepts, beliefs, values, content and language; and contemporary Māori opinions about current issues in the care and education of intellectually disabled people, both Māori and Pākehā.

Methodology

The research was a small exploratory study consisting of a literature review and interviews with 16 people involved in working or living with Māori who were intellectually disabled.

Literature review

Written sources on intellectual disability in pre-European times are

---

2   Bray, 2003, is a user-friendly publication that gives multiple answers to the question 'What is intellectual disability?' and provides an excellent discussion of the controversy involved. It can be accessed at http://www.donaldbeasley.org.nz/publications/NHC_Definitions.pdf

non-existent, and so I drew on traditional stories, values, customs and practices; whakapapa information; early ethnologies (Anderson, 1931; Makereti, 1938; Best, 1952); and the work of respected Māori writers to hypothesise about traditional Māori concepts of and attitudes towards ID. A range of contemporary written sources, including the Royal Commission on Social Policy (1988), were consulted to answer other research questions.

Interviews and data analysis

Sixteen in-depth, face-to-face interviews were conducted. Although participants were given a formal questionnaire beforehand, the process itself was very informal: "we talked, laughed and cried, ate, looked at photo albums, reminisced, ate and talked some more" (Bevan-Brown, 1994, p. 207). The interviews, which ranged from 1 to 5 hours, were audio-taped and later transcribed. Analysis consisted of summarising data and presenting it in tables, quotes and précis form under the respective questions.

Participants

The eight male and eight female participants ranged in age from 32 to 67. They represented a variety of socioeconomic and educational backgrounds, tribal affiliations and semi-rural, suburban and urban residence. All participants were well respected in the Māori community and had experience of knowing, dealing with or caring for intellectually disabled people, either in their own home, the hospital, school or a work situation. The majority had family members or friends who are intellectually disabled.

Results

Traditional concepts and attitudes

From the literature review two opposing hypotheses regarding ID emerged. On the one hand, Māori in pre-European times appear to have had little tolerance and sympathy for people who were disabled in any way. As Best (1952) reported, "Deformed persons, who were not common, met with little sympathy and often received a name descriptive of the deformity" (p. 8). Intellectual disability, along with physical and sensory disability, was regarded by some Māori as punishment for a tapu infringement, either by the disabled person or by a close relative.

As such, the disability was accepted with an air of fatalism (Royal Commission on Social Policy, 1988).

In traditional times Māori believed that the wairua or soul leaves the body during sleep and wanders about, and the memory of its wanderings constitutes a dream. A person should never be wakened suddenly for fear of the body being awake before the wairua returns, leaving the person "half-witted" (Anderson, 1931). This idea of spiritual influence is echoed by Durie (1985, p. 483): "Without a spiritual awareness the individual is considered to be lacking in well-being and more prone to disability or misfortune."

On the other hand, the opposing hypothesis of a tolerant, sympathetic, accepting and inclusive attitude towards ID is also supported in the literature. Arguments mainly centre around the Māori holistic perspective of health which focuses on collective wellbeing rather than emphasising personal dysfunction (Durie 1977; 1985; Marsden, 1986; Murchie, 1986; Pomare, 1986; Rankin, 1986). Furthermore, in the past whānau were socially and morally obliged to look after all their members, including children, the elderly and those with disabilities. Ill health reflected on the whānau and it was held accountable for any harm that came to one of its members. This is reflected in the practice of muru raids, which could take place following a death. If there was any evidence of neglect then the whānau of the deceased could be plundered as punishment for their negligence (Durie, 1977).

Similarly, data from the interview participants supported opposing hypotheses about ID. On the positive side, participants recalled stories showing intellectually disabled people being revered as taonga, being accepted with amusement and being valued as an integral part of the community. They also mentioned that in earlier times children with an ID were often in the special charge of kaumātua.

Negative attitudes were linked to the breaking of tapu:

> Sometimes a family didn't only have one with this sort of disability but two or three … I would consider it as heredity but in the old days it would be considered that they had done something *really* wrong, probably broken a tapu or something like that, so this was 'hitting back' at them 'cause that's how it used to work in the old days.

However, the most frequently mentioned attitude related to the acceptance and inclusion of intellectually disabled people into the community. This was based on the premise of whanaungatanga, whereby all members are accepted and have a role to play within the whānau and iwi according to their skills and abilities.

Interestingly, there appears to be no traditional Māori word that equates to ID, although the term *hinengaro hauā* has entered into modern usage. Participants mentioned *pōrangi* and *wairangi*. Some believed that these words may encompass aspects of ID, but the general interpretation, supported by Māori dictionaries, relates to mental illness, insanity, confusion and similar concepts rather than ID.

Contemporary concepts and attitudes

Participants were asked about their own understanding of ID. The general picture that emerged was that of slow thinkers, doers and learners who had limited ability to look after themselves and cope with everyday life. Also discussed were differences between mental and chronological age, degree of disability and possible causes. When the similarity between general Pākehā understanding of ID was noted, one person remarked:

> When we talk about intellectual handicap and disability those are Pākehā terms ... we have formed those tabs without us really understanding the Māori perspective of them and we take them for granted. We have taken on the Pākehā understanding and we now, as Māori, have to go back and change our cogs, go backwards to clear our minds ... there are a whole lot of word labels that have been learned from childhood right through. We think it is part of us but really it isn't and we don't know when to chop them off.

In discussing possible differences between Pākehā and Māori understanding of ID, the nine participants who believed that differences existed, mentioned differences in: degree of severity ("We don't seem to consider people handicapped unless they are *really bad*"), spiritual component ("To some Māori, spirituality plays a part in their understanding of ID. I'm not sure it does in the Pākehā sense"); and the concept of time and development:

> People need to come to different stages of development through their own time ... Māori do not measure that time as Pākehā do ... Māori

children are classified as intellectually disabled when in fact they are not … they are classified through a different cultural perspective.

This quote alludes to the disparity between chronological age and mental age that is an indicator of ID in the Pākehā world. The participant noted that this disparity is not relevant in a culture where personal development is not conceived as fitting into a time frame.

While the literature does not discuss differences between Pākehā and Māori understanding of ID *per se*, it does comment on differences between the concept of wellbeing in general. The Māori approach, described by Durie (1985) as Te Whare Tapa Whā, encompasses the physical dimension (te taha tinana); the spiritual dimension (te taha wairua); the thinking, emotional dimension (te taha hinengaro); and the family dimension (te taha whānau) (Durie, 1985; Pomare, 1986). This holistic, all-embracing notion of good health will necessarily result in an understanding, emphasis and treatment of ID that is different to the more narrow Pākehā concept of health. Similarly, Durie (1985) discusses differences in modes of thought, communication and social status. He maintains that the Pākehā mode of thought and communication is essentially cognitive and analytical, and that social status is gained by a person's earning capacity, which is often related to their intellectual ability. On the other hand, "Māori thinking could be described as holistic" (Durie, 1985, p. 484), with emotional and spiritual awareness being integral components, and command and appreciation of taha Māori playing a greater role in social status than one's earning capacity (Marsden, 1986; Pomare, 1986). Such differences will, in turn, have an impact on concepts of and attitudes towards ID.

Participants' attitudes towards people who are intellectually disabled revealed a range of emotions and beliefs. The most frequently mentioned view, prevalent among younger participants, was that ID is a fact of life. People with ID are accepted on an equal basis as fellow human beings deserving equal opportunity and having just as much mana as non-disabled individuals. The older age group spoke more often of sympathy, relief at not being disabled and willingness to help whenever they could. Thirteen of the sixteen participants reported feeling comfortable among intellectually disabled people, two were uncomfortable, while the other participant chose neither but added, "I would be quite happy if an intellectual disabled person came up to me and the kids at the park as I think it is good for kids to be around them. It teaches them to know difference."

By and large, these personal views were echoed in answers to a question relating to Māori and iwi attitudes to ID. The most commonly mentioned attitude was that of non-judgemental acceptance both by individuals and by the Māori community. Three aspects of acceptance were referred to: ID as a fact of life; intellectually disabled people having value and mana; and greater acceptance of human difference among Māori. Other common attitudes were those of caring, aroha, tolerance and support, as exemplified in the following quote:

W.P. is a real identity at home. He wanders around at all hours, has access to everyone's homes. It is amazing what he can remember— whakapapa and that. If you get him on track he is good, but he has things generally mixed up in conversation. He dribbles a lot. He has the freedom of the village, goes to all the hui and is invited in to eat. No one can remember him ever being sick. At Christmas time he is always welcome. He'll eat and sleep at someone's house then he disappears and ends up at someone else's! He has been doing that all his life and no one ever says anything.

However, it was noted by other participants that attitudes are changing. Whereas in the past Māori may have been likely to support intellectually disabled people within the whānau and community, it was becoming increasingly difficult to do so in urban situations, especially where resources are scarce.

Three participants supported the traditional belief that the breaking of tapu could cause ID, four people denied it, and the rest provided qualified answers. In reference to the tapu belief, the Royal Commission on Social Policy (1988) reported that some whānau were not diligent about therapeutic treatments away from hospital because they felt they could not change the order of things. The mixed view about tapu exemplifies one participant's warning: "You can't generalise … there is a range of attitudes towards ID just as in the Pākehā world."

Māori content in the care and education of intellectually disabled Māori

There was unanimous agreement among interview participants that Māori concepts, beliefs, values, subject matter and te reo should be included in the care and education of intellectually disabled Māori. People felt strongly that a Māori identity is just as important to an intellectually disabled Māori as it is to a non-disabled Māori:

> Yes, because if they are Māori their beliefs, values and attitudes are there whether they are intellectually disabled or not … If you are in a positive environment and the values that you have are seen to be OK, are valued and all that, then you are more likely to make the most of your capacity and in fact improve.

> Whatever we want for our non-handicapped children should also be taught to the intellectually disabled up to what they are capable of learning.

Te reo Māori

Similarly, there was unanimous agreement about the inclusion of te reo Māori. In fact everyone agreed that intellectually disabled Māori children are better off in a "good" bilingual or total immersion situation than in a monolingual class. It was pointed out that cultural values are part of te reo and that you could not have one without the other: "If we appreciate that language is essential to our cultural identity then it is just as crucial for the identity of the disabled Māori."

However, five participants qualified their answers by saying that the child's degree of disability would be a limiting factor in what was taught. One suggestion was a programme specifically geared to intellectually disabled Māori, while another involved using te reo naturally in the child's environment rather than 'teaching' it as such.

A further point with respect to including te reo was:

> The reo is important but the manaaki from people caring for that person is more important. If you can combine them both, it's ideal. Kōrero is no good without rapport. Te reo is important, but it depends on how it is implemented.

Māori curriculum

In addition to te reo, other Māori content specifically mentioned included: legends; history; customs, traditions and tikanga (both every-day and marae protocols); whakapapa; karakia and traditional Māori spiritual beliefs; art and craft, such as flax weaving, tāniko and carving; music, from modern action songs to waiata tawhito; and Māori values, such as aroha-ki-te-tangata, manaakitanga, whanaungatanga and an appreciation of nature and care of the environment. Whānau grouping, tuakana–teina relationships, strength-based teaching, co-operative learning, consensus decision making and power sharing were all mentioned as effective and appropriate teaching strategies and approaches.

Many people stressed the importance of all Māori content being included and/or taught with the correct wairua and in the right context. For Māori values to have real meaning, they should be an integral part of the person's daily life. Not only must they be acknowledged in educational and caring provisions, but they should also be practised by all concerned.

People who work with Māori children need to be aware of cultural practices such as reluctance to make eye contact and concepts such as whakamā. One participant supported this view with a story of an able child who was put in a special class because her extreme shyness and upbringing of being "seen but not heard" was misinterpreted as "not knowing." There was a concern that these quiet Māori children missed out on needed help because they did not "speak out".

Additional points were that parents, whānau and the Māori community should be involved in setting Māori curriculum, and that Māori content should not be taught in isolation, limited to the classroom nor focused solely on the past:

> How it's taught and where it's taught has to be in a way that you get total immersion and the community is involved, the students are involved, everybody is involved and that opens up the opportunities to have things taught anywhere. It could be on the marae, in a school, at university, at health camp, anywhere … It should be given the widest possible coverage.

> [The curriculum] must include all the things that make a holistic person—social, physical, cultural, intellectual—using all the latest technology. For economic reasons the intellectually disabled must be helped and advanced. If we just give whakapapa and things from the

past we are still on the wrong canoe!

The majority of participants believed that Māori content, including Māori values, should be included in the care and education of all people who are intellectually disabled, not just Māori. It was thought that doing so would improve tolerance and understanding, which in turn would lead to greater racial harmony and acceptance of disability. The suggestion was also made that intellectually disabled Māori who have cultural knowledge could be involved in sharing this with their peers.

Issues in the care and education of intellectually disabled people

Inclusion

The majority of participants believed children with intellectual disability should be taught in ordinary classrooms:

> Yes, yes, the mainstreaming of those kids is more in line with Māori community values, I think, being part of the whole and not separated.

> Intellectually disabled children must not be excluded. I think we are just a little too quick to remove kids from the class. Invariably Māori kids end up being the little hīanga kids in the classroom and teachers want them out as quickly as possible, but we just have to persevere with them in the class and change our attitudes towards them so that they become part of the class instead of, 'Zap, out you go!'

The benefits of inclusion are that it promotes aroha-ki-te-tangata; raises teachers' and children's expectations, leading to increased achievement; provides opportunities for role modelling; and fosters social interaction, which is valuable for all those involved. As one participant explained, "Having ID children at school improves the attitudes of the other kids. They are around and it's no big deal, whereas in my day they freaked you out."

A mother of a disabled son reflected:

> I regret that [R] wasn't in an ordinary class but there didn't seem to be much open for him in those days. [K] and I always said we'd look after our own kids, 'He's ours, we'll do that for him, we don't need anybody,' but you do!

Participants noted that for inclusion to be successful, intellectually disabled children must feel totally accepted by their peers and teachers must feel comfortable about having them in their classes. Whānau grouping was suggested as the best way of including intellectually disabled children. Some participants believed that short withdrawal periods might be required for additional tuition. The need for extra resources and preparation was widely emphasised:

> It depends on the resources, the support and the capability of the teacher, how many are in your class, if there's a teacher aide … A lot of work has to be done before disabled children even come to school to prepare other children, teachers and parents of that child.

> Yes, if everything else is geared up then no problems. If teacher training, the community at large, boards of trustees are geared up, if the powers that be are knowledgeable, in terms of the legislation, then there should be no problem.

Support for inclusion, however, was not unanimous. Two people believed that the demands of teaching intellectually disabled children could be better met in segregated settings. They also voiced a concern about potential disruption in the regular classroom.

Whānau issues

Wide-ranging whānau issues were discussed. The most frequently mentioned related to consultation, involvement, empowerment and assistance. Similar to the previously discussed situation in education, participants believed that whānau consultation and involvement were equally essential in the health sector. Speaking specifically of hospitals and institutions, one participant noted that if whānau were not permitted to be involved, there was a risk of them becoming "divorced" from their disabled member:

> The networking from the hospital needs to be backwards and forwards with the whole lot involved … Māoris should be encouraged to participate fully in programmes. Māoris should be leading programmes.

All participants believed that intellectually disabled people are best cared for in their own homes, but added that the family would need additional assistance because of the economic, physical and emotional stresses involved. A mother who had cared for her disabled son from birth explained:

> In their families are where they feel safe, loved and secure, but because of the stress level it can become really difficult from my own experience. Parents can get run into the ground depending on the degree of disability the child has … It is a real struggle … There should be some part of the day they [the intellectually disabled person] can go out to work. It gives them some sense of self worth.

Many participants believed that the extra help needed could be provided by the wider whānau with the aid of community facilities and organised around a whānau concept. Others added that in cases of severe ID, institutions may also need to be utilised to give whānau a break. A warning was sounded about the stress placed on whānau who felt a responsibility to care for disabled members but had limited resources to do so:

> A hell of a lot of us are living in nuclear families with all the social and economic pressures that go with it, and because we are not living around the marae and supporting one another and all that, we just have not got the capacity to support people as we would in the past.

One participant suggested a means of addressing the financial demands many whānau experience:

> Taxes should be returned to the family to enable them to care [for] and educate their intellectually disabled children. What happens with the funding in New Zealand? The funding is to pay for the administration of a 50 grand person to get into their bloody car, to burn off to see me, the parent, who doesn't give me any enskilling whatsoever, says, 'How's Mary?' and pisses off again and writes a report! Now, if they gave me 10 grand, a retainer for me, the parent, to be enskilled into how to manage and educate my own child, then that 50 grander would be out of a job … Why can't every parent who has a child like this have one day a week attending a course, fully funded, where they are trained?

In a discussion of Māori over-representation in special education, older participants cited possible reasons as: socioeconomic; indifferent parental attitudes; lack of support for education and recognition of its importance; lowered parental expectations; educational inadequacy of parents; ignorance of supporting services; and lack of confidence in attaining them:

Parents care but they don't know how to go about it, they're not sure. They don't know where to go for help. Pākehā people are on the ball so they get into social welfare and IHC. Also Māori people are quite shy. They tend to stand back unless someone they know can awhi them, can come with them and take them and talk, and explain to them that there are these things available to help their children learn, but other than that they tend to stand back. Definitely I would say it was because they don't understand.

Concerns and content

Concerns about the quality of education and care provisions were most often voiced by younger participants. In particular, people mentioned: misplacement in special classes because of prior family history; low professional expectations; misdisagnosing hearing problems (prevalent among Māori) as ID; Pākehā-centric teaching; conflicting home and school value systems; and incorrect assessment and classification because of differing cultural perspectives. One participant elaborated on the last concern:

It depends on who is doing the judging. These people only get into the box because someone thinks they should be in it, and if these people are psychologists and Pākehā ... I think we are talking about partnership. There ought to be a Māori and a Pākehā psychologist every time there's any assessment of a Māori child ... There ought to be affirmative action programmes to get a whole lot more Māori people trained to do these assessments.

The need for more professional Māori staff was poignantly highlighted in the following story:

Participant: Palmerston sent him to Queen Elizabeth hospital for assessment when he was four or five. He was there for a month, and at the end of it I went and had an interview with the therapists from each department, you know, occupational and all the rest of that rubbish, and they said we should institutionalise [R] because there was nothing for him. He'd never be able to do anything you know. I mean they were adamant. They said he'd never be able to speak or feed himself, or go to the toilet like he is doing now, or shower himself, or do anything like that ever.

Jill: Was there anyone who said, 'Yes, he could?'

Participant: Yes, the domestic staff did. They worked around his bed and that and they said [R] talked to them, pointed to anything he wanted if they couldn't understand him or that sort of thing, but they said when the doctors came, the faces of them so long, looking at him, in their long white coats, they watched and they said, 'No wonder that kid didn't want to talk to them!' They said, 'Hey listen Mrs [R], he'll do anything, he can communicate and that's all that matters.'

Jill: Were those domestic staff Māori or Pākehā?

Participant: Māoris. Māoris they will talk to anybody and they will get people talking to them. They used to clean around him, talk to him and give him lollies and what have you, and as soon as he saw the doctors coming, brmmm, he'd just close up completely because that is what they told us. We never went back.

People believed that in addition to more professional Māori staff, improved services require more culturally competent Pākehā staff, especially at "ground level;" increased funding; more resources; greater iwi advocacy; and increased flexibility of timetabling and thinking. The latter is explained in the following participant's quote:

Māori belief is that people are forever learning. It doesn't matter what stage of life they are at, learning always goes on, no-one actually reaches the end of learning in a lifetime. [This] means that people who are intellectually disabled are still able to learn. You know, they are not regarded as not having the ability to learn, but the important thing is that they are given the right environment where they can learn, the right sort of curriculum if you like, to fit their needs, is put in place and the time, they are given the time. Each kid is different, they have a different time-of-learning scale, and one will learn today and another one mightn't learn till next year the same sort of skill. But I mean, that is their time, that is their individuality, so you have to accept that and fit around that instead of saying, 'Well OK, I'm going to make the time scale. I am going to say what you are going to learn, what you must learn in this time and what you must learn in that time and it's on your head if you don't!' I mean that is really stupid. So what I am saying is a lot of what we do in schools is wrong. It shouldn't be done. If we stop categorising kids like that, we might find that these people who are labelled as slow or handicapped are not really.

Concerns mentioned by interview participants were supported in the literature with respect to disabled Māori in general. For example, the Royal Commission on Social Policy (1988) noted a lack of recognition of cultural diversity and called for disability services to be presented in a culturally acceptable way, for more Māori workers, and for organisations to keep records of the ethnicity of their clients. They also reported the need:

> for service organisations and others working in the disability area to consult widely with Māori people to determine servicing lacks and needs and for a fairer allocation of resources. This could result in Māori people having control of their own resources and programmes. (p. 777)

While a few interview participants advocated "Māori control" of the education and care of intellectually disabled Māori, most supported the idea of an equal partnership, citing the Treaty of Waitangi as justification.

Participants all agreed that care and education services should be available from birth till death, as and when they are needed. In addition to the previously discussed Māori content, participants believed that social and self-care skills should take top priority in educational programmes, while care services should place emphasis on the skills intellectually disabled people need in order to live as independent a life as possible. However, one participant noted:

> You have to be careful not to be too patronising here. I think it has to be on a consultation basis involving the person themselves. They must feel they are part of the decision making. An intellectually disabled person might want to spend more time on the academic skills and less on the work skills, social and self-care skills. It might be a particular phase in the person's development—well then, that's the programme. It must be a partnership, a negotiation with the person concerned. I think that is crucial to the whole process. They must feel empowered. I think that is really important.

Discussion

The literature review and participant interviews revealed a wide spectrum of traditional and contemporary concepts of and attitudes towards ID. What was consistent, however, was the influence other cultural concepts, beliefs and values had on Māori people's understanding, attitudes, and educational and care requirements, which, in turn, resulted in some distinct Māori views and preferences. Following are the recurring priorities.

1. Māori identity is just as important to an intellectually disabled Māori as it is to a non-disabled Māori. Because of this, they are entitled to have Māori content and te reo included in their care and education.

2. All Māori content should be included and/or taught with the correct wairua. Values must not only be acknowledged but also practised by all concerned.

3. Consultation with and involvement of whānau in educational and care provisions for intellectually disabled Māori are paramount. They should be empowered and enskilled in the process.

4. Intellectually disabled Māori are best raised in their own homes. To enable this, parents and wider whānau members will need additional assistance and support because of the economic, physical and emotional stresses involved.

5. Māori should be involved at all levels in decision-making related to the care and education of intellectually disabled Māori.

This research provides a snapshot of Māori understanding of ID and opinion about the education and care of intellectually disabled Māori. No generalisations are possible from such a small sample and limited literature review. However, despite the limitations of the study, it was significant in that it raised awareness and issues at a time when research in this area was scarce. Now, almost 25 years later, the study's relevance rests on whether subsequent research has supported its findings.

Unfortunately, published research focusing specifically on Māori perspectives and experiences of ID is still very limited. This is not surprising given that research on ID in general in Aotearoa / New Zealand is also lacking. For example, a recent report (Ministry of Health, 2013) noted that

There is only a small literature on the delivery of health care services for people with intellectual disability in New Zealand. In part because of the small sample size there is limited analysis by different population sub-groups such as Māori or older people. (p. 19)

This note in the Appendix was the only mention of Māori in the entire report.

However, one significant study was published by the National Advisory Committee on Health and Disability (NAC) in 2003. Over a two-and-a-half year period researchers interviewed a number of intellectually disabled people, including Māori, their whānau and service providers. They reported that kaupapa Māori services with a strong cultural component were strongly supported by intellectually disabled Māori, but that, in general, these were underfunded and not available, especially to Māori living with their whānau in rural areas. Three Māori-specific recommendations were made.

- Māori adults with an intellectual disability should have access to "the same initiatives and opportunities as the rest of the Māori population, including access to Māori housing initiatives" (NAC, 2003, p. 42).

- Needs assessment, service co-ordination and service provision should be made relevant to the lives of Māori adults with an intellectual disability.

- Māori with intellectual disability should have the "option of referral to adequately resourced Māori service providers" (NAC, 2003, p. 43).[3]

Although research specifically on intellectually disabled Māori is still limited, there is a considerable number of relevant, more widely focused, research-based reports, articles, action plans, strategies and theses available.[4]

In the health sector, of particular note is *He Korowai Oranga: Māori Health Strategy*, which sets the direction for Māori development in the

---

3   Details about how these recommendations can be achieved can be found at http://nhc.health. govt.nz/archived-publications/nhc-publications-pre-2011/have-ordinary-life-kia-whai-oranga-noa.

4   This is based on the fact that intellectually disabled Māori represented 50.9 percent of disabled Māori identified in the 2006 New Zealand Household Disability Survey. (Office for Disability Issues and Statistics New Zealand, 2010). At the time of writing Māori disability statistics from the 2013 census have not yet been released.

health and disability sector (Ministry of Health, 2002), and *Whāia Te Ao Mārama: The Māori Disability Action Plan for Disability Support Services 2012–2017* (Ministry of Health, 2012). The latter was developed in consultation with over 200 Māori who participated in focus groups, hui and interviews throughout the country, a Māori disabled leadership group, and disability organisations such as Te Piringa, the Māori Disability Provider Network. This extensive background research was conducted over an 18-month period. It identified clear, consistent messages from disabled Māori, who reported feeling disconnected from their whānau and culture as a result of their past disability experiences. Consequently, they wanted:

- every opportunity to have leadership, choice and control over their lives (te rangatira),
- to be supported as both Māori and as disabled to thrive, flourish and live the life they want,
- to be able to participate in te ao Māori (the Māori world),
- to have their whānau valued as their primary support system,
- to be connected to natural support networks, including Māori and disability communities,
- a holistic approach to their disability that also values the beneficial effects of Māori cultural views and practices on spiritual, mental, physical, emotional and whānau wellbeing (Ministry of Health, 2012, p. 3).

These wishes were supported by whānau members. Anecdotal evidence indicated that:

> Māori whānau commonly take care of their disabled whānau members without accessing the supports by the Ministry of Health-funded disability support services. (Ministry of Health, 2012, p. 5)

This would seem to be corroborated by statistics showing that in June 2011 only 19.7 percent of disability support services funding for Māori disabled was allocated to home support. Sixty-four percent went on residential care and 5.2 percent on day programmes.

Taking heed of Māori disability statistics and consultation feedback, *Whāia Te Ao Mārama: Māori Disability Action Plan for Disability Support Services 2012–2017* contains a vision, guiding principles and priority areas focused on achieving the identified aspirations of disabled Māori, and reducing barriers they and their whānau face.[5]

Other health-related studies that concur with the *Whāia Te Ao Mārama* consultation data include research by Collins and Wilson (2008); Nikora, Karapu, Hickey and Te Awekotuku (2004); Ratima and Ratima (2007); and a recently completed study conducted by the Donald Beasley Institute in collaboration with Ngā Kete Mātauranga Pounamu Charitable Trust and the University of Otago School of Physiotherapy.[6] This year-long project consulted with 29 disabled Southland Māori and their whānau. A news release noted that "participants felt they were not being valued". Also reported were:

> negative impacts of discrimination, colonisation and disconnection, and lack of self-worth ... All participants wanted to be valued, to participate and did not want to be judged by their disability. (McDougall, 2013)

In the education sector Māori children are still over-represented among those with special needs. IHC (2012) reports that nearly 3,000 of these children have an ID. Since the research reported in this chapter the author has interviewed hundreds of parents, whānau and Māori children with special education needs in a wide variety of research projects. The most substantial study was her PhD research, conducted over a 5-year period. One component of this study involved individual and focus-group interviews with 92 participants, many of whom had a child/whānau member with ID. These interviews identified eight general factors and nine cultural factors that were considered essential to culturally appropriate, effective service provision. They included requirements to:

- involve parents and develop a good home–school relationship
- empower parents and whānau
- employ cross-culturally competent staff conversant with Māori culture, te reo Māori, and total immersion and bilingual education

---

5   More information about *Whāia Te Ao Mārama: Māori Disability Action Plan for Disability Support Services 201–2017* can be accessed at http://www.health.govt.nz/publication/whaia-te-ao-marama-Māori-disability-action-plan-disability-support-services-2012-2017

6   This research is now available at http://www.otago.ac.nz/physio/research/ageing/otago065884.html

- provide whānau-based services
- include Māori staff members
- include Māori content, reo and resources
- utilise culturally appropriate, relevant identification and assessment measures, procedures and teaching strategies
- incorporate Māori values, perspectives and perceptions of special needs (Bevan-Brown, 2002).

These findings are supported in other educational research which has consulted with parents and whānau of Māori children with special education needs; for example, Berryman et al., 2002; Berryman & Woller, 2011; Massey University, 2002; Wilkie, 2001; along with other relevant publications, such as Fortune, 2013, and Phillips, 2000.

The implications of research findings for people who work with intellectually disabled Māori and their whānau

As is evident in the discussion above, subsequent research in the health and education sectors concurs with the findings of the author's original study. Issues of cultural identity, culturally responsive care and education, and parental and whānau involvement, empowerment and support are timeless. It is beyond the scope of this chapter to examine progress made in these areas over the intervening years, but it has been considerable. Evidence of the progress made includes:

- the large number of Māori provider organisations that offer culturally relevant services to intellectually disabled Māori (see http://www.health.govt.nz/our-work/disability-services/Māori-disability-support-services)
- online cultural competency training for health professionals (see http://www.health.govt.nz/news-media/news-items/foundation-course-cultural-competency-continues-be-available-online-free)
- documents such as *Uia Tonutia: Māori Disability Research Agenda* (Ministry of Health, 2011), *Guidelines for the Cultural Assessment of Intellectually Disabled Māori* (Ministry of Health, 2004) and the *Māori Education Strategy: Ka Hikitia—Accelerating Success 2013–2017* (Ministry of Education, 2012).

However, the *IHC Submission: Inquiry into the Determinants of Wellbeing for Māori Children* (IHC, 2012) shows that there is still a long way to go.

First and foremost, people who work with intellectually disabled Māori and their whānau need to be aware that their own understanding of ID and attitudes towards it may differ significantly from that of people with ID and their whānau. No assumptions can be made. Because understanding, beliefs and attitudes influence the nature and type of care and education preferred, the onus is on professionals to investigate these factors. For example, if the person with ID and their whānau adhere to Durie's Whare Tapa Whā concept of wellbeing mentioned earlier, then provisions will necessarily be holistic in nature.

Consequently, from the outset professionals must consult with the person with ID, their parents and whānau. This consultation should include questions about Māori identification and the desire for cultural and reo content. This raises three points. Firstly, from the author's experience, Māori are sometimes reluctant to request cultural input in care and special education provisions, not because they don't want it but because they fear that by requesting this input they may jeopardise their chances of receiving quality services—or in some cases, any service at all! Therefore, it should be made clear that cultural input is an available entitlement that will enhance the provision being offered.

Secondly, this should not be a question that is asked at the beginning of service provision and never again. People's wishes change with time and experience. It could be that when parents first learn that their child is intellectually disabled the matter of cultural input is the last thing on their minds. However, in time, and as they become comfortable dealing with professionals, the offer of cultural input may have more meaning for them.

Thirdly, because of the nature of ID there is a tendency not to consult with intellectually disabled people themselves, especially if they are young. While young age is a limiting factor regardless of whether the child has ID or not, professionals are encouraged to look for ways and means of including the intellectually disabled child in all decisions that affect them, as early and as often as possible.

As research indicates, involving parents and whānau should be much wider than merely consulting with them. It should be an empowering experience, where they are included in decision-making, enskilled and supported to participate in whānau-based programmes at a level of their choosing.

Finally, and obviously, cultural input can only be offered if health and education provisions incorporating it are actually available. This places responsibility on professional associations, training institutions, government departments, disability organisations and service providers to lobby for, develop and provide relevant training, resources and programmes. Also needed is a commitment from professionals to develop the skills, attitudes and cultural competence required to contribute to improving the life chances of the intellectually disabled Māori with whom they work. As the whakataukī states: "Ehara taku toa i te toa takitahi, engari he toa takitini" (My strength is not that of a single warrior but that of many)—the combined efforts of many are needed.

Study questions

1. Why did the author's research include traditional concepts of ID? What concurrence was found between traditional and contemporary concepts?

2. While acknowledging a diversity of understanding about and attitudes towards ID among Māori today, nine participants and some literature supported a difference between Māori and Pākehā understanding and attitudes. What were these differences based on? Do you believe that differences exist? Justify your answer.

3. In the author's research, in what areas was there unanimous agreement among participants? What findings in subsequent research have supported their opinion, and what progress has been made in these areas?

4. What are the major concerns in the care and education of intellectually disabled Māori? From research and your own experience, what are some strategies for addressing them?

References

Anderson, J. (1931). The Māori and religion. In P. Jackson (Ed.), *Māori and education or the education of natives of New Zealand and its dependencies.* Wellington: Ferguson and Osborn.

Berryman, M., Glynn, T., Walker, R., Reweti, M., O'Brien, K., Boasa-Dean, T., et al. (2002). *SES sites of effective special education practice for Māori 2001: Draft report to the SES board and executive team.* Wellington: Specialist Education Services, Poutama Pounamu Education Research and Development Centre.

Berryman, M., & Woller, P. (2011). Early intervention services: Effectively supporting Māori children and their families. *Kairaranga, 12*(1), 3–9.

Best, E. (1952). *The Māori as he was.* Wellington: Government Printing Office.

Bevan-Brown, J. (1989). *Intellectual disability: A Māori perspective.* Unpublished master's project, Massey University.

Bevan-Brown, J. (1994). Intellectual disability: A Māori perspective. In K. Ballard (Ed.), *Disability, family, whānau and society* (pp. 205–230). Palmerston North: Dunmore Press.

Bevan-Brown, J. (2002). *Culturally appropriate, effective provision for Māori learners with special needs: He waka tino whakarawea.* Unpublished doctoral thesis, Massey University [Palmerston North].

Bray, A. (2003). *Definitions of intellectual disability: Review of the literature prepared for the National Advisory Committee on Health and Disability to inform its project on services for adults with an intellectual disability.* Wellington: National Advisory Committee on Health and Disability. Retrieved from http://www.donaldbeasley.org.nz/publications/NHC_Definitions.pdf

Collins, A., & Wilson, G. (2008). *Māori and informal caregiving: A background paper prepared for the National Health Committee.* Retrieved from http://www.nhc.health.govt.nz/moh.nsf/pagescm/7552/$File/Māori-informal-caregiving-apr08.pdf

Durie, M. (1977). Māori attitudes to sickness, doctors, hospitals. *New Zealand Medical Journal, 86,* 483–485.

Durie, M. (1985). A Māori perspective of health. *Social Science Medical, 20*(5), 483–486.

Fortune, K. (2013). The impact of policy and legislation on Māori children with special needs in Aotearoa / New Zealand. *Support for Learning, 28*(1), 41–46.

IHC. (2012). *IHC Submission: Inquiry into the determinants of wellbeing for Māori children*. Retrieved from http://www.ihc.org.nz/downloadsihc188

Kaa, W. (1987). Ethnic and cultural considerations. In *The draft review of special education* (pp. 81–83). Wellington: Department of Education.

Makereti. (1938). *The old time Māori*. London: Victor Gollancz.

Marsden, M. (1986). *Māori illness and healing in mental health: A case for reform* (pp. 1–21). Auckland: Legal Research Foundation, University of Auckland.

Massey University. (2002). *Special Education 2000: Monitoring and evaluation of the policy*. Final report to the Ministry of Education, Wellington, New Zealand. Palmerston North: Institute for Professional Development and Educational Research, Massey University.

McDougall, N. (2013). *Valuable look at disability*. Retrieved from http://www.stuff.co.nz/southland-times/news/8992962/Valuable-look-at-disability

Ministry of Education. (2012). *The Māori education strategy: Ka hikitia—Accelerating success 2013–2017*. Retrieved from http://www.minedu.govt.nz/theMinistry/PolicyAndStrategy/KaHikitia.aspx

Ministry of Health. (2002). *He korowai oranga: Māori health strategy*. Retrieved from http://www.health.govt.nz/publication/he-korowai-oranga-Māori-health-strategy

Ministry of Health. (2004). *Guidelines for cultural assessment—Māori*. Retrieved from http://www.health.govt.nz/publication/guidelines-cultural-assessment-Māori

Ministry of Health. (2011). *Uia tonutia: Māori disability research agenda*. Retrieved from http://www.health.govt.nz/system/files/documents/publications/Māori-disability-research-agenda-feb2011.pdf

Ministry of Health. (2012). *Whāia te ao mārama: The Māori disability action plan for disability support services 2012–2017*. Wellington: Ministry of Health. Retrieved from http://www.health.govt.nz/publication/whaia-te-ao-marama-Māori-disability-action-plan-disability-support-services-2012-2017

Ministry of Health. (2013). *Innovative methods of providing health services for people with intellectual disability: A review of the literature*. Wellington: Ministry of Health.

Murchie, E. (1986). The Māori Women's Welfare League's health survey and programme. In M. Abbott & M. Durie (Eds.), *The future of mental health services in New Zealand: Māori perspectives* (pp. 7–12). Auckland: Mental Health Foundation of New Zealand.

National Advisory Committee on Health and Disability (NAC). (2003). *To have an 'ordinary' life: Kia whai oranga 'noa'.* A report to the Minister of Health and the Minister for Disability Issues from the National Advisory Committee on Health and Disability. Retrieved from http:// nhc.health.govt.nz/archived-publications/nhc-publications-pre-2011/ have-ordinary-life-kia-whai-oranga-noa

Nikora, L. W., Karapu, R., Hickey, H., & Te Awekotuku, N. (2004). *Disabled Māori and disability support options.* A report prepared for the Ministry of Health, Hamilton Office. Hamilton: Māori Psychology Research Unit, University of Waikato.

Office for Disability Issues and Statistics New Zealand. (2010). *Disability and Māori in New Zealand in 2006: Results from the New Zealand disability survey.* Wellington: Statistics New Zealand.

Phillips, H. (2000). Te ata hāpara: Educational provision for Māori students with moderate to high needs. In Ministry of Education (Ed.), *Draft report of the literature review for the Enhancing Effective Practice in Special Education Research Programme* (pp. 81–156).Wellington: New Zealand Government.

Pomare, E. (1986). Māori health: New concepts and initiatives. *New Zealand Medical Journal, 99,* pp. 410–411.

Rankin, J. F. A. (1986). Whai ora: A Māori cultural therapy unit. In M. Abbott & M. Durie (Eds.), *The future of mental health services in New Zealand: Māori perspectives* (pp. 19–26). Auckland: Mental Health Foundation of New Zealand.

Ratima, K., & Ratima, M. (2007). Māori experience of disability and disability support services. In B. Robson & R. Harris (Eds.), *Hauora: Māori standards of health IV.* Wellington: Te Rōpū Rangahau Hauora a Eru Pōmare.

Reid, P. (1986). Te waiora. In M. Abbott & M. Durie (Eds.), *The future of mental health services in New Zealand: Māori perspectives* (pp. 13–18). Auckland: Mental Health Foundation of New Zealand.

Royal Commission on Social Policy. (1988). *Future directions: Social perspectives: The April reports.* Wellington: Author.

Wilkie, M. (with Berryman, M., Himona, T., & Paul, T.). (2001). *Mātauranga motuhake.* Wellington: NZCER.

Wylie, C. (1988). How fair is New Zealand education? In *Part 1: NZCER research: Report of the Royal Commission on Social Policy: Future directions, Vol. 3.* Wellington: The Royal Commission on Social Policy.

Chapter 9

Māori and autism spectrum disorder

Jill Bevan-Brown

Ko Waitaha ngā tāngata,
ko kawe kē tō ngakau.

All men of the Waitaha tribe,
but all differing in inclinations.

Introduction

This chapter briefly introduces autism spectrum disorder (ASD) and then reports on a study in which parents and whānau shared their experiences of raising a child with ASD, noting the cultural issues that arose, the people, services and strategies they found helpful, and the barriers they faced.[1] Similarities between subsequent research are discussed, as are the implications for professionals who work with Māori children with ASD and their whānau.

---

1   This chapter draws substantially on Bevan-Brown, 2004. Due to the size constraints of this chapter, only limited information could be included. The reader is urged to consult the original report to gain a greater appreciation of the participants' opinions and experiences. It can be accessed at http://www.educationcounts.govt.nz/publications/special_education/5479

What is autism spectrum disorder?

ASD refers to a group of developmental disabilities that can cause significant communication, social and behavioural challenges. Considerable controversy exists over how ASD should be defined, with the two most common diagnostic classification systems, the *Diagnostic and Statistical Manual, Version 5* (DSM-5) and the *International Classification of Diseases, 10th Edition* (ICD-10), differing in how they classify ASD. There is also debate over whether ASD is a disorder, a condition or a neurologically based difference in the way people with ASD think. To add to the confusion, no single cause of ASD has been identified, with both genetic and environmental factors being proposed.[2]

What is certain, however, is that a person's ethnic culture has an impact on how ASD is experienced and managed. Acknowledging this and being committed to providing appropriately for Māori children with ASD, the Ministry of Education commissioned me to conduct a small exploratory study. The purpose of this research was to investigate parents' experiences of raising Māori children with autism, to discover what had been both helpful and unhelpful over the years, and to find out how services could be improved in the future. This research was conducted over a 7-month period in 2004.

The research

There were no existing publications on Māori and ASD, and so no literature review could inform the research. Even prevalence figures for Māori with ASD could not be obtained, as information on the incidence of ASD is not presently collected in Aotearoa / New Zealand. However, based on United Kingdom prevalence figures, it has been estimated that there are approximately 40,000 people in this country with ASD (Ministry of Health and Ministry of Education, 2008). On a pro rata basis, this means there are approximately 6,000 Māori with ASD. With indications of an increase in the incidence of ASD internationally, it is likely that this figure could be even higher.

---

2   To learn more about ASD, readers should consult the many excellent websites available . A wealth of information can be gained from the following site and from the links within it: http://www.minedu.govt.nz/NZEducation/EducationPolicies/SpecialEducation/OurWorkProgramme/SupportingChildrenWithASD.aspx

Methodology

Advisory group input and interview pilot

After gaining ethical approval from Massey University's Human Ethics Committee, an advisory group was established to provide guidance and feedback. This group consisted of two parents of Māori children with ASD, and a kaumātua who had a whānau member with ASD. The kaumātua also provided advice on Māori protocols relevant to the research process. The advisory group recommended that a formal list of questions not be used, but instead participants should be invited to simply tell their stories of raising their children with ASD. This approach would allow them to share their most meaningful experiences. To ensure that a wide range of information was obtained, an interview schedule/prompt sheet was used. The interview process and schedule were trialled with the parents on the advisory group and proved an effective data gathering approach.

Participants

Prospective participants were identified by paediatricians, Ministry of Education (Group Special Education) staff and from my own networks. All those contacted agreed to participate, and subsequently 17 face-to-face interviews were conducted with the parents and whānau of 19 Māori children with ASD.[3] In total, 51 people were present during all or part of these interviews. This included 15 mothers, seven fathers, one grandmother, one friend, 14 siblings and 13 of the 19 children with ASD. Of the latter, only one person, a 15-year-old youth with Asperger syndrome, took an active part in the interview. Similarly, while siblings contributed the occasional comment, they did not participate to any great extent. Although up to 51 people were present in the interview situation, other whānau members contributed indirectly. In a number of cases participants specifically mentioned consulting with their partners and seeking their input prior to the interview.

Of the 51 people, five were Pākehā: the Pākehā partners of four Māori men and one Pākehā grandmother. Of the 17 families involved, 13 were two-parent and four were single-parent families. They were all located in the central and lower North Island region. However, as a number of families had shifted from other areas in Aotearoa / New

---

3 Two families had two children with ASD.

Zealand, their experiences related to a much wider geographical area in both the North and South Islands. Participants lived in the city, suburbs and rural locations.

The children

The 19 children involved were all diagnosed with ASD or ASD "tendencies". This included those with mild, moderate and severe autism and Asperger syndrome. In addition, a number of the children had other disabilities and medical conditions. They ranged in age from 2 to 19 years. Five were preschoolers, nine attended primary school and five were at secondary school.

The five children under 5 years of age attended fully integrated early childhood education facilities (ECEF). Of the nine primary children, six were in the mainstream, two were in special classes/units and one was being home-schooled. Three of the five secondary students were in special units, one was in a residential special school, and one was at a mainstream school. Four children had previously attended kōhanga reo, one was presently at a kura kaupapa Māori, one had previously been in a bilingual unit, while another had attended a kura kaupapa Māori but had moved on to a secondary school immersion unit. A further student, although in a special unit at a secondary school, was also a valued member of the school's whānau class.

Data collection and analysis

Fifteen interviews were conducted in people's homes and two were held in my office. They varied between 1 and 5 hours in length. Notes were taken in one interview and the remainder were taped. After being transcribed, the interview transcripts were returned to participants for verification, possible amendment, and approval to include the information provided. Interview transcripts were coded and analysed using a thematic approach. In writing up the data, priority was given to including the participants' voice, and multiple quotes were included. A draft summary report was given to the participants, advisory group members, Ministry of Education personnel and members of their ASD advisory committee for consideration and comment. Amendments based on the feedback received were made, and a final report submitted to the Ministry of Education. Copies were also given to all research participants.

Results

Past experiences and present understanding

The majority of parents became aware that their child/ren had difficulties before age two. However, actual diagnosis of ASD or ASD tendencies did not come until some time later due to a range of factors, including:

- difficulty identifying ASD in young children
- a cautious wait-and-see attitude among medical personnel
- long waiting lists
- parents' concerns not being taken seriously
- the existence of other confounding disabilities or medical conditions
- an initial, inaccurate diagnosis
- delays caused by red tape and rural location.

Parents' experiences at diagnosis varied from no help and information given at all, to informative explanations and support. The written information given at diagnosis varied in its usefulness. There was strong support for having a person visit parents to explain the nature of ASD and what services and entitlements were available, and to assist in obtaining these. As one participant explained:

> **Participant:** When you initially get diagnosed you get a million things thrown at you, and which all just goes 'arrrgghhh'. I guess for me I would have liked to have had someone come along and make me a cup of tea, and say to me 'look', and then have your little booklet. Because I think we are great orators, we love our kai and we love to talk.

> **Jill:** So it is a Māori process?

> **Participant:** Exactly! Yes, I really wouldn't want a book given to me, 'Here you go,' because I have had enough stuff thrown at me, whereas it is somebody to come along and ... just to sit with me and really to have a physical support ... I think there needs to be something, physical—somebody.

The concept of ASD that was described and discussed by parents was the generally accepted triad of impairments, heavily influenced by the medical model. Only one participant had knowledge of ASD prior to their child being diagnosed. However, understanding had developed through their experiences of raising their children, talking to medical personnel and teachers, reading and, for 11 out of 17 families, consulting the Internet. While their present knowledge of ASD varied from vague to expert, most parents had a good understanding and six had in-depth knowledge. These people had attended conferences, read widely, sought out relevant research and were active members of various parent organisations.

Issues relating to Māori culture

Parents varied in their desire for professionals to include cultural input into their child's education and service provision. This ranged from substantial to minimal input. Not surprisingly, those parents whose children were in total immersion or bilingual education were the staunchest supporters of cultural input. However, the great majority wanted some degree of cultural content included. Involvement in kapa haka and noho marae were specifically mentioned. Characteristics associated with ASD were identified as hindering involvement in these cultural activities, but successful accommodations were also reported. For example, one child who found the noise and number of people at kapa haka distressing wore ear muffs in performances. A further strategy was described by one mother:

> He was in the kapa haka—over exuberant … I had to take him out, calm him down cos they were kinda losing the plot with the rest of the group. They were getting out of sync because of Raymond[4] and a few of his little mates [with special needs] … They just take him out for a little while and then bring him back in.

At a noisy noho marae, a separate 'kaumātua room' was available when/if the child with ASD needed some quiet time.

In discussing te reo Māori, many parents mentioned that although they would have liked their child to learn to speak Māori, they were concerned that learning a second language might prove too confusing given the communication difficulties associated with ASD. A couple who did speak Māori to their son at home described a problem that arose and how they dealt with it:

---

4   Pseudonyms have been used throughout this chapter.

I still remember one time at kindy when I was watching Karlos looking at the fish tank and he was pointing to the fish and he was saying 'ika, ika', and I still remember his kindy teacher thinking that he was just speaking garbage and trying to correct him saying 'No, it's a fish, it's a fish'. He was right. As far as he knew, that's what it was because that's all we used to call it.

When he got funding from about four, I think, we started getting a teacher aide for him and one of our stipulations was, like, 'Could you look further afield and find somebody that speaks Māori,' because his language skills were very, very limited until he was six, but with that situation he does understand Māori and words that come out, you've got to be able to try and interpret it whether it's gibberish or English or Māori. When he started school we had a book to write up in the front anything that happened at school to give us an idea, and in the back I put the vocab of common Māori words that we used for them to be aware of and listen out for.

Children with ASD could also be disadvantaged because of difficulties meeting cultural expectations and participating in culturally valued practices, such as group activities and whakawhanaungatanga. One mother advised:

An education approach, therefore, would have to take these factors into consideration because these are cultural expectations that most Māori are socialised into … To develop these children is to go with what they have and work with them towards meeting 'cultural needs'.

Other suggestions for meeting cultural needs included whānau involvement in teaching, taiaha lessons, individual education plan (IEP) meetings in the home, inclusion of karakia and Māori myths, legends and stories, a holistic approach that included life skills, and upskilling of teachers. It was believed that to ensure cultural and spiritual safety, teachers must find out about the values, practices and priorities of the child's family and then incorporate these, where appropriate, into the school and ECEF programme. Parents also expressed a wish for more culturally appropriate assessment measures and procedures, and for more Māori services, service providers and professionals.

Māori-medium education and Māori services were seen to have

both advantages and disadvantages for children with ASD. On the one hand, the cultural content, wairua, inclusive philosophy and supportive attitude of staff and children in Māori-medium facilities and the friendly, approachable style of many Māori service providers were seen as beneficial. On the other hand, there was considerable concern at the lack of ASD expertise among some Māori educators and service providers.

On the other hand, concern was expressed about the lack of whānau support. This ranged from 24/7 help to none at all. Wonderful examples were provided of whānau acceptance and assistance, although three participants pointed out some concomitant disadvantages:

> Māori … depend too much on their own families. They don't know what's out there and nor do the families to get help. I've found with a lot of Māori families, that's why a lot of women are too timid, because they know Mum is around the corner or Mum-in-law. They know Nanny is up the road, they come from big families, like all of us, there's always someone there. The extended family can be a pleasure, but it can also be a hindrance in a lot of things.

> They say, 'Don't worry,' and I agree with that, but I have to explain to them that I'm looking long term … There are things that are funny now but would you laugh if he was 15 and doing it. So he has got to know.

Reasons cited for little or no acceptance included no family living nearby, whānau avoidance because they felt uncomfortable, lack of interest, denial, and concern about the "destructiveness" of the child with ASD.

It was quite typical for support to vary within the whānau. Also typical was a general lack of understanding of ASD among whānau members. This ignorance lead to some hurtful comments. One couple explained:

> No they don't understand anything at all. Like typical family, they always say the wrong things. 'So and so's got children, they're only one and two and they are worse behaved than yours!' and 'Look at Lee, she's so pretty, what a shame!' And it's both of our families—like saying, 'They're still ill? Are they still sick?' No, no, they've got autism!

Consequently there was strong support among participants for whānau members in particular, and Māori people in general, to learn more about ASD. As one mother noted, "I look at our different kids, and I think, 'You know, if your parents were a little bit more on to it, they might have actually picked this [ASD] up'."

Another mother made the point that in order for whānau members to provide assistance in various areas they need to receive training. An example was given:

> They showed everyone—whoever who was willing. They showed me and then a paediatric nurse came to the house and she brought round the little dummy to teach the family CPR and teach the family how to put a tube down.

Other examples of whānau involvement were inclusion in the MAPS[5] process and in IEP meetings. A mother explained how her son's school changed the IEP date so that Nana, who was coming down from Auckland for a holiday, could be included in the meeting. They also offered to send her copies of her grandchild's IEPs. Siblings were variously reported as being helpful, protective, embarrassed, annoyed and sometimes "left out" as a result of having a brother or sister with ASD.

Organisational involvement

The parents from 10 families either had been or still were members of parent organisations. Some attended meetings, while others only used the organisations as information sources. Reasons for limited or non-involvement were generally of a practical nature, although a concern was voiced about Māori parents feeling uncomfortable in Pākehā-dominated organisations where their culture was not understood or catered for. There was some support for Māori-focused groups, which would involve whānau, fun, cultural activities, shared experiences, hands-on strategies and operate according to Māori kawa.

Helpful people

Parents acknowledged many medical, educational, special educational and support personnel who had provided outstanding service over the years. Particular professionals were praised for their aroha, support,

---

5   MAPS is a personalised plan of action. For details see http://www.inclusion.com/artcommon-sensetools.html

assistance, advocacy, advice, resources and expertise. Many examples were given of service above and beyond the call of duty. The following description of a special education advisor is a good example:

> We had Susan, absolutely marvellous, all the years I've been under SES [Specialist Education Services] I could never fault her. She was good. It wasn't only work from 9 to 5, she would come around at the weekends. She'd ring me up at night and she came out during the day, and if I was looking tired or Karl looked a bit touchy, she'd ring us up and say, 'What's going on? You two don't look very happy.' Karl has still got his desk that she gave him. She gave us a little school desk. She was lovely … Her friendly attitude, she didn't come in with the, 'I'm SES and I know'. She came in and made herself part of the family, which relaxed Karl. I think that's really what I liked. There was no reading text books and saying, 'That child should not be doing this, the child should be doing this.' No looking down at us saying, 'It's not normal, it's not this, it's not that.' She let us do it our way and supported us.

One of the most frequently mentioned sources of support and information was other parents of children with ASD. In particular, they were goldmines of information about various services, resources and entitlements. They also provided genuine understanding, empathy, and tried-and-true advice and advocacy.

Helpful services, entitlements and strategies

A wide range of services and entitlements were cited as being helpful. These included a variety of recreational, support, financial, assessment and educational provisions and resources. The most frequently mentioned helpful service was respite care (also known as care and relief), which was used by 12 of the 17 families. The majority used family members; firstly, because the children and parents knew and trusted family members, and secondly, because respite providers outside the family were often difficult to find. One couple told of going through three different providers, none of whom lasted long because of the challenges involved in caring for a child with ASD.

After family members, the most frequently used respite-care providers were present or past teachers and teacher aides. Many of these people had become firm family friends over the years and children looked forward to staying with or visiting them. People also appreciated the flexibility of the respite-care entitlement which was used: to have children cared for by friends, family members and caregivers; as payment for residential, daily and holiday care facilities and programmes; and to fund extra teacher aide and education support worker hours.

Similarly, parents described a wide range of different strategies as being particularly helpful in the education and care of their children. The top nine were: careful preparation and transition activities; visual strategies; firmness and perseverance; activities involving music and rhythm; computer use; one-on-one assistance; social stories; preparatory class and school visits; and involvement in selecting ancillary staff to assist the children. The following quote explains how one mother combined two of these strategies:

> What we did was muck around with the social stories concept and set things to music, because that is what worked best for him, and that is an idea that I got from someone else ... I made up little songs for Rawhiti instead of stories because that didn't grab him and ring his bells, so we had a get up in the morning song, we had a getting into the shower song, we have that going on, and that worked. And, I just put rhyming words and that, because Rawhiti likes playing with words and we had nonsense words in there and silly words in there—I modified it to suit him.

Barriers

Parents also described a variety of barriers they had encountered. Following are 10 of the main barriers, with a small selection of the many examples shared.

(1) A shortage of services and qualified personnel

Parents mentioned long waiting lists, inconsistency between services offered in different regions, a high staff turnover rate, and burn-out resulting from heavy workloads. When one mother was near breaking point, she was told the waiting time for crisis intervention services was 1 month, while another was told that the waiting time for a speech–language therapist to see her son with severe language difficulties was 1 year to 18 months. A third mother, who was concerned about her daughter being hit by another child in the class, noted, "[the behaviour specialist] has still not helped with my daughter like he was supposed to last year. He still hasn't got there, so she is still getting hit."

(2) Difficulty accessing services

Parents complained that even when appropriate services existed, they were not always able to access them. This was attributed to a number of causes, including organisational rules and regulations, gatekeeping, rural location and the poor health of the child.

(3) Funding issues

Insufficient funding, lack of transparency in funding, ineffective funding systems, disparities and funding cuts were all issues that caused parents considerable concern. A number mentioned that they lived under the threat of their child's funding being cut. A message given to parents was that, for safety reasons, if their child did not have teacher aide time, they could not attend school or early childhood facilities:

> They didn't want Leon left alone, so if the teacher aide couldn't be there I had to be there but I wasn't allowed to take Ameria [my pre-school child] with me. I don't know what I was going to do with Ameria, leave her in the car or something! It was horrid.

In some cases teacher aide hours were being topped up by the school and/or parents.

(4) Lack of information

Limited, incorrect or no information about services and entitlements were frequent complaints:

> In terms of what you are entitled to, it took me forever just to get hold of the [organisation] … We floundered really. We still are floundering along, not really sure where you fit, or who you really see.

> It is hard work, the amount of times where I have just wanted to say, 'Okay, I can't do this anymore!'

One mother reported reaching crisis point at one stage. After physically hurting her son, she made a number of desperate phone calls to find help.

> **Participant:** Yes, now I know how to deal with it, how to cope with it, I know who to get hold of if it gets to the point where it gets too

much, and I have got someone on call 24 hours if I do get to that crunch time. Even Support Services said, 'If it gets to the point where you can't cope with him, ring us and we will come and get him, and we will just take him away for the night.'

Jill: And, that is what you needed to know before you came to that situation?

Participant: Yes, that is all I needed—there is help there—why didn't you say that before?

(5) Financial strain

A strong theme was the financial strain having a child with ASD placed parents under. While various types of financial assistance were available and appreciated, they came nowhere near to covering the extra cost involved in raising a child with ASD. Also, the effort, explanations, bureaucracy and waiting time involved in accessing financial assistance were described as off-putting and sometimes upsetting: "It's just being constantly reminded that there's something wrong with your child and there's not a damn thing you can do about it."

(6) Assessment hassles

A variety of problems relating to assessment were mentioned. These included: inadequate time to assess properly; inappropriate assessment tools, procedures and venues; inexperienced assessors; the subjectivity of assessments; and "waste of time" assessments. A few parents told of incorrect diagnoses as a result of inadequate testing.

(7) Organisational, system and procedural hassles

Parents reported a variety of organisational barriers, such as red tape, inflexible rules and timetabling, competition for clients, administrative delays, inappropriate resources, and unhelpful work styles and scheduling. An example of the latter was teaching schedules that involved frequent changes of teacher aides. Children found this confusing and unsettling: "People would come and go and disappear ... and Ronald wasn't shown properly where they fit in."

Problems with the taxi services to and from school were frequently reported. One instance was described by a father:

Tama [qualified for the taxi service but] we'd still have to go to school to take his sister anyway so there didn't seem any point. We even suggested that maybe they take both of them either to school or home from school and we do the other trip ... We would have been quite happy to do this, but they said they couldn't take special needs kids and non-special needs kids in the same vehicle. I don't know why. There must be some law or rule. So we ended up not using that service.

(8) A lack of knowledge among professionals

Parents complained of professionals not appearing to have the necessary expertise and of making incorrect, unwise, unreasonable and sometimes bizarre decisions and statements. The doctor who told parents not to give their son apples or he would grow too tall is a case in point! Parents frequently mentioned the lack of ASD knowledge among teachers and teacher aides and the inappropriate programmes their children were receiving. Many examples were given. One parent was concerned that teachers who did not understand ASD misinterpreted ritualistic behaviour as misbehaviour and consequently used discipline inappropriately. A further observation of three parents was that teachers always blamed the children and never looked at school factors that might contribute to their misbehaviour.

(9) Detrimental attitudes

Parents reported a variety of detrimental attitudes among professionals and the public at large. With respect to professionals, the major complaints were not being listened to, being disbelieved, or having their opinions and suggestions undervalued.

Negative attitudes relating to children's behaviour were also frequently reported. Parents talked of their children being stared at, growled at, feared, ignored and excluded, while they themselves were often subject to insensitive, insulting and sometimes downright rude remarks. Taking their children shopping was particularly challenging: "One time he threw a massive tantrum in PAK'nSAVE. He was screaming away and this old guy says, "Oh God, will you just shut up!"

Incidents of prejudice, detrimental cultural stereotyping and patronising attitudes were also reported, the most blatant being the social worker's comment below:

'We're only here because there's enough ignorant little Māori girls like you that want to play happy families and don't cope and with your son being autistic on top of it … so more than likely he is a prime candidate to be abused …' He had expectations that I was a typical solo mother and on top of that, the typical solo Māori mother that didn't know anything … Kenny was actually home from school, he'd finished school for the day, and he said, 'Typical Māori, why isn't that kid at school?' I said, 'Go and find me a school that will have him from nine till three and then you can say it.'

(10) Parental stress

Having a child with ASD is by its very nature challenging. Parents told stories of having to cope with destructive, unsafe, violent, demanding, self-injurious and frustrating behaviours. In addition to coping with these behaviours, parents also had to contend with the many barriers described above. The need to fight for services emerged as one barrier that proved particularly stressful for parents:

> People say to me, 'You have to fight for blah blah,' and 'You have to fight for…' I spend enough energy getting through the day with this child, please don't tell me I have to fight! But you do, and it is a reality, and there are so many times.

One parent who had gone public with her fight told of being pressured into remaining quiet:

> 'This is not in the best interest of your son to be going public like this.' It was emotional blackmail. 'You are humiliating our organisation and you have nothing to gain from it.'

Physical stress was mentioned in relation to sleepless nights and having to be constantly vigilant about dangerous situations. Similarly, instances of psychological and emotional stress and stress on marital, family and friendship relationships were reported. Finally, concern about what will happen to their child 'when they grow up' caused considerable worry to a number of parents—the teenage years, adulthood and when the parents died were particular areas of anxiety.

Social interaction

Typical of children with ASD, those in the study had difficulty initiating and maintaining social interactions, learning appropriate social skills and developing friendships. The latter was exacerbated by circumstances such as having to travel out of the neighbourhood to attend schools that had appropriate special education programmes and an ASD-friendly, safe environment.

Bullying was mentioned by a few parents:

> Yes, he [got bullied] a while there in his first year at school, because if you hit him and say, 'Sorry' it is okay, so what the kids at school were doing was hitting him and saying, 'Sorry,' and then kicking him and saying, 'Sorry,' and he was accepting that that was okay because they had said, 'Sorry'.

However, the most frequently mentioned cause of distress for parents was seeing their children socially isolated:

> I don't go to the school if I can help it. I stay away from the school because I know he will always be on his own, sitting on his own, playing on his own, or playing watching the other kids, and it breaks your heart to watch him playing on his own.

A number of strategies were being used both at school and at home to facilitate social interaction. Some of these were: the formal teaching of social language and skills; buddy systems; involving other children in therapies; community experiences; providing opportunities for socialisation with family and friends through outings, visits and family gatherings; and fostering an interest and involvement in sports, games and other recreational activities. The success rate of these strategies varied.

Interaction with other Māori children in bilingual classes, whānau classes and kapa haka groups was seen as having socialising benefits, both in and out of the school environment. For example, a mother explained how her son's involvement in kapa haka and visit to the bilingual class helped other children realise that "He's not really scary, he does some funny things, he's not bad. Then it spread within the whānau classes."

Past, present and future wishes and dreams

Parents were asked about their past, present and future wishes and dreams for their children. Wishes for the past fell into two categories:

- the provision of more information and personal support at diagnosis
- the provision of ongoing support, information, services and

equipment that would have met their child's changing needs and circumstances.

Behavioural support and an emergency phone contact in times of crisis; car restraints, locks, nappies, home help, a "safe room", information about appropriate schools, respite care, access to appropriate programmes, speech therapy and financial assistance were all mentioned, as were provisions that were needed but unavailable in the past.

Requests for the present were similarly centred around services and equipment that were needed but unavailable. Invariably parents' dreams for their children's future were for them to be as happy and independent as possible. Parents' perceptions of independence and the means of obtaining it varied—usually according to the severity of their child's ASD.

Update

The research above was conducted 10 years ago. Since then I have kept in contact with a number of the whānau involved. Also, in preparation for writing this chapter, people were asked about changes in the intervening period. There was general agreement that services and education had improved over the years and that there was now a much greater societal awareness of ASD and cultural issues. However, there were also stories of a continuing struggle to have children well provided for and included. Problems related to personnel, policies and provisions.

There are still too many professionals who lack knowledge about ASD and/or have negative attitudes about working with children with ASD and their whānau. The Ministry of Education-supported ASD endorsement in the Post Graduate Diploma (Specialist Teaching) offered by Massey University and the Tips for Autism programme were both commended for their work in upskilling professionals. However, it was believed that additional measures are needed to make a widespread difference. An increased focus on ASD in initial professional training and readily available in-service education were seen as priorities. Such courses could focus on familiarising students with the *New Zealand Autism Spectrum Disorder Guideline* (Ministry of Health & Ministry of Education, 2008) and the wealth of useful ASD assessment, teaching and research information now available on the world wide web.

On the policy front, one parent had high praise for the Ministry of Education's Success for All— Every School, Every Child vision and supported inclusion for her child, although putting this into practice was proving a major challenge. The mother noted that *all* professionals involved had to support the initiative for it to work. Similarly, the Ministry's Intensive Wrap Around Service was appreciated, but also criticised because of a lack of collaboration with the Ministry of Social Development. While definite progress has been made, there still appears to be an abundance of bureaucratic red tape causing unacceptable delays in service and resource provision, especially in times of crisis.

Discussion

Subsequent research

Unfortunately, Māori-focused ASD research is still scarce. Although a small number of studies include Māori students with ASD among the participants (e.g. Bevan-Brown, Carroll-Lind, Kearney, Sperl, & Sutherland, 2008) or their families as informants (e.g. Bevan-Brown, 2010;[6] Bevan-Brown et al., 2011), I am aware of only one other research study that focuses solely on Māori with ASD. This was conducted by the Ministries of Health and Education to provide information for the *New Zealand Autism Spectrum Disorder Guideline* (Ministry of Health & Ministry of Education, 2008). Five hui were conducted throughout Aotearoa / New Zealand to enable Māori to contribute their views and experiences of ASD. Approximately 150 people attended these hui, answering set questions on the themes of:

> factors influencing representation; assessment and diagnosis; post-diagnosis support; the need for kaiārahi; education; services and on-going support; information; guideline development; other ASD related issues. (p. 203)

A descriptive summary of the material gathered is presented in Part 7 (pp. 203–214) of the *New Zealand Autism Spectrum Disorder Guideline* (2008).

---

6   In the Bevan-Brown (2004) research a need for an explanatory DVD to share with whānau and others was identified. Subsequently two mothers from the research and I formed the PAI4ASD Trust (2008), which produced the DVD *In My Shoes*. To date 22,000 free copies of the DVD have been distributed in Aotearoa / New Zealand and overseas (see http://www.inmyshoes.co.nz). An online questionnaire answered by 137 individuals informed the content of this DVD, which includes a specific Māori section.

Complementary findings and recommendations

There is a high degree of concurrence between the findings of the Guideline research and the study reported above (Bevan-Brown, 2004). Both reported parents and whānau struggling to manage because of a range of factors. To address these challenges, the Bevan-Brown research made recommendations to:

- increase the number of personnel in existing services and expand provisions for parents, whānau and children with ASD, to ensure they have readily available, ongoing assessment, information, assistance and support

- increase ASD-related financial assistance available to parents

- adopt friendly, personal approaches to service provision, which include providing information to parents, helping them to access resources and entitlements, and supporting them during transition periods, such as beginning, changing and leaving school

- financially assist parent organisations to enable them to effectively perform their dual function of informing and supporting parents

- listen to and be guided by parents (Bevan-Brown, 2004, pp. xii & xiii).

Despite the findings of the Guideline research strongly supporting the recommendations above, only three Māori-specific recommendations were made in the *New Zealand Autism Spectrum Disorder Guideline*. The first is a recommendation that "ASD information in English and te reo Māori should be provided and distributed through Māori and mainstream providers of health, education and disability services" (p. 198) and via a variety of other Māori and mainstream organisations and media.

A second strong point of concurrence relates to Māori cultural input. Both studies identified a shortage of culturally appropriate professionals, services and contexts. To address this, the Bevan-Brown research made recommendations to:

- increase teachers' and other professionals' knowledge of ASD and Māoritanga to enable them to provide culturally appropriate, effective programmes and services

- upskill personnel employed in existing Māori provisions, and increase and expand these services

- increase the bicultural and bilingual expertise of personnel in mainstream services (Bevan-Brown, 2004, p. xiii).

Participants in the Guideline research also called for cultural upskilling of professionals, but the only formal recommendation made was that "the appointment of a kaiārahi (guide) should be considered. The kaiārahi would work in conjunction with, and be supported across, the health, education and disabilities sectors involved with ASD (Ministry of Health & Ministry of Education, 2008, p. 198). Additionally, participants in the Guideline research suggested: the implementation of cultural protocols such as pōwhiri, karakia, whanaungatanga and manaaki into all services provided; the involvement of kaumātua and kuia; taking cognisance of Māori world views and using a holistic frame of reference, including emotional support and a spiritual dimension; by-Māori-for-Māori and kaupapa Māori services; marae-based support and training; encouraging more Māori to train in specialist ASD services; community wānanga about ASD; and the development of Māori respite-care services.

Both studies suggested a range of measures to improve the general quality and accessibility of provisions and to raise awareness and understanding of ASD. The Bevan-Brown research included recommendations for:

- the provision of more ASD-friendly, safe assessment and learning environments
- the reduction of red tape involved in accessing relevant services, and the development of user-friendly, culturally appropriate administrative and funding procedures
- the introduction of media programmes to facilitate awareness and understanding of ASD and to improve detrimental attitudes among the general public
- the provision of services and facilities for adults with ASD to enable them to live with dignity and as much independence as possible (Bevan-Brown, 2004, pp. xii & xiii).

Participants' suggestions in the Guideline research aligned with these recommendations. In addition, they wanted: fewer personnel involved in assessment, professionals' roles to be clarified and jargon to be avoided. Guideline participants emphasised the important role whānau play and suggested a range of measures to empower, support and include them. These included: allowing whānau to take ownership of ASD processes; providing them with workshops and information packs on ASD, the range of service and educational options available, funding opportunities, entitlements and eligibility criteria; supporting iwi-based ASD advocacy services; and ensuring that services provided are both person and whānau centred.

The implications of research findings for people who work with Māori with ASD and their whānau

The third Māori-specific Guideline recommendation was, "A programme of empirical research that would provide baseline information about Māori and ASD should be developed" (Ministry of Health & Ministry of Education, 2008, p. 198). Unfortunately, this has not happened. Because of the lack of research and other information specific to Māori with ASD, it is difficult to gauge what progress has been made in the last 10 years and what still needs to be done. However, from my experience in this field, and the research update provided earlier, the previous recommendations are still relevant today, although it should also be noted that many improvements have been made over the intervening years.

Although the power to increase ASD funding does not rest with professionals in the field, they do have a role to play in advocating for needed money, services and resources and can contribute to raising awareness and understanding of ASD among their colleagues and society at large. They also have the following responsibilities.

1. Professionals in the field have a responsibility to develop the cultural competency and professional expertise that will enable them to work with Māori children with ASD and their whānau in an effective, culturally sensitive and responsive manner. Although resources specifically focused on Māori children with ASD are limited, an Internet search will reveal a wealth of online material to help professionals develop their Māori cultural knowledge and ASD competencies. Gaining cultural and ASD knowledge, however, is just the first step. Given the characteristics of children with

ASD, professionals need to be creative and to consult with whānau about what adaptations and accommodations are needed to successfully incorporate cultural input.

2. Professionals in the field have a responsibility to listen to, be guided by and support parents and whānau of Māori children with ASD. Parents know their children best. Research has also shown that strategies parents report as effective are those supported by ASD research in general (Bevan-Brown, 2010). Therefore professionals would do well to take note of parents' concerns, requests, suggestions and wishes in respect to their children with ASD.

3. Finally, professionals in the field have a responsibility to make the services they provide as user-friendly, whānau-focused, relevant and accessible as possible.[7]

In conclusion, it should be noted that, apart from the culturally specific research findings, recommendations and suggestions, the balance of this chapter is equally applicable to all children with ASD and their families, regardless of ethnicity. Knowledge of ASD among professionals and the general public is limited. Hopefully, with greater awareness and understanding will come improved attitudes and services. This cannot happen soon enough for Māori children with ASD, their parents and whanau.

Study questions

1. There is a suggestion that Māori children are under-represented among those diagnosed with ASD. Why might this be? What are the implications of under-representation?

2. A number of accommodations were made so that children in this study could participate in different cultural activities. What were they? What other cultural activities might be particularly challenging for children with ASD, and what adaptations or accommodations could help them participate?

3. Parents mentioned 10 main barriers to raising their children with ASD. Choose three you think would be the easiest to eliminate and

---

7 A questionnaire providing guidance to parents in selecting a culturally effective school for their children with ASD can be found at http://www.massey.ac.nz/massey/fms/Colleges/College%20 of%20Education/ Documents/C&P/Kairaranga/Volume%208_Issue%202_2007.pdf

state how this could be done.

4. A huge cause of distress for parents was seeing their children with ASD socially isolated. In educational and care facilities, what can people do to increase social interaction between children with and without ASD? What can parents and family members do to encourage and facilitate social interaction during out-of-school hours?

References

Bevan-Brown, J. (2004). *Māori perspectives of autistic spectrum disorder.* Wellington: Research Division, Ministry of Education. Retrieved from http://www.educationcounts.govt.nz/ publications/special_education/5479

Bevan-Brown, J. (2010). Messages from parents of children with autism spectrum disorder (ASD). *Kairaranga, 11*(2), 16–22.

Bevan-Brown, J., Bourke, R., Butler, P., Carroll-Lind, J., Kearney, A., & Mentis, M. (2011). *Evaluation of the Tips for Autism professional learning and development programme: Final report.* Wellington: Ministry of Education.

Bevan-Brown, J., Carroll-Lind, J., Kearney, A., Sperl, B., & Sutherland, M. (2008). Making assumptions vs building relationships: Lessons from a participatory action research project to identify effective practices for learners with ASD. *Kairaranga, Special Issue, 9*, 22–31.

Ministry of Health and Ministry of Education. (2008). *New Zealand autism spectrum disorder guideline.* Wellington: Ministry of Health. Retrieved from http://www.health.govt.nz/ publication/new-zealand-autism-spectrum-disorder-guideline

PAI4ASD Trust. (2008). *In my shoes: An everyday look at autism spectrum disorder* [DVD]. People Media.

Chapter 10

Hei Āwhina Mātua: A kaupapa Māori response to behaviour

Mere Berryman

Ko ōu hīkoinga i runga i tōku whariki,
Ko tōu noho i tōku whare,
E huakina ai ōku tatau ōku matapihi.

Your steps on my mat,
Your respect for my home,
Opens doors and windows.

Introduction

Hei Āwhina Mātua (strengthening parents and other adults), a kaupapa Māori research and development project, sought to capitalise on the strengths available within both whānau and teachers so that both groups could take joint responsibility for students' learning and behaviour. This required professionals trained in delivering learning and behavioural programmes for individual students working in culturally responsive and collaborative ways with adults, whānau, teachers and community members. This chapter returns to this study to reconsider the key findings.

Parental involvement in education

In terms of parental involvement in their children's education, Durie (2006) contends:

> [f]or many whānau, contact with school only occurs when there is a crisis or a problem, or funds to raise or a hāngi to prepare. Parents are often placed in a defensive position which all too often leads to a deteriorating relationship with school. The crisis approach to whānau involvement is not one that will induce a sense of whānau enthusiasm for learning or for education. While it is important that parents are kept informed of difficulties, it is more important that parents are also able to work with schools to identify potential and then to jointly construct pathways that will enable promise to be realised. (p. 10)

More frequently, parents are participating either in fund raising, as assistants or other teacher-support activities, or participating as elected representatives on the school's board of trustees. Although important and worthwhile, these forms of participation do not provide effective or respectful contexts for sharing information about the behaviour and learning of individual students, nor do they provide collaborative learning opportunities for parents and teachers as a way to reinforce and build on learning that occurs in both home and school settings (McNaughton, 2002). Rather than co-construct potential pathways or learn from each other, it is more likely that students' learning and behavioural difficulties in one setting (home or school) are being too quickly attributed to the perceived inadequacies of the other setting (Bishop & Berryman, 2006). This can be even more problematic when teachers whose ethnicity is different to that of their students do not understand that, for all individuals and groups, culture counts (Bishop & Glynn, 1999; Macfarlane, 2004; Villegas & Lucas, 2002). The teacher's culture counts, as does that of their students, but the impact of one culture on another is often determined by relationships and power.

Without prior connections or respectful relationships with families, teachers may too readily blame students' failure to learn at school on perceived inadequacies in students' home backgrounds, their cultural differences, their ethnicity and their parents' lack of motivation or commitment to help them achieve (Bishop, Berryman, Tiakiwai, & Richardson, 2003). Meanwhile parents may just as readily blame their children's low achievement and behavioural difficulties on teachers' ignorance of students' cultural and ethnic origins, and on teachers growing increasingly out of touch with the financial and emotional stresses and strains of contemporary parenting.

The genesis of Hei Āwhina Mātua

Hei Āwhina Mātua emerged when a group of Māori teachers and kaumātua expressed an urgent need for more positive and effective behaviour management strategies and educational resources focused specifically on the needs of students learning in Māori-language settings. In particular, teachers sought strategies and resources to work with whānau and children in their own communities to improve their own responses to students' behaviour.

Local special educators provided a professional development programme focused on how behaviour was learned and how to respond more appropriately to the most challenging student behaviours. The professional development programme was adapted from the Assertive Discipline programme (Canter & Canter, 1992a, 1992b) that was being widely used at the time in many mainstream schools. Following the intensive 3-day programme, evaluations from teachers expressed their need for further and continuing input into managing challenging student behaviours. Importantly, these teachers signalled that they had difficulty accepting the behavioural concepts, principles, rewards and sanctions as they were packaged in the Assertive Discipline programme, given there had been little or no regard for the cultural values and preferences of Māori students and their whānau.

Schools were also requesting support for teachers to help them work more effectively with Māori students and their whānau, and at the same time there was an urgent challenge to develop culturally appropriate and responsive learning and behaviour resources for these students. A small group of Māori whānau, educators and a Pākehā academic undertook to research and develop such a resource. Effective solutions to these challenges were seen to lie with increased Māori ownership and control of the research, as well as in the development of behavioural and learning programmes that recognised and incorporated Māori cultural values as essential components of the programme. This group won a Ministry of Education contract for the research and development of a collaborative behaviour management programme for teachers and whānau, and as a result established themselves as a research whānau known as Poutama Pounamu.

Participation by kaumātua ensured that appropriate Māori cultural values, beliefs and practices were followed in all aspects of planning and decision making. Adherence to kaupapa Māori principles ensured that the ownership and control of the research questions, methodology and procedures, the data generated, and how those data were understood and interpreted remained clearly within the research whānau. Critical power issues between the researcher and the researched— related to control over questions of initiation, benefits, representation, legitimation and accountability (Bishop, 1996)—were thus defined and resolved from within frameworks that came from a Māori world view. This approach contrasted strongly with the majority of educational research at the time that sought to address the educational achievement of Māori students with solutions that were largely imposed from a Western world view. Hei Āwhina Mātua would aim to address these concerns by connecting directly to Māori at both the personal and the epistemological levels.

The research and development

Adhering to all of the ethical procedures required, the research whānau proposed to develop and trial a set of resources with teachers and their Māori community in one school, then further trial and test these resources in two other schools. These activities, in each of the schools, are discussed next.

School 1

School 1 was a large, urban intermediate, with over 300 students, of whom 30 percent were Māori. This school had a Māori-medium syndicate and two English-medium syndicates. The Hei Āwhina Mātua resources were developed with the three classes in the Māori-medium syndicate, where 90 percent of students were Māori and there were five Māori staff, including a kuia and a male kaiāwhina.

The first task for researchers and School 1 staff was to develop three behavioural checklists to identify the:

- settings where students may get into trouble
- challenging behaviours that may be occurring
- positive behaviours to be most valued.

Data from the checklists in School 1 would then be used to produce the behavioural scenarios in a Hei Āwhina Mātua video resource.

Students as researchers

Inspecting the behavioural checklists as they were being drafted provided students with their first opportunity to reflect on what was happening in the research. Student input was sought to verify the street credibility of the language and item content in the checklists. The seriousness and depth of the students' responses to this invitation was impressive. Students affirmed and extended the colloquial language used in the checklists and identified important behavioural settings they considered to have been omitted from the 'settings' checklist. Their suggestions were welcomed and adopted by the research whānau, who soon came to appreciate that ongoing consultation with these experts (the students) would remain important if accurate information was required. From this point on these students were fully recognised as partners in the research. Students in this school had a clear understanding of the role of the checklists:

> It all began with filling out the checklists. There were three different checklists. One was about when and where we might get into trouble, the next one was about behaviour that bothers us, and the last one was about behaviour that we like. (Troy)

Whānau members responded to the checklists at a meeting called in the school hall to farewell one of their teachers. Students put on a brief kapa haka performance, ensuring a full turnout of whānau and kaumātua, who came to see their children perform, to farewell their teacher, to hear the Hei Āwhina Mātua project introduced by the research whānau, and to complete the three behavioural checklists.

Each of the checklist items allowed responders to rate how frequently specific behaviours and contexts were of concern to them. They rated each item on a four-point scale (0, never; 1, sometimes; 2, often; 3, always). Responses to the checklists were collated separately for students, whānau and school staff. From the individual responses to every item, a mean score for each responder group (students, school staff and whānau members) was calculated. Item mean scores were then ranked from highest to lowest for each responder group.

The completed checklists from students, teachers and parents generated valuable information for collation and analysis. We identified the top 10 settings or situations in which problem behaviour occurred, the top 10 challenging behaviours, and the top 10 positive behaviours as selected by teachers, parents and students. These nine sets of data were then presented back to the students in their own cultural meeting space, within which students were able to set up an open and frank dialogue with the research whānau about their behaviour at school, at home and in the community. For example, they volunteered one after-school setting (a shopping mall) as a context for problem behaviour that neither their parents nor their teachers were aware of. Together with the students, the whānau determined which were the key settings and which were the specific behaviours that needed to be included in the video resource that was to be developed.

Next, 10 skits were devised to represent these behaviours and settings in the video. The skits were discussed with a wider group of students, together with the teachers of the immersion classes. Teachers and whānau encouraged students to role-play various situations to show how the specific behaviours occurred at home, at school and in the community, and how teachers and parents and other adults responded to these behaviours.

Role-playing assisted the gathering of language appropriate to the people and to the situations in the scripts. A clear example of this occurred when a dangerous head-high tackle during rugby practice was identified as a setting event for trouble. Students identified swearing as an essential part of this scenario, and that this language needed to appear in the video. The resulting skit shows a convincing outburst of swearing that has street credibility with many viewers. For the students who participated in this discussion, however, this was an important event in the research process. It affirmed for them that their views would be listened to and taken on board. For us, it was an invaluable lesson in the power of an inclusive culturally responsive learning and teaching process where the working relationship embodied genuine participation and power sharing.

Draft video scripts were prepared. These were read and volunteer actors negotiated specific roles for themselves. Although filming was in the school holidays, there was an impressive voluntary attendance by students. Students were not required to memorise and rehearse specific dialogue. What was more important was to convincingly convey the messages contained within each skit.

> We found out what the checklists had identified as the problems. From here we talked about what would be in the skits and who would want to be in a video. (Troy)

> After the researcher listed the 10 main problem areas, the teachers, parents and kids were asked their ideas about the different situations, what we thought of the wording and how everything happened. (Bronwyn)

Following this meeting, skits were further developed and confirmed by a group of students and teachers. Students were encouraged to role-play various situations in order to show how specific behaviours occurred at home, at school and in the community, and how teachers, parents and other adults responded to these behaviours.

> We talked about the scripts and we were allowed to change whatever we thought didn't seem realistic ... We asked if we were allowed to swear in the video. (Tara)

> We were allowed to change some of the parts that we thought didn't seem real. (Danielle)

> We went through each script changing stuff we thought wasn't right. That was a good thing to do because some of the words ... used in the scripts would not have been used in real life. At least, not by most kids. So the skits we did in the holidays last year were based on what we thought about the problems ... We were the bosses and directors. (Bronwyn)

The research whānau heeded the students' advice and this is reflected in the *better but not perfect* approach taken in all of the alternative response versions of the scripts:

> It was our choice to decide to do this video because we held the meetings and did the acting during our holidays. And that was just hard luck giving that time up. But, I wanted to do the acting and all the hard work because I was excited about being a part of the skits. (Tama)

While not all students turned up at the time required for their assigned roles, there was always someone willing to step in. Students were given outlines of each skit just before the filming began.

> When I started to act I was just being my usual self, doing an everyday thing. (Tama)

> We were allowed to say whatever came naturally, so that it would be more realistic and therefore more helpful to those who would use it in the future. (Bronwyn)

The continuing process of consultation and collaborative production of the skits with the students ensured credible performances set in realistic scenarios. By now the whānau had really begun to understand the meaning of "participant driven" research (Bishop, 1996). The film production concluded with a shared meal to celebrate the outcome of months of successful planning, collaboration and learning.

Soon after, the first milestone report to the Ministry of Education advisory committee was due. Five students volunteered to write about specific aspects of the research project and to present their reports in person at this meeting. Their presentations were delivered so confidently and competently that the Ministry of Education provided additional funding to allow them to travel to Dunedin with the research whānau to participate in editing the video. There they viewed the many hours of videotape and they selected specific 'takes' as their preferred choices for use in each skit. Their contribution was essential to editing the video interviews as three of them were among those interviewed. While in Dunedin they were interviewed by local newspapers and featured as a news item on Southern Television.

On their return to Tauranga some of the students were again interviewed by the local newspaper and on talkback radio. They then helped to write and present information about Hei Āwhina Mātua at a national and then an international education conference. They rose to the occasion every time, coming across as informed experts, capable of expressing their own views, and knowledgeable about the project. The strong and productive working relationship that was established between students and researchers ensured that the students continued to offer their sound and constructive critique throughout the project, and continued to do so. Without a doubt the research project benefited from the voices of these students, which at the time (1996) was a very new research experience.

Assessing the programme

The next phase of our work involved assessing the effectiveness of the Hei Āwhina Mātua concept and resources within a professional development programme for teachers and whānau members in two new schools. The programme that had been developed, but not trialled, in School 1 comprised workshop activities based on exploring the data collected in the research development phase. It also involved understanding 10 different strategies for changing behaviour evident within the various skits presented in the video. Four of these were 'antecedent' strategies, which change behaviour by altering the settings and contexts in which it occurs. The remaining six were 'consequent' strategies, which change behaviour through refining the timing, frequency, positivity and cultural responsiveness of its consequences. Workshop activities focused on matching behavioural strategies with particular skits, and inventing and presenting new skits to demonstrate how the strategies might be effectively applied in new situations.

The decision to match behavioural strategies to what was going on in the skits, rather than constructing the skits to demonstrate specific behavioural strategies, resulted from our interactions and discussions with the students in School 1. They convinced us that this approach would focus attention and learning on their actual behaviours in real-life contexts. This was a decision to move from observation to theory, rather than the reverse. The students' notes were incorporated into the training manual and workshop materials, along with the 10 behavioural principles they had identified as being best able to help others to consider ways to improve their own behavioural interactions. The 10 principles were:

1. model what you want

2. contingent positive consequences

3. get in early

4. a little and often

5. give clear instructions

6. take the time to plan ahead

7. change the setting

8. accept gradual improvement

9. find positive ways to reduce unacceptable behaviour

10. use effective sanctions for unacceptable behaviour.

Schools 2 and 3

Staff and whānau from both trial schools had connections with the research whānau and had volunteered their participation. School 2 was a small rural kura kaupapa Māori. Trialling the checklists in this kura required presenting the checklists in Māori. A member of the research whānau who was a native speaker undertook the challenging task of expressing the wide range of behavioural concepts in traditional Māori style through the use of appropriate metaphors. In this school four further resources were developed to complete the professional development package for teachers and whānau. These included a playground observation tool, a classroom observation tool, and Māori-language assessment tools for literacy and numeracy.

School 3 was a small, bilingual, semi-rural primary school. At the end of Year 6 students from this school transitioned to the intermediate school previously identified as School 1. This school therefore included many who were whānau to the first group of students.

Working with the kura and whānau

Hei Āwhina Mātua began in School 2 with a hui so that whānau and school staff could learn about the programme and the expectations for the research, then decide whether they would participate or not. Once each community had agreed to participate, they were asked to fill out the checklists. Next, time-sampled observations of 10 randomly selected students were gathered in each classroom. Playground observations, recording zone-by-zone, on a time sample basis, antecedent information (time, location, number and gender of students present, number of teachers/adults present), behavioural information (categories of behaviour), and information on immediate consequences of the observed behaviour (if any) were also gathered. These observations were subsequently carried out after the implementation of the professional development and then after 10 weeks of the schools' maintaining the programme on their own. Assessments of reading, writing and maths performances were also made, with samples taken pre- and post-programme.

Developing relationships with teachers and whānau to involve them in the programme taught the research whānau a major and fundamental lesson. In the first school (the kura kaupapa Māori), the research whānau again chose to let the school staff lead the process. After reporting the checklist findings to the combined group, teachers suggested they would meet at the school while whānau members could work in their homes. At this point the historical protocols, procedures and power bases embedded in the school context had begun to dominate. Although Māori protocols (such as karakia and mihimihi) were followed, the research whānau had gone along with engaging the home and school community as two separate groups and without kaumātua guidance. This did not allow the time or space to acknowledge the mana and experience of each group of participants (parents, teachers and students).

Soon it was clear that rather than create a space to share information with and between the groups and thus learn from one another, this move had provided each group with a space to deficit theorise the other. In other words, the research whānau had cut across the important cultural relationships that connected these groups with each other, with their marae and with their kaumātua. This resulted in the professional development showing little attitudinal or behavioural change in the home or in the school, and the perpetuation of a situation where both groups were talking past each other.

After 6 months it was clear that the programme was not working in School 2; nothing had changed. The research whānau looked at their own processes to find where they had gone wrong. Rangiwhakaehu Walker, the kuia whakaruruhau for the research whānau and also to many in these school communities, advised that the professional development needed to begin again by working with staff and whānau combined, and also from the two schools combined. Rangiwhakaehu's advice was simple and effective: begin the checklists and baseline work in School 3, then bring both groups together.

After the initial work was completed she called a hui of teachers, whānau and students from both schools. She called this hui on the marae of the kaumātua who had supported the initial development of Hei Āwhina Mātua in School 1. The hui was preceded by a traditional pōwhiri that was led by these kaumātua. The mana of all groups present was acknowledged and respected, as were their connections to this marae and to this programme. Kaumātua advice led to the workshop activities taking place in the wharenui itself. In this context a space was created where all concerns could be raised for discussion in a setting that was culturally safe and empowering for all.

Professional development on the marae

Accordingly, the two schools and their home communities met for the interactive professional learning sessions in the place where other important cultural events take place. Kaumātua, some of whom were grandparents of the students, helped to run the sessions. The 11 skits in the Hei Āwhina Mātua video were used to provide examples of problem behaviours and problem settings, and to illustrate more effective ways of responding to them. Supporting people to develop a clear understanding of the 10 Hei Āwhina Mātua principles underlying the specific procedures for changing behaviour was essential, as this understanding would be crucial if the attitudes and behaviours of parents and teachers were to change. Being able to theorise the new principles would ensure more effective behavioural change. This was illustrated in the following incident that occurred when one of the kuia sat watching breakfast being cooked by the mothers. She remarked that even though the gas cookers had been in the marae kitchen for quite some time now she had not yet learned how to use them. The mother quickly remarked, "Can't you see I'm modelling what you need", at which the kuia grinned and affirmed that the mum was indeed doing this, but she'd better keep on modelling because the kuia hadn't quite learned yet.

Throughout the training each of the principles was role-played in contexts where the problem situations or typical responses were presented. Each example was responded to with an improved response based on the 10 specific principles. Small groups presented their role-plays to the workshop as a whole, and the whole group then discussed and analysed these ideas. These discussions often generated even more effective and appropriate ideas for responses. For example, in one instance, where a skit included inappropriate hitting, the wider group was able to note the impact of this behaviour being modelled for children; it had been copied and applied by the children to their younger siblings.

Following the workshops, parents and teachers returned to their homes and schools ready to negotiate and plan for more informed and effective collaborative behaviour change across both settings. Parents and whānau at home and teachers at school would be implementing strategies based on the same 10 principles. Further, teachers and parents planned to share information on students' behaviour more openly and regularly, with the encouragement and support of kaumātua.

Inside the wharenui, several generations had been present—grandparents, parents, children and grandchildren—as well as their tūpuna, who were represented in the carvings and photographs. Various distinct groupings had participated in the workshop exercises. These included kaumātua and kuia, teachers, parents and whānau members, students, researchers and trainers. However, whānau and whanaungatanga ties binding these groups proved far stronger in this cultural context than the occupational or generational ties within each group. These two factors—strong whānau links and the marae context—ensured that Māori language and cultural protocols prevailed, providing both a culturally responsive and relations-based framework for all the learning and teaching that occurred, some of which was planned and some of which had emerged from the cultural contexts and settings.

In this culturally responsive conversational space, kaumātua and kuia were able to assume their cultural leadership roles and assist anyone who needed cultural support or guidance—even the senior teachers present. Seeing a teacher being gently but clearly instructed by a kuia provided a powerful cultural statement for students, parents and researchers alike. Seeing teachers and parents inventing and acting in skits in which they portrayed themselves getting things hilariously wrong, and laughing at themselves, had a powerful and positive impact on the students and on the researchers. Students came to see their own behaviour in quite a different light in terms of its impact on other people. Working with groups together in appropriate and responsive cultural contexts had a pervasive and positive impact, and required a lot less time to accelerate the learning outcomes. All groups focused their energy and knowledge on improving the wellbeing of the students. There was learning by doing, learning by sitting and watching, learning by listening, and learning by laughing and crying. Learning was driven by the many intergenerational relationships opened up and validated in this indigenous Māori space. The experiential learning on this marae also served to extend and deepen the powerful cultural relationships.

Findings

After two terms, all measures (classroom observations; playground observations; reading, writing and numeracy) were repeated in both schools. These results showed that when parents, teachers and students exercised responsibility and ownership of the Hei Āwhina Mātua principles and programme, a range of positive behavioural and achievement outcomes occurred. The full set of behaviour and academic results for both schools is presented in the final report (Glynn, Berryman, Atvars, & Harawira, 1997), but this chapter presents the playground and classroom observation results from School 2 only.

The school playground was separated into two sections. Within each section all zones listed were clearly visible from one observation point. Table 10.1 shows the percentage of students actively and appropriately engaged in each zone and the number of teachers or adults present in each section, before and after the Hei Āwhina Mātua programme. Inappropriate and appropriate behaviours had been defined and agreed to by communities through the checklist activity. Inappropriate behaviours related to activities such as fighting, bullying, damaging property, arguing and swearing. Appropriate behaviours related to pro-social activities such as sharing, playing and working together, as well as caring for and listening to each other. Data in Table 10.1 are mean data across three separate pre- and post-observation samples within the same zones.

Table 10.1. Playground observation data

School 2	PRE		POST	
Section 1	% students appropriately engaged	Teachers interacting with students	% students appropriately engaged	Teachers interacting with students
Zone 1: Netball courts	50		100	
Zone 2: Big field	81	2	98	7
Section 2	% students appropriately engaged	Teachers interacting with students	% students appropriately engaged	Teachers interacting with students
Zone 3: Right of the quadrangle	92		85	
Zone 4: Back verandah	60		100	
Zone 5: Left of the quadrangle	93		100	
Zone 6: Front verandah	55	4	99	15

Pre-programme observation data revealed a wide variation in appropriate student engagement, with three zones in particular showing low levels of appropriate student engagement. Higher rates were observed on the big field and at the right and left of the quadrangle. At pre-programme, only two teachers were observed interacting with students in section 1 and four in section 2.

Post-programme data showed an improvement in student engagement across five of the six zones, and, importantly, even though the same number of teachers remained officially on duty, there were many more observed instances of teachers interacting with students (from 6 instances at pre-programme to 22 at post-programme). Thus teachers had taken a proactive stance of playing with and being available to students at recess times.

Table 10.2 presents results from the observations of on-task behaviour in each classroom, with a mean on-task behaviour level as well as an individual on-task level for particular target students from the time sample. Pre and post data are averaged over three separate observations.

Table 10.2. Classroom observation data: School 2 on-task behaviour

classroom 1	PRE	POST
Class mean	76	76
Target student 03	80	100
classroom 2		
Class mean	43	86
Target student 01	20	60
classroom 3		
Class mean	68	93
Target student 02	63	73
classroom 4		
Class mean	77	82
Target student 04	40	70
Target student 05	97	*60
Target student 06	60	67

* Student going through change of medication for epilepsy.

Classroom 1 was a new entrant class with a long-term relief teacher. A reasonably high level of on-task behaviour was maintained from pre- to post-programme. The mean on-task behaviour of target student 03, which was already above the class average at 80 percent, rose a further 20 percent to 100 percent.

Classroom 2 was a junior class with a Year 1 teacher. The low class average at pre-programme, which indicates high levels of student off-task behaviour, had improved by post-programme to 86 percent. Furthermore, the average on-task behaviour of target student 01 at pre-programme also showed a marked improvement.

Classroom 3 was a middle-school class with a long-term relief teacher. This classroom on-task behaviour began at a reasonable level, yet improved to 93 percent by post-programme. The on-task behaviour of target student 02 began a little below the class average, and although his on-task behaviour had improved by post-programme, it was still below the class average.

Classroom 4 was a senior school class with a mature long-term relief teacher. Students' on-task behaviour improved slightly throughout the programme. Target student 04's on-task behaviour was well below the class average at pre-programme but improved by 30 percent. Target student 06 began well below the class average and remained below the class average. Target student 05 showed a major decrease in on-task behaviour between pre- and post-programme, which is most likely explained by a change in medication for epilepsy.

Even though the mean behaviour levels varied considerably across the classrooms, there were either marked gains at post-programme or reasonably high levels were maintained. On-task behaviour gains between pre- and post-programme were also observed for all but one of the target students. While the behaviour changes on their own were impressive, these improvements were further reflected in gains in learning across all literacy and numeracy scores. Although a direct causal link to Hei Āwhina Mātua cannot be made, these data are consistent with those that followed in School 3. Therefore, it seems highly likely that the programme may well have contributed to these positive gains.

New connections

As part of the Ministry of Education's work programme, Meyer, Taiwhati and Hindle (2011) undertook an evaluation of Hei Āwhina Mātua. Their report identified Hei Āwhina Mātua as a programme designed specifically in accordance with Māori cultural values that had the potential to be a school-wide framework approach consistent with Positive Behaviour for Learning (PB4L). They suggested, however, that additional supports to this framework would be required if it were to address students with severe behavioural challenges. Accordingly, in 2012 the Ministry of Education contracted the University of Canterbury to develop a kaupapa Māori intervention framework within the PB4L work. Working in partnership with Te Tapuae o Rehua, and extending on the principles of Hei Āwhina Mātua and Hui Whakatika, a programme called Huakina Mai was developed. Huakina Mai uses the four values of kotahitanga, whanaungatanga, manaakitanga and rangatiratanga to guide the implementation within schools and classrooms, and in collaboration with whānau, hapū and iwi. This programme will be piloted and evaluated in two Hawke's Bay schools in 2014 and 2015.

Implications for others

Hei Āwhina Mātua has demonstrated the effectiveness of teachers, students, whānau and community working constructively and collaboratively to address challenging student behaviours at school and at home. For these Māori students, their whānau and teachers, it was clear that effective solutions stemmed from activating culturally preferred values and practices for engaging school and community, and from establishing a more equitable sharing of responsibility, expertise and accountability among these groups.

Both schools confirmed the effectiveness of the school collaborating with its Māori community to resolve behavioural challenges in a culturally competent and responsive manner. Parents, whānau and teachers alike celebrated the improvements because they were seen as positive outcomes of their collaborative efforts. Instead of looking to blame each other for the behaviour of students at school, these whānau and teachers asserted collective ownership of both the problems and the solutions, and in the process learned to show increasing respect for the level of expertise and commitment of the other. While the voices and experiences of these communities defined the problems, they also generated the solutions.

After more than a decade, components of Hei Āwhina Mātua are being applied within a new programme. How power will be maintained, so that collaboration and culture can be truly determined by the very communities in which the programme is being introduced, is still the greatest critical questions.

Study questions

1. How were the Hei Āwhina Mātua behavioural principles legitimated in this context?

2. Schools are told that they should work with Māori whānau and their communities; what were the benefits of doing so in this study?

3. What can schools learn about engaging with whānau from this study? Why is power so important in these contexts?

References

Bishop, R. (1996). *Whakawhanaungatanga collaborative research stories.* Palmerston North: Dunmore Press.

Bishop, R., & Berryman, M. (2006). *Culture speaks: Cultural relationships and classroom learning.* Wellington: Huia.

Bishop, R., Berryman, M., Tiakiwai, S., & Richardson, C. (2003). *Te Kotahitanga: The experiences of Year 9 and 10 Māori students in mainstream classrooms*. Wellington: Ministry of Education.

Bishop, R., & Glynn, T. (1999). *Culture counts: Changing power relations in education*. Palmerston North: Dunmore Press.

Canter, L., & Canter, M. (1992a). *Assertive discipline: A take-charge approach for today's educator*. Santa Monica, CA: Lee Canter & Associates.

Canter, L., & Canter, M. (1992b). *Assertive discipline: Positive behaviour management for today's classroom*. Santa Monica, CA: Lee Canter & Associates.

Durie, M. (2006, October). *Whānau, education and Māori potential*. Keynote presentation at the fifth Hui Taumata Māturanga, Taupō.

Glynn, T., Berryman, M., Atvars, K., & Harawira, W. (1997). *Hei Āwhina Mātua: A home and school behavioural programme*. Final report to the Ministry of Education. Wellington: Ministry of Education.

Macfarlane, A. (2004). *Kia hiwa ra!: Listen to culture*: *Māori students' plea to educators* Wellington: New Zealand Council for Education Research.

McNaughton, S. (2002). *Meeting of minds*. New York, NY: Richard C. Owen Publishers.

Meyer, L. H., Taiwhati, M., & Hindle, R. (2011). *Research and evaluation of kaupapa Māori behaviour programme: Hei Āwhina Mātua*. Wellington: Victoria University of Wellington.

Villegas, A. M., & Lucas, T. (2002). *Educating culturally responsive teachers: A coherent approach*. New York, NY: State University of New York Press.

Chapter 11

Gifted Māori children: Nurturing sturdy kauri

Jill Bevan-Brown

> Kīhai i taka te parapara a ōu tūpuna: tuku iho ki a koe.
>
> *You cannot fail to inherit the talents of your ancestors: they must descend to you.*

Introduction

This chapter begins with a brief discussion of terminology, the concept of giftedness, and giftedness in pre-European times.[1] It then reports the results of a research study into giftedness from a Māori perspective. Subsequent research, publications and gifted initiatives are discussed and the chapter concludes with a section on how people who work with gifted Māori children can nurture 'sturdy kauri'.

Gifted, gifted and talented, exceptional, special abilities—these and other terms are used worldwide to describe people whose ability

---

1   This chapter draws substantially from the original research on which it is based, and on subsequent publications relating to it, in particular Bevan-Brown, 2011.

in some valued area is considerably superior to others of a similar age. The concept of exceptional ability and people who exhibit it can be found throughout history and across all cultures. Certainly Māori have long-standing words in te reo that encapsulate various aspects of giftedness; for example, ihi, wehi, wana, parapara, mana, tohunga. Likewise, there are many Māori across time and iwi who have manifested giftedness in a variety of fields: Māui-tikitiki-a-Taranga, Apirana Ngata, George Nepia, Whina Cooper, Kiri te Kanawa, and many more.

An understanding of giftedness in pre-European times can be gleaned from the nature and role of tohunga, which means both 'an expert' and 'one who is chosen' (King, 1977; Marsden, 1975; Metge, 1976). Tohunga were chosen by tutelary atua, who endowed them with knowledge and expertise. Advanced abilities, therefore, were gifts from the gods, and people possessing these gifts were merely vehicles through which atua could communicate and create. Along with these gifts came a responsibility not to use them for self-aggrandisement, but rather for the benefit of others. In fact, if gifts were not used wisely, they could be withdrawn (Marsden, 1975; Mead, 1993; Puketapu-Hetet, 1993; Te Awekotuku, 1991).

There were three different types of tohunga: tohunga ahurewa (experts in esoteric knowledge), tohunga taura/whiāwhia (occult experts), and tohunga (experts in more earthly knowledge). This last group had qualifying adjectives added to their title to denote their field of expertise. There were tohunga in whaikōrero, art and craft, rongoā, fighting, whakapapa, history, composing and performing waiata and haka, building whare and waka, cultivating, fishing and hunting, understanding and interpreting the physical elements, and so forth (Buck, 1950; Marsden, 1975).

As well as having exceptional 'subject' knowledge, tohunga were also experts in associated kawa and tikanga, which required advanced spiritual, cognitive, social and affective abilities. They were outstanding members of their hapū and iwi—tall poppies, who were not only allowed to bloom but who were encouraged to do so (Best, 1924).

The research

As part of my Master of Education (Bevan-Brown, 1993) I conducted research into giftedness from a Māori perspective. This study investigated both traditional and contemporary concepts of giftedness, and also what Māori considered to be effective, appropriate means of identifying and providing for gifted and talented Māori students.

Methodology

A two-pronged approach was used: first, a literature review and documentary analysis, and then informal, exploratory interviews with 33 Māori participants.

Literature review

An extensive literature search was undertaken over a period of 5 years. This involved consideration of:

- history books
- biographies of famous Māori
- te reo for relevant terms and whakataukī
- oral literature, especially ngā moteatea and legends
- Māori writing—fiction and non-fiction
- traditional lifestyle and educational practices
- arts, crafts and music
- Māori values and tikanga
- Māori social structure and organisations
- religious beliefs and practices
- whakapapa
- television programmes and videos
- previous academic writing about Māori and giftedness.

Participants

A whānau network system was used to obtain 33 participants, ranging in age from teenagers to a kaumātua of 70-plus years. There were 10 males and 23 females: six kaumātua, 12 educators and 15 others. The educators were teachers from kōhanga reo, kura kaupapa Māori, mainstream primary and secondary schools, a polytechnic, a college of education and a university. 'Others' refers to people who identified themselves as Māori and had a demonstrated commitment to their Māori culture. The participants came from a variety of educational and socioeconomic backgrounds, were urban, suburban or rural dwellers, and represented many different hapū and iwi. One outcome of using whānau suggestions to guide participant selection was that the eventual sample included a relatively large number of very able people. Their talents included artistic, musical, academic, sporting, organisational, spiritual and cultural expertise.

Data collection and analysis

Interviews were held in Porirua, Paekakariki, Otaki, Palmerston North, Masterton, Gisborne and Ruatoria over a period of 8 months. The majority of interviews were conducted in the participant's or friends' homes. Interviews in te reo Māori were an option, but all participants chose to speak in English. The interviews were informal, social, enjoyable occasions that lasted between 1 and 3 hours. An interview schedule was used to guide conversation in three targeted areas: gifted people from the past; gifted people in the present; and catering for able and talented Māori children.

Interviews were audio-taped and transcribed, and the data were analysed using a coding and summarising system within a conceptual framework. A wide variety of analytical strategies were used to draw and confirm conclusions.

Results

A Māori concept of giftedness

Data from both prongs of the research revealed that while some changes have occurred over time, generally traditional and contemporary concepts are very similar. They have eight distinctive components in common (see Table 11.1).

Table 11.1. Components of a Māori concept of giftedness

1. Giftedness is widely distributed in Māori society. It is not bound by social class, economic status, lineage or gender.
2. Giftedness can be exhibited by both individuals and groups. Also, an individual's gifts and talents can be 'owned' by a group.
3. The recognised areas of giftedness and talent are broad and wide ranging.
4. Importance is placed on both 'qualities' and 'abilities'.
5. The concept of giftedness is holistic in nature and is inextricably intertwined with other Māori concepts.
6. There is an inherent expectation that a person's gifts and talents will be used to benefit others.
7. Māori culture provides a firm foundation on which giftedness is grounded, nurtured, exhibited and developed.
8. Mana tangata is frequently accorded to gifted people, especially in the areas of traditional knowledge and service to others.

1. Giftedness is widely distributed in Māori society. It is not bound by social class, economic status, lineage or gender

Both the documentary analysis and the research interviews revealed a wide variety of people considered to be gifted. In the interviews, for example, 56 national figures, 32 iwi figures, 48 whānau members and nine groups were nominated as being outstanding. They were people from many different walks of life—ranging from national heroes to cousin Hinemoa next door. Overall, the number of men and women chosen was very similar, although men dominated in the national and iwi groups and women in the whānau group.

It was noted that there was a greater tribal expectation for people from certain rangatira families to succeed, and that being from a whānau acknowledged for expertise in a particular field gave members greater access to associated knowledge. However, while these two factors might influence expectation and opportunity, there was unanimous agreement that whether or not a person succeeded depended on their ability rather than on their whakapapa.

2. Giftedness can be exhibited by both individuals and groups. Also, an individual's gifts and talents can be 'owned' by a group

Both in the literature review and in the research interviews a number of groups were cited as being gifted. Individual members were not named; rather, they were perceived as belonging to a collective of people who together demonstrated a particular talent or quality. Given the group orientation of Māori society, this citing of group expertise is not surprising.

An associated belief is that of group ownership of giftedness. This could be in the sense of a person possessing a particular quality or ability their whānau or hapū are celebrated for, or it could be the acknowledgement of the contribution others have played in nurturing and enabling a person's giftedness to develop. One participant noted that the 'self-made man' did not fit into Māori philosophy. While individual effort was applauded, especially if this involved battling against adversity, individuals themselves were viewed within the context of their whānau. People were conceived and raised and their abilities recognised and nurtured by others. Often personal sacrifices were made by whānau members to provide opportunities for a person's gifts and talents to be developed. As one participant explained,

The talent in a person is the talent you see encapsulated in that individual, but it is a talent that belongs to the group and that's the difference. It's just the perception, how you actually view the thing. (Bevan-Brown, 1993, p. 122)

3. The areas of giftedness and talent recognised are broad and wide ranging

Many different abilities and qualities are valued. These include spiritual, cognitive, affective, aesthetic, artistic, musical, psychomotor, social, intuitive, creative, leadership and cultural abilities and qualities.

Two examples illustrate this component. For a start, *Te Ao Hou* (1961 to 1975) contained articles celebrating gifted and talented people: cultural performers, carvers, orators, whakapapa and tikanga experts, academics, architects, boxers, rugby and league players, wrestlers, gymnasts, ballroom dancers, agriculturalists, sculptors, artists, writers, entertainers, dress designers, fencers, linguists, members of Parliament, educationalists, doctors, armed services personnel, lawyers—and the list goes on!

Second, in the research interviews, a multitude of different abilities, qualities, areas of excellence and descriptors of gifted people were cited:

- service to Māori (at the national, tribal and whānau levels)
- Māori knowledge (e.g. whakapapa, whaikōrero, waiata, healing, tikanga, tribal history, carving, weaving and other traditional arts and crafts)
- spirituality
- language ability, communication and negotiation skills
- musical, literary and artistic ability, and aesthetic appreciation
- leadership and visionary ability, initiator/pioneering spirit, missionary zeal, 'people skills', teaching ability
- mana
- sporting prowess, and, in the past, military/fighting ability
- intelligence, 'thinkers and doers', 'good all rounders with holistic understanding', good memory, academic ability, scientific analysis, love of learning, and Pākehā knowledge
- pride in Māori/tribal identity, and strong whanaungatanga

- outstanding knowledge and appreciation of nature
- cooking ability
- outstanding personal qualities and high moral values, including a raft of specifically mentioned qualities such as patience, aroha, honesty, integrity, openmindedness, manaakitanga, humility, bravery, serenity, reliability, selflessness, and sensitivity to and respect for others; particular gifted individuals were described as having moral courage, strength of character and a good sense of humour, being energetic, well organised, determined, motivated, responsible and hardworking.

Such a broad and wide-ranging concept of giftedness fits comfortably with the multi-categorical approach advocated by Gardner (1993), Gagné (2003) and others. However, differences lay in the level of detail attributed to cultural talents, traditions and values, and in the interpretation of various gifts. 'Leadership' is a case in point. While many definitions mention this general ability, its interpretation from a Māori perspective includes Māori-specific components. Three different styles of leadership emerged from this research. There is the 'up-front' brand of leadership, similar to that recognised in the Pākehā world, but also a quieter leadership-by-example genre. A third style is a 'behind-the-scenes' variety exemplified by the following quote:

> People who have and hold this type of mana are not always seen in the public eye, but are often consulted and approached within the privacy of their own kinship group. Today, people from other cultures often approach Māori people who appear to be carrying leadership roles within the formal context of the marae-atea, only to be told to approach someone else who is working quietly behind the scenes. People familiar with this type of mana have little or no difficulty recognising or 'feeling' it within other people. (Pere, 1982, p. 32)

4. Importance is placed on both 'qualities' and 'abilities'

In the context of this research, 'qualities' are perceived as being positive personal attributes such as aroha, bravery and manaakitanga. They are intangible attributes that are manifested in a person's behaviour, particularly as this behaviour relates to others. 'Abilities', on the other hand, relate to a person's skills in a particular area (e.g. artistic and academic ability). A strong emphasis was placed on intangible 'qualities', mainly in the affective, interpersonal and intrapersonal domains.

5. The concept of giftedness is holistic in nature and inextricably intertwined with other Māori concepts

No ethnic group's concept of giftedness and talent can stand alone. Rather, it is affected by the myriad attitudes, beliefs, needs, values, customs and other concepts that are the essence of the culture itself. For example, for Māori, manaakitanga, aroha-ki-te-tangata, whanaungatanga, wairua and āwhinatanga are all very strong cultural values, and this is reflected in the importance placed on personal qualities and service to others.

6. There is an inherent expectation that a person's gifts and talents will be used to benefit others

Gifts bring with them inherent responsibilities and a commitment to reciprocate (utu) (Timutimu-Thorpe, 1988). Consequently, the traditional belief that god-given gifts should be used to benefit others continues today. Participants provided numerous examples of gifted individuals who were sharing their talents at the national, tribal and local levels in a wide variety of service areas.

Apart from being an important category in its own right, 'service to others' is a strong common thread in many other categories. An examination of all the 'personal qualities' cited shows that the majority are related to caring for and helping others. The 'language abilities' mentioned are also generally service-oriented, as are the visionaries, thinkers and doers in the 'intellectual' category. In the category of 'traditional knowledge', many specific skills have inbuilt tikanga that embody the ethos of service (e.g., when learning to weave the first article produced must be given away). One participant who is very knowledgeable about the world of Māori art mentioned the obligation to share artistic talents with younger Māori. He said this was not something that was stated, but rather an obligation that was felt by most Māori artists he knew. It was an obligation that, when acted upon, raised the mana of the artist in the eyes of other Māori. He went as far as saying that a person could be the most talented artist in the world and produce wonderful works of art but, if their motivation is merely for self-gain and they do nothing to help others or support Māori kaupapa, then that person would not be acknowledged as a gifted Māori artist but rather recognised as a gifted artist who just happens to be Māori.

7. The Māori culture provides a firm foundation on which giftedness is grounded, nurtured, exhibited and developed

- The vast majority of gifts and talents considered in this research have Māori culture at their foundation in some way or other. Language ability is a good example. Contemporary Māori cited as gifted in this area demonstrated three distinct types of language ability:
- an outstanding competence and confidence in te reo Māori
- the ability to present an argument or point of view in a convincing, even inspirational, way, which was usually related to supporting a particular Māori cause
- the ability to interest, amuse and entertain an audience.

Again, the examples given usually related to Māori story-telling, or to engaging and inspirational whaikōrero.

Similarly, many other abilities and qualities were demonstrated in a Māori context. Even the service component, while acknowledging service to all people, more often than not referred to service that supported Māori causes.

8. Mana tangata is frequently accorded to gifted people, especially in the areas of traditional knowledge and service to others

A common thread throughout the research was mana. There are four different types of mana: mana atua, mana tūpuna, mana whenua and mana tangata. It is this last type that has particular relevance to giftedness.

Buck (1950), discussing the subject of chiefly mana in traditional times, notes that "It was not a mysterious, indefinable quality flowing from supernatural sources; it was basically the result of successive and successful human achievements" (p. 346). The fact that outstanding individuals were often accorded mana tangata is evidence of the value and importance of giftedness in pre-European Māori society. The highest reward a person could be given was not wealth, in terms of possessions, but rather mana. Wealth, in fact, was not accumulated, but shared, thus earning more mana for the giver (Metge, 1976; Schwimmer, 1966).

Nowadays mana continues to play an important role in Māori culture, and it is still regularly accorded to people with outstanding gifts and talents (Tauroa, 1989). This fact was supported by the interview data: national, iwi and whānau figures were often cited as possessing mana. Frequently, this mana was gained for their in-depth traditional knowledge and their outstanding service to others. Where mana is accorded, a person so endowed must reciprocate with a commitment to be accountable (Timutimu-Thorpe, 1988). This adds a further obligation to use one's gifts and talents for the benefit of all.

Identifying and providing for gifted and talented Māori students

Research participants and writers at the time of the research (Cathcart, 1994; Reid, 1992; White, 1994) believed gifted Māori learners were not being adequately identified and provided for in our schools. Consequently, the study sought Māori opinion about effective and appropriate means of addressing this problem. Participants made numerous suggestions, many of which are equally applicable to all students regardless of ethnicity. For example, teachers were advised to observe students carefully in a range of environments and not to disregard those whose behaviour was challenging. A wide range and abundance of resources were recommended, as were developing good child–teacher relationships and a warm, friendly, flexible environment, utilising outside expertise, and providing a broad, challenging curriculum.

A number of Māori-specific recommendations were also made, including the following.

- Educators should consult with Māori and work in partnership with them to identify and develop the potential of gifted Māori students.
- Strong networks between the whānau and early childhood education providers or schools should be developed to support and encourage gifted Māori learners.
- Methods and programmes used to identify and provide for gifted Māori students should take account of Māori concepts of giftedness, be culturally appropriate and challenging, and be delivered in a culturally responsive environment.

- Teachers, parents and whānau should work together to raise the aspirations and self-esteem of all Māori students.

- Gifted Māori students should be encouraged and developed in their Māoritanga. Educational provisions should: incorporate cultural content, focus on both qualities and abilities, and provide opportunities for students to enhance their mana tangata and use their gifts and talents in the service of others.

- Teachers and other professionals who work with Māori need to be better trained to provide appropriately for Māori students in general and gifted Māori students in particular.

Associated issues

A number of issues emerged in relation to the recommendations above.

Parental, whānau, peer and self-nomination

With respect to identification, parents may be reluctant to identify their children as gifted for fear of appearing whakahīhī. The same factor can work against successful self-nomination. Parents may also be reluctant to approach the early childhood education provider/school because of bad memories of their own schooling, or they may have a concern about nominating their children for placement in inappropriate programmes. Although parents may feel too whakamā to nominate their own children as being gifted, it is quite acceptable for other whānau members to do so. Kaumātua, in particular, have a lifetime's experience of caring for young children and can readily identify their gifted mokopuna. Kōhanga reo kaiako and whānau, cultural and bilingual support group members and rūnanga personnel can also play a role in advising teachers about gifted and talented children they know of—if they are asked.

Reid (1992) argued that in identifying gifted Māori learners, negative peer pressure acts against successful peer nomination. He stated that Māori children who show any special gifts or leadership are "criticised, ridiculed and alienated by their peers until they conform" (p. 55). Data from this research did not support Reid's opinion. Māori students' willingness to share their gifts and talents with their peers was frequently mentioned. The talented artist was asked to decorate peers' projects, the able sportsperson was nominated for and supported in school teams, and the gifted academic was sought out to provide help with homework. Giftedness was acknowledged and enjoyed by all; the sharing of gifts and talents added to the mana of the individual and the group. Consequently, peer nomination was supported as a useful form of identification. The qualification was made, however, that the person asking for nominations must be someone the students know and trust. If this is not the case—if the person's motives are suspect, or if nomination will lead to gifted Māori students being isolated from their peers—then peer nomination will probably not be effective.

Raising expectations and aspirations

Research participants called for teachers and whānau members to work together to raise the aspirations of gifted Māori students. This can only be done if teachers, parents and whānau themselves have high expectations of these children. It was believed that many teachers did not expect Māori children to be gifted, and that this creates a double disadvantage. Not only are potentially gifted Māori students remaining unidentified, but due to the 'golem effect'[2] they are not extending themselves. Rather they are performing down to expectation.

A number of participants mentioned a belief among certain Māori that they were 'dumb'. It was thought that this low racial self-esteem has emerged as a result of the colonisation process. To the contrary, participants believed that Māori came from "very talented stock." This was reflected in their migration and adaptation to the environment in Aotearoa, in their legends ("How did Māui know the North Island was shaped like a fish?") and in their art, craft and waiata. There was a call for the message of Māori ability and potential to be widely disseminated by teachers, parents and whānau alike.

Further misconceptions are that Māori society does not encourage tall poppies, and that gifted Māori children are actively discouraged from standing out. This research revealed the opposite to be true. In pre-European times, when a child's talents were recognised, the child was taken under the wing of a kaumātua or tohunga so that their gifts could be nurtured and developed (either in a mentor-like relationship or in a specialised whare wānanga). Because outstanding people used their talents to benefit the whole tribe, they were encouraged and

---

2   The effect whereby the lesser the expectation placed on someone, the poorer they perform.

celebrated. Similarly, today, gifted Māori are celebrated and admired for their ability, and whakapapa connections to talented individuals are recited with pride.

It can be argued that two factors may have led to these misconceptions. The first is a misinterpretation of the concepts of whakaiti and whakahīhī. In Māori culture there are strong sanctions against boasting. As one proverb says, "It is not for the kūmara to say how sweet it is!" Consequently, Māori children who boast about their talents may quickly be reprimanded. It should be noted, however, that this reaction is to discourage boasting, not to discourage or deny the child's ability. Similarly, as has already been mentioned, parents may be reluctant to nominate their child as being gifted. They may even play down any compliment a teacher makes about their child just in case agreement is interpreted as being whakahīhī. This parental reaction, however, is usually reserved for 'outsiders'. Within the whānau parents can often be heard to praise and encourage their children in their endeavours. Within the whānau there is not the same fear of being considered whakahīhī. Because whānau members know the parents well, their positive comments about and to their children are not at risk of being misconstrued. Their comments are accepted for what they are: genuine praise and pride in their children's achievements. The second half of the previously quoted whakataukī supports this: the kūmara cannot mention its sweetness, the proverb continues, "but I can make it known, I can speak about it."

A second factor that may have led to the erroneous belief of gifted Māori children being discouraged from standing out is a misinterpretation of the group ethos in Māori culture. While whanaungatanga and kotahitanga are both deep-seated Māori values, group solidarity does not mean group sameness, and 'individuals' can exist within a group. Being a strong individual and a co-operative member of a group are values that did not clash in pre-European times and, despite arguments to the contrary, do not today (Timutimu-Thorpe, 1988).

Withdrawal vs inclusion

A fervent plea was made against enrichment and acceleration programmes that isolate gifted Māori children from their peers. Stories were told of gifted children who failed, misbehaved or opted out of programmes in which they felt isolated, uncomfortable and unfamiliar with the teaching methods used. The following quote illustrates this situation poignantly.

> Te Aomarama, one of our girls, a very Pākehā-looking girl, went on a science course with all the able kids from each primary school and we thought she'd do very well. She pulled out. She didn't like the learning environment. She couldn't get on with the children, they wouldn't try to say her name, so she was asked by the teacher to revert back to a Pākehā name. When they went to an overnight camp they were expected to get up and get their own breakfast. Well, she doesn't do that sort of thing. She just felt she didn't know the place. She didn't feel comfortable going to a strange place and helping yourself. She's quite a capable kid, she could help herself if she felt comfortable. She didn't know anyone. I felt terrible when I realised what I'd done. I'd sent her there on her own. She had no one to play with or be with during intermission. If we send someone next time, we are going to send two girls or two boys otherwise we are not interested. (Bevan-Brown, 1993, pp. 107–108)

Another participant added that withdrawal classes sent an unspoken message to those left behind that they were not bright. He noted that individualised programmes could operate successfully "within a group context". Students could be given challenges pitched at their individual levels of ability but still work together supporting each other's learning.

The importance of cultural input

Participants believed that children who have strong cultural identities also have heightened self-esteem and confidence, and consequently are more likely to develop their potential. A further benefit was that when these gifted Māori students were in a situation where their culture was valued, they were less likely to succumb to negative peer pressure against achieving. A number of examples were given of children who appeared to 'bloom' in many different areas once their Māoritanga had been tapped into and developed. Therefore, it was considered import-ant that not only must Māori students be provided with a supportive and culturally valuing environment where their gifts would 'surface', but they must also be offered extension and enrichment programmes in te reo Māori and cultural skills and abilities.

However, it was noted that there was a lack of reo and cultural expertise among teachers who work with gifted Māori students. Participants believed that teachers needed to:

- increase their Māori cultural and reo knowledge

- learn about teaching methods appropriate for Māori children in general

- in particular, increase their understanding of Māori concepts of giftedness and of identifying and providing for gifted Māori students.

Discussion: Subsequent research, writing and gifted initiatives

From the outset it should be emphasised that every gifted Māori student is a unique individual. Some will identify strongly with their Māori culture and incorporate Māori concepts, values, beliefs and practices into their everyday life. At the other end of the spectrum are gifted Māori students who have little knowledge of Māori culture and even less about their whakapapa and iwi connections. The research findings and discussion in this chapter must not be used to stereotype gifted Māori students. Rather, they are presented to raise awareness of possibilities professionals need to consider. Gifted Māori students, their parents and whānau should be consulted to ascertain the degree to which research findings are relevant to them.

Identifying and providing for gifted and talented Māori learners

Since the research above was submitted in 1993, a considerable amount has been written about gifted and high-achieving Māori students in literature reviews, book chapters, student assignments, Ministry reports, master's and PhD theses, and journal articles. While the degree of research informing these publications varies, a consistent message across the years is that gifted Māori students are being inadequately provided for. Predominant among the reasons given are:

- an over-reliance on monocultural concepts, practices and educational provisions

- the use of a narrow range of identification strategies

- a shortage of people with the cultural expertise required to identify and provide for gifted Māori students

- a lack of culturally relevant resources
- low teacher expectations of Māori children
- giftedness being a low priority in low-decile schools where there are high numbers of Māori students (Bevan-Brown, 2000, 2002, 2005; Education Review Office, 2008; Hattie, 2000; Jenkins, 2002; Macfarlane & Moltzen, 2005; Macfarlane, Webber, Cookson-Cox, & McRae, 2014; Mahuika, 2007; Ministry of Education, 2012; Rawlinson, 1999; Riley, Bevan-Brown, Bicknell, Carroll-Lind, & Kearney, 2004; Scobie-Jennings, 2012; Webber, 2011).

The majority of the literature cited above also contains suggestions, research findings and recommendations to improve the situation for gifted Māori students and their whānau. These unanimously confirm and support the Māori-specific recommendations made by participants in the author's initial research. Three particularly strong themes to emerge from later research are:

- the importance of including Māori cultural input in the education of gifted and high-achieving Māori students
- the need for teachers to increase their knowledge and ability to provide culturally appropriate identification and programmes for gifted Māori students
- the need for, and benefits of, consultation, collaboration and empowerment of parents and whānau in their gifted child's education.

With regard to the associated issues discussed earlier, a divergent finding emerged from Galu's (1998) research. He found that despite accelerated classes not meeting the cultural needs of the 10 gifted Māori students in his study, the majority "enjoyed their time in the gifted programme and felt that they had benefited academically from the experience" (Riley et al., 2004, p. 135). One explanation for this difference in findings is that the students in Galu's study had other Māori in their gifted programme, whereas the examples in my research were all the *only* Māori student in the class/activity.

One can also speculate as to why there was no Māori content in Galu's student's programme. It is likely that there were no staff with the prerequisite knowledge to provide this input. This speculation is supported by Riley at al.'s (2004) finding that Māori students in main-stream schools who are gifted in cultural abilities and qualities are seldom extended in these areas because of their teachers' lack of Māori cultural knowledge. A further reason was that cultural giftedness was given a low priority in many schools. However, it must be noted that despite this finding, and the previously outlined inadequacies in the education of gifted Māori students, there has been considerable progress made since my research was reported in 1993. Certainly, professionals nowadays are a great deal more aware of the need to provide culturally responsive gifted education, Māori resources have increased, and there has also been an increase in Māori enrichment and extension classes, with shining examples being various programmes emanating from government-funded projects such as the Extending High Standards Across Schools and the Talent Development Initiatives (2003–2005) (see Riley & Moltzen, 2010). There are also excellent examples of Māori-initiated programmes, such as Tū Toa (Hapeta & Palmer, 2009) and the Waikato kura kaupapa Māori programme described by Herewini, Tiakiwai and Hawksworth (2012); and an increase in the Māori-relevant professional development being offered, such as Helping Gifted Learners Soar: Kia Rewa ki Runga, the 2012/13 programme run by Te Toi Tupu, and sessions on 'Māori Giftedness within Ka Hikitia' and 'Chess as a Game Plan for Māori Intelligence', offered at the 2014 Tairawhiti REAP Working Together Symposium.

Tairawhiti REAP is in fact initiating and/or supporting a range of exciting projects for Māori students with high potential. These include the 2011 Poutama Tamatane project, which taught mau rākau to Māori youth identified by their schools, in Sunny Bush's words, as:

> underachieving, disinterested students, who possessed latent potential. The premise behind the initiative was to tap into this covert talent and then give them some tools to openly explore pathways to future success.

Other initiatives include a GATE Art programme in Hicks Bay, and the 2011 Eastbay REAP project in which Māori students scripted and filmed a local Māori legend (Sunny Bush, personal communication, 26 April 2014).

Similarly, gifted Māori students and Māori topics have also starred in the Future Problem Solving and Community Problem Solving pro-grammes offered in a number of Aotearoa / New Zealand schools. A highlight of this programme was the team from Kerikeri High School, who, in 2012, came second in an international Future Problem Solving competition with their investigation of ways in which learning and usage of Māori language could be increased in their school and community.[3]

Māori concepts of giftedness

Although there has been a pleasing increase in research related to gifted Māori students, research specifically focused on Māori concepts of giftedness is still limited. Participants in Jenkins's (2002) research also identified a broad concept of giftedness, including an emphasis on qualities such as manaakitanga, aroha-ki-te-tangata, whanaungatanga, wairua and āwhinatanga. Similarly supported were the attribution of mana for Māori forms of leadership; collective support, acknowledge-ment, ownership and celebration of giftedness; and a requirement to share one's gifts for the benefit of others.

Mahuika's (2007) literature review calls for future research to clar-ify variations in the Māori concept reported by Bevan-Brown (1993) and Jenkins (2002). In particular, she notes the need for research into "potential iwi or hapū divergences, gender considerations as well as dif-ferences of opinion and experience for gifted Māori who do not strongly adhere to their Māoritanga" (p. 9). Similarly, Herewini et al. (2012) add that "Māori perspectives of giftedness are not finite and static, but rather dynamic and evolving" (p. 41). They highlighted the need for literature and resources that reflect Māori-medium, English-medium, bilingual and immersion settings. They also reported consulting with respected kaumātua about their perspectives of giftedness, to inform their kura kaupapa goal of nurturing Māori concepts of giftedness that reflect tikanga Māori. Unfortunately these perspectives were not elab-orated on.

Macfarlane et al. (2014) took an important step forward in their study. Although not specifically identified as "gifted" research, two of their research questions focus on Te Arawa perceptions of educational

---

3   This can be viewed at https://www.youtube.com/watch?v=QPGiJty9XZM&feature=em-share_video_user

success and how the traits of successful students align to "Te Arawa distinctiveness" (p. 53). The findings showed that eight identified strengths and characteristics of Te Arawa icons and tūpuna—identity, diligence, relationships, innovation, wellbeing, scholarship, humility, and values—continue to guide today's high-achieving Māori youth.

Finally, a further aspect of Māori views on giftedness was revealed in special education research I conducted (Bevan-Brown, 2002; Cullen & Bevan-Brown, 1999). This research showed that giftedness was considered to be just one of the many categories of special education needs. The special need associated with giftedness arose because

> the processes, services, expertise and resources needed to challenge and extend gifted children were considered to be lacking in our present education system—both in English-medium and Māori medium education. (Bevan-Brown, 2002, p. 280)

The implications of research findings for people who work with gifted Māori

Nurturing sturdy kauri

Native to Aotearoa / New Zealand, the kauri towers above all other trees in the forest. For Māori, kauri traditionally had chiefly status, which is reflected in the whakataukī: "Kua hinga te kauri o te wao nui a Tane" (The kauri has fallen in the sacred forest of Tane), a saying that is used whenever a great person dies. Nowadays, kauri are valued not only by Māori but by all New Zealanders.

Professionals who work with gifted Māori children have a responsibility to help these small kauri grow into sturdy, well-developed adults. The research shows that this can be achieved by ensuring the following factors are addressed.

1. *Māori perspectives are included in the definition of giftedness adopted by early childhood education providers and schools.* This equates to a broad, wide-ranging concept that includes spiritual, cognitive, affective, aesthetic, artistic, musical Ecef facilities, psychomotor, social, intuitive, creative, leadership and cultural abilities and qualities. Māori ways of perceiving and demonstrating these various components also need to be taken into consideration (e.g., group giftedness and differing leadership types).

2. *Identification measures and procedures are culturally appropriate, effective and include all areas of giftedness in the early childhood education provider's/school's definition.* Space constraints prevent a detailed consideration of identification, but helpful information on observations, checklists, rating scales, products, processes and performances, nominations and tests can be found in Bevan-Brown, 2009.[4] This article also contains a checklist of Māori-specific cultural abilities and qualities. Also helpful are the Māori-specific identification tools at http://gifted.tki.org.nz/For-schools-and-teachers/Cultural-considerations/Māori-students/Toolbox. A combination of identification strategies is recommended. However, whatever methods are chosen, in order to be effective they must be used within the context of a culturally responsive environment (i.e. a place where gifted Māori students' culture is valued, affirmed and developed).

3. *Educational provisions are culturally appropriate, effective, linked to identified strengths and interests, and take Māori needs, aspirations and concepts of giftedness into account.* Again discussion of this requirement is constrained by space limits, so readers are referred to the previously mentioned article for suggestions relating to culturally appropriate provisions. There should be three layers of cultural input: curriculum-wide Māori content that contributes to creating the all-important culturally responsive environment; specific content to extend students who are gifted in Māori cultural abilities and qualities; and relevant cultural content in programmes to extend Māori students with gifts and talents in other areas. Ideally, educational provision should be holistic, include a service component, and be provided in an environment where the gifted student feels comfortable and well supported by both peers and teachers.

4. A further point that bears highlighting is that schools should not give priority to certain areas (usually academic) while neglecting others (usually affective), as was found by Riley et al. (2004) in their survey of New Zealand gifted education provisions. Although extending children in the spiritual domain and in the much-valued qualities mentioned by participants in my research may be

---

4   Available at http://www.giftedchildren.org.nz/apex/v15no1.php.

difficult, a few suggestions for meeting this challenge are included in Bevan-Brown, 2009. Also, it is recommended that teachers consult with their community for ideas and guidance. This approach was reported as being successful by Herewini et al. (2012): "We embraced this new learning and continue to meet with pakeke, whānau and other interested gifted communities to grow our understanding and knowledge in appropriate ways" (p. 47).

5. *Parents, whānau and the Māori community are consulted, involved, supported and empowered in the education of gifted Māori students.* The requirement to collaborate with parents has become widely accepted in Aotearoa / New Zealand, and teachers are often reminded that "parents know their children best". However, consulting with parents of gifted children and Māori parents is doubly threatening to some teachers, who consequently avoid it. They hold a stereotyped view of parents of gifted children as being pushy and overestimating their children's ability. While this may apply to a small minority of parents, research indicates that the opposite is usually true. Robinson, Shore and Enersen (2007) report that parents of gifted children are very accurate in identifying giftedness, and that involving them in their child's education leads to more successful outcomes for the child. With respect to Māori parents of gifted children, as discussed earlier, reticence is most likely due to a fear of being considered whakahīhī rather than indicating their inability to recognise or encourage giftedness in their child. Being aware of and sensitive to this situation will contribute to building effective home–early childhood education facility (ECEF)/school relationships. All ECEFs and schools were provided with a copy of the book *Nurturing Gifted and Talented Children: A Parent– Teacher Partnership* (Ministry of Education, 2008). Sharing this with parents is a good strategy for further developing a good working relationship.[5]

6. *Professional development focused on gifted education and Māori education in general, and teaching gifted Māori children in particular, is given priority.* In addition to the variety of relevant courses offered by universities, wānanga and private providers, there are

---

5   It can also be accessed online at http://gifted.tki.org.nz/For-schools-and-teachers

also valuable online resources that educators can access to upskill themselves to effectively teach gifted Māori students. The TKI gifted website[6] and the Ministry of Education (2012) publication *Gifted and Talented Students: Meeting Their Needs in New Zealand Schools*[7] are worthy of special mention. They both contain helpful information and resources relating to teaching gifted Māori students. "Shortage of staff with the prerequisite knowledge and skills to provide culturally appropriate programmes for gifted Māori students" is no longer an acceptable excuse for a lack of relevant educational provisions.

7. Widespread application of the five requirements listed above will contribute to the growth of many proud and sturdy kauri in our ECEFs, schools and homes.

Study questions

1. What differences are there between the Māori concept of giftedness outlined in this chapter and any of the widely known Western concepts? (Some of these can be accessed at http://gifted.tki.org.nz/For-schools-and-teachers/Definitions.)

2. In your opinion, what is the greatest barrier to the development of 'sturdy kauri'? How can it be overcome?

3. Describe ways the service component could be included in educational programmes at early childhood, primary and secondary school levels.

4. Go to http://gifted.tki.org.nz/For-schools-and-teachers/Cultural-considerations/Maori-students/ and download and complete the '25 questions to ask your school'. How well did your school fare? Celebrate the areas of strength, and develop and implement a plan to rectify any weaknesses identified.

6　In particular, http://gifted.tki.org.nz/For-schools-and-teachers/Cultural-considerations/ Māori-students

7　Which can be downloaded at http://gifted.tki.org.nz/For-schools-and-teachers

References

Best, E. (1924). *The Māori as he was.* Wellington: Government Printer.

Bevan-Brown, J. (1993). *Special abilities: A Māori perspective.* Unpublished master's thesis, Massey University [Palmerston North].

Bevan-Brown, J. (2000). Running the gauntlet: A gifted Māori learner's journey through secondary school. In *Proceedings of Now is the Future: The Gifted Student in Today's Secondary School Conference.* Auckland: George Parkyn Centre.

Bevan-Brown, J. (2002). *Culturally appropriate, effective provision for Māori learners with special needs: He waka tino whakarawea.* Unpublished doctoral thesis, Massey University [Palmerston North].

Bevan-Brown, J. (2005). Providing a culturally responsive environment for gifted Māori learners. *International Education Journal, 6*(2), 150–155.

Bevan-Brown, J. (2009). Identifying and providing for gifted and talented Māori students. *APEX, 15*(1), 6–20.

Bevan-Brown, J. (2011). Gifted and talented Māori learners. In R. Moltzen (Ed.), *Gifted and talented: New Zealand perspectives* (3rd ed., pp. 82–110). Auckland: Pearson.

Buck, T. R. H. (1950). *The coming of the Māori.* Wellington: Whitcombe and Tombs Ltd.

Cathcart, R. (1994). Exceptionally able children from minority cultures. In *They're not bringing my brain out* (pp. 184–200). Auckland: REACH Publications.

Cullen, J., & Bevan-Brown, J. (1999). *Resourcing special education in early childhood: Database and best practice validation.* Final report to the Ministry of Education. Palmerston North: Institute for Professional Development and Educational Research, Massey University,

Education Review Office. (2008). *School's provision for gifted and talented students.* Wellington: Author. Retrieved from http://www.ero.govt.nz/ National-ReportsSchools-Provision-for-Gifted-and-Talented-Students-June-2008%20

Gagné, F. (2003). Transforming gifts into talents: The DMGT as a developmental theory. In N. Colangelo & G. Davis (Eds.), *Handbook of gifted education* (3rd ed., pp. 60–74). Boston, MA: Allyn & Bacon.

Galu, M. (1998). *Gifted and talented perceptions of Māori and Polynesian students educated in segregated classes.* Unpublished master's thesis, University of Waikato.

Gardner, H. (1993). *Multiple intelligence: The theory in practice*. New York, NY: Basic Books.

Hapeta, J., & Palmer, F. (2009). Tū toa—Māori youth 'standing with pride as champions' in sport and education. *Journal of Australian Indigenous Issues, Special Issue: World Indigenous Peoples' Conference on Education (WIPCE), 12*(1–4), 229–247.

Hattie, J. (2000). What's so special about gifted education? In *Proceedings of the Now is the Future: The Gifted Student in Today's Secondary School Conference*. Auckland: George Parkyn Centre.

Herewini, L., Tiakiwai, S. J., & Hawksworth, L. (2012). Gifted and talented. *set: Research Information for Teachers, 2*, 41–48.

Jenkins, H. (2002). *Culturally responsive pedagogy: Embracing Māori giftedness*. Unpublished master's thesis, Waikato University.

King, M. (1977). *Te Puea*. Auckland: Hodder & Stoughton.

Macfarlane, A., & Moltzen, R. (2005). Whiti ki runga!: Gifted and talented Māori learners. *Kairaranga, 6*(2), 7–9.

Macfarlane, A., Webber, M., Cookson-Cox, C., & McRae, H. (2014). *Ka awatea: An iwi case study of Māori students' success*. Unpublished report to Ngā Pae o te Māramatanga.

Mahuika, R. (2007). Māori gifted and talented education: A review of the literature. *MAI Review, 1*. Intern Research Report 5.

Marsden, M. (1975). God, man and universe: A Māori view. In M. King. (Ed.), *Te ao hurihuri: Aspects of Māoritanga* (pp. 118–138). Auckland: Reed Books.

Mead, H. M. (1993). Ngā timunga me ngā paringa o te mana Māori. In W. Ihimaera (Ed.), *Te ao marama: Regaining Aotearoa: Māori writers speak out* (pp. 199–209). Auckland: Reed Books.

Metge, J. (1976). *The Māoris of New Zealand: Rautahi*. London: Routledge and Kegan Paul.

Ministry of Education. (2008). *Nurturing gifted and talented children: A parent–teacher partnership*. Wellington: Learning Media.

Ministry of Education. (2012). *Gifted and talented students: Meeting their needs in New Zealand schools*. Wellington: Learning Media.

Pere, R. R. (1982). *Ako: Concepts and learning in the Māori tradition*. Working paper No. 17. Hamilton: University of Waikato.

Puketapu-Hetet, E. (1993). Māori weaving. In W. Ihimaera (Ed.), *Te ao marama: Regaining Aotearoa: Māori writers speak out* (pp. 282–286).

Auckland: Reed Books.

Rawlinson, C. (1999). *Teachers' recognition of children with special abilities: A change in direction!* Paper presented at the NZARE/AARE conference, Melbourne, VIC. Retrieved from http://www.tki.org.nz/r/gifted/pedagogy/rawlinson_e.php

Reid, N. (1992, July). *Correcting cultural myopia.* Paper presented at the Guiding the Gifted conference, Auckland.

Riley, T., Bevan-Brown, J., Bicknell, B., Carroll-Lind, J., & Kearney, A. (2004). *The extent, nature and effectiveness of planned approaches in New Zealand schools for providing for gifted and talented students.* Report to the Ministry of Education. Palmerston North: IPDER, Massey University. Retrieved from http://www.educationcounts.govt.nz/publications/assessment/5451

Riley, T., & Moltzen, R. (2010). *Enhancing and igniting talent development initiatives: Research to determine effectiveness.* Report to the Ministry of Education. Wellington: Ministry of Education.

Robinson, A., Shore, B., & Enersen, D. (2007). *Best practices in gifted education: An evidence-based guide.* Waco, TX: Prufrock Press.

Scobie-Jennings, E. (2012). *An investigation into how Māori students who are gifted and talented are identified in mainstream schools.* Unpublished master's thesis, Massey University [Palmerston North].

Schwimmer, E. (1966). *The world of the Māori.* Wellington: A. H. and A.W. Reed.

Tauroa, H. (1989). *Healing the breach: One Māori's perspective on the Treaty of Waitangi.* Auckland: Collins.

Te Ao Hou. (1961–1975). *Te Ao Hou: The Māori Magazine* (36–76).

Te Awekotuku, N. (1991). *Mana wahine Māori.* Auckland: New Women's Press.

Timutimu-Thorpe, H. (1988, November). *E āwhi, e manaaki, e tiaki he tamaiti hunga haua.* Paper presented at the Conference on Community Integration for People with Intellectual Handicaps, Dunedin.

Webber, M. (2011). Look to the past: Stand tall in the present: The integral nature of positive racial-ethnic identity for the academic success of Māori students. In W. Vialle (Ed.), *Giftedness from an indigenous perspective* (pp. 100–110). Wollongong, NSW: University of Wollongong Print Press.

White, S. (1994). Te wero: The challenge. *APEX, 7*(2), 10–16.

Chapter 12

Conclusion: Relationships of interdependence—Making the difference together

Mere Berryman

E koekoe te tūī, e ketekete te kākā, e kū kū te kererū.

The tūī squawks, the kākā chatters, the kererū coos.

Korihi ake ngā manu. Tākiri mai te ata. Ka ao, ka ao, ka awatea!
Tīhei mauri ora.

The birds call. The day begins and I am alive.

Introduction

This chapter begins by taking a brief look at New Zealand history. It then presents two different Māori whakataukī as metaphors, both to reconnect to the beginning of the book and also to make connections throughout the book as a whole. These metaphors are used to bring the chapters together and to consider how *inclusion*, a term that is often highly contested and poorly understood (Wearmouth, 2009), might begin to be better understood and applied when working with Māori children and young people with disabilities, or special education needs, or both, and with their families.

Considering our colonial past

As has happened with other indigenous peoples around the globe, competing discourses and practices founded on unequal power relations (Bishop & Glynn, 1999) have continued to pathologise the condition of Māori people in Aotearoa / New Zealand society (Shields, Bishop, & Mazawi, 2005). These discourses and practices have continued since the initial impact of colonisation (Consedine & Consedine, 2005; Smith, 1999), generating an education system imposed on Māori by the state; or, as Walker suggests (1990, p. 10), an education system that has contributed to "a structural relationship of Pākehā dominance and Māori subjection". This has been problematic for many Māori, but especially so for Māori students and young people with disabilities, or special education needs, or both, many of whom, together with their whānau, have experienced the impact of being doubly disadvantaged, both within and by the very systems set up to provide them with access and benefits.

In New Zealand's formal education system, principles derived from colonial images have served to guide teachers' actions and explain the basis for those actions. From this pattern of images and principles, educational policies and rules of practice were developed that have required Māori students to, metaphorically, leave their culture at the school gate in order to participate in education (Bishop, Berryman, Tiakiwai, & Richardson, 2003; Macfarlane, 2004). In other words, Māori language, values, beliefs and practices have not been represented and legitimated within Aotearoa / New Zealand's classrooms and schools. This has resulted in the education provided by the state playing a major role in destroying the Māori language, culture and iwi identities, and replacing them with those of the colonisers.

This situation has created the need to construct new metaphorical spaces in which people from indigenous or minority cultural backgrounds can feel safe to bring their own cultural toolkit (Bruner, 1991, 1996) or prior knowledge and experiences to mainstream educational contexts so that they can more effectively relate to, interact with and learn with and from each other. Accordingly, knowledge and understanding from te ao Māori, including the use of whakataukī, pepeha and metaphors from Māori, have all contributed to the overall theorising and shape of this book.

Sense-making through the use of metaphors and discourses

Heshusius (1996) describes the use of metaphor as "a deeply creative act, an act that gives rise to our assumptions about how reality fits together, and how we know" (p. 4). She explains that metaphors are used to "make sense out of reality and construct reality … people's lives, their thoughts, actions, and experiences, are generated by metaphorical images, the very vehicle for shaping the content of consciousness" (p. 5).

Within contexts such as these, Parker (1992) highlights the importance of the "system of statements which constructs an object" (p. 5), for these are the discourses that we draw upon to explain and understand our everyday practices. Burr (1995) asserts that a discourse refers to "a set of meanings, metaphors, representations, images, stories, statements and so on that in some way together produce a particular version of events" (p. 48). Fundamental to discourses is power (Burr, 1995), given that the discourses within which we are positioned, or maintain as real, may see some discourses privileged over others in our development of relationships and interactions with others (Berryman, 2008).

Particularly relevant in the context of a colonial education system is Foucault's (1972) seminal contention that when the language and metaphors from the majority discourse are able to dominate, then the minority discourse will be understood in deficit terms. Foucault suggests that discourses, rather than being understood as merely linguistic systems or texts, should be understood as discursive practices where power relations are extolled in the sets of rules and conditions that are established between groups and institutions. These power relations become embedded and are explicit in economic and social practices and other patterns of behaviour. Indeed, these assumptions of superiority are both explicit and implicit in the metaphors and discourses of the colonisers, many of which have continued to theorise Māori in deficit terms up to the present day. For example, aspects of Māori culture such as kapa haka, prowess in warfare and, today, prowess in sport were and still are being used to reinforce the colonial metaphor of 'savage other' (Consedine & Consedine, 2005; Hokowhitu, 2001).

In their work, Bishop, Berryman, Powell and Teddy (2005) and Bishop, Berryman, Cavanagh and Teddy (2007) have applied the concept of discourse as being the sets of ideas, influenced by historical events, which in turn influence one's practices and actions, and thus how one relates and interacts with others and then understands and explains those experiences. They have shown that discourses are a major influence on the images and experiences that teachers and Māori students have of each other, and therefore on the relationships and interactions that exist between them. The writers in this book would contend that this is also very true for the Māori students, young people and whānau this book is concerned with.

Whakataukī as metaphor for the future

Accordingly, each chapter in this book has been prefaced by a different whakataukī or whakatauākī[1] as the writers of this book seek to discursively position this book within metaphors that will take us more legitimately into a Māori-focused future that Māori have been able to define. The *nothing about us without us* discourse that provided a strong theoretical foundation for the disabilities movement (Charlton, 2000), and which has also been taken up by indigenous and other groups, underpins our support of a kaupapa Māori movement towards greater self-determination. The first whakataukī in this chapter, "E koekoe te tūī, e ketekete te kākā, e kū kū te kererū", speaks literally of three different native birds that frequent the Aotearoa / New Zealand landscape. Metaphorically, this whakataukī speaks of diversity. It recognises and values the special attributes that we each maintain: the genealogical and whānau connections, the attributes and the talents that make us who we are and that give us our own voice. As discussed in Chapter 1, it also reminds us that each individual and each whānau are different, and culturally specific information cannot be assumed to apply in every situation, or from one situation to another.

The second whakataukī, "Korihi ake ngā manu. Tākiri mai te ata.

---

1   According to the teachings of renowned elder and academic Wharehuia Milroy, from Ngāi Tūhoe, both whakataukī and whakatauākī are adages or metaphorical sayings. However, unlike whakataukī, whakatauākī can be attributed back to their original source.

Ka ao, ka ao, ka awatea! Tīhei mauri ora", again uses the metaphor of birds, but this time to speak literally of the multitude of birds—each contributes to the dawn chorus with its own voice. Metaphorically, it is from this diversity that the richness of the dawn chorus ensues. While each bird is able to determine its own voice, together they work in relationship with all others, and by working interdependently they enhance the combined result—the concept of what we can do together being more powerful than what any one of us can do on our own. It is from contexts such as these that new understanding and learning can emerge; thus, 'Tīhei mauri ora' (Let new life and wellbeing emerge).

Relationships of interdependence

This concept of relational interdependence for wellbeing was first introduced in Chapter 1 of this book with the metaphor 'He kura ngā tāngata' (People are precious). In this whakatauki, Mead and Grove (2003) highlight not only the value of people, but also, importantly, the added value that people can contribute to the wellbeing of the group. Likewise, it is important to acknowledge that this book represents the coming together of a group of Māori women who are mothers and nannies and who are also researchers and scholars. Members of this group have all undertaken research in the area of special education and disability, and all want to give back to the whānau and communities in which they have worked. By sharing their experiences and knowledge in this book with other educators and specialists, the intention is that more relational, culturally responsive and authentic pathways may be incorporated and applied in people's practices. In turn, more Māori children, especially those with special education needs, and their whānau, can be provided with greater opportunities to access more of the benefits that the education system has to offer.

The Treaty of Waitangi mandated this promise to all New Zealanders: equity and social justice without compromise to one's cultural knowledge and integrity. This is a promise that for many is still to be fulfilled.

Cultural distinctiveness and understanding

The centrality of culture in the contemporary world—to living and learning—continues to be very perplexing for many New Zealanders,

Māori and non-Māori alike. While there has been a plethora of research about Māori (Smith, 1999), research-based information by Māori, about Māori and for Māori has been far less common, especially research by Māori about children and young people with special education needs. This is not to say that it does not exist; rather that it has often been marginalised, overpowered and overlooked in favour of the abundance of Western research—research that is usually located offshore and undertaken with other populations and then brought to Aotearoa / New Zealand and applied in interventions to Māori and the general population. Such research is often legitimated in the name of cultural neutrality, and theorised as therefore being able to apply to people of any culture regardless of their whakapapa or genealogy.

In the first chapter, rather than simply accept interventions as capable of being culturally neutral, Jill Bevan-Brown highlights the influential role culture plays in the perception and management of special education needs. This contention is played out again and again throughout the chapters of this book. For too long special education has remained dominated by the culture of the school. Many schools continue to be challenged by the idea of acknowledging the cultural capital that families bring with them to the school setting. Failure to see the cultural knowledge of whānau as a valuable resource for the process of educating children perpetuates schools as dominant white spaces (Milne, 2013; Skrtic, 1991), with policies, approaches and protocols that continue to be informed and legitimated by Western medical models. Although many families and whānau with children who are referred to special education may not be from the dominant group, we find that their own cultural practices and customs are not seen as a source of legitimate knowledge and are often marginalised; family, whānau and parental knowledge is routinely belittled, dismissed or at best marginalised by knowledge from medical experts (Ferguson, 2008).

In Chapter 2 Sonja Macfarlane reinforces the hegemonic policies, systems and practices that continue to privilege Western perspectives over indigenous Māori knowledge, creating a default setting that regularly relegates Māori cultural practices and evidence to the margins, despite its relevance or potential to inform (Tooley, 2000). Sonja highlights the many conventional special education perspectives and policies that continue to be at odds with those held by Māori, and respectfully suggests a more inclusive pathway for Māori students with special education needs with the whakataukī she has chosen: "Whaia ki te ara tika, whaia te kotahitanga o te wairua, mā te rangimārie me te aroha e paihere" (Pursue unity of spirit, which is bound together by peace and compassion).

From the voices of Māori researchers, special education practitioners and whānau, Sonja identifies the importance of respecting the fact that Māori are able to determine more effective responses to their own issues through the use of evidence that has meaning and relevance for them, and through their understanding and application of Māori knowledge. To support this, she provides a number of models for more effective, Māori-informed practice for Māori.

Self-determination

Being able to be more self-determining often requires the more powerful partner to be prepared to relinquish some of their power. This begins by their being able to understand personal agency and share power. In Chapter 3 we learn about inclusion from four kura rumaki, where the metaphor demands a focus on strengths rather than weaknesses. Rather than be distracted by weaknesses, this metaphor, "Waihoa ko ōku whengu, mauria mai ko ōku painga", urges us to focus on and nurture our strengths. Rather than supporting the medical model that traditionally begins from the position of establishing individual need, whānau in these kura consistently identified the need for holistic and inclusive responses that are culturally located within the whānau, and that are strengths-based. The model that emerged from this research suggests a balanced and holistic approach, with the child embedded in both their whānau and their culture. This chapter explores some of the implications for learning from and engaging with such a model.

In Chapter 4 Huhana Hickey uses the metaphor "whānau hauā" to demonstrate the embedded nature of the child, nested within the nuclear and wider whānau. Not only is the culture of the child important: Huhana reminds us that if self-determination is to be a reality, then we must recognise and emphasise the importance of learning from, by listening to, Māori children, parents and wider whanau— the whānau hauā. The metaphor chosen by Huhana, "He waka eke noa" (A canoe which we are all in with no exception), reminds us that whānau such as these do not have a choice. The challenge for others working in these contexts is how might whānau hauā help them as professionals to position themselves to make a real contribution to the whānau from inside the waka, rather than engaging from outside as an objective professional, and what are the implications of both positions?

Like other writers before her, Huhana presents a number of Māori models, among them tātau tātau, which is offered as a whānau hauā model of wellbeing. She links to the need for whānau hauā to have greater input at the level of practice as well as policy. Huhana reminds us that if we do not include whānau hauā in the setting of policy direction, we will continue to see this group suffer the consequences of marginalisation and invisibility. It seems clear that if self-determination is to be a reality for whānau hauā, their inclusion needs to be sought at the local and national levels, and also at international levels through forums such as the United Nations. Again, this theme is maintained consistently throughout the chapters in this book.

In Part II of the book a number of different disability categories are examined, and new themes are considered.

Mahi tahi—working as one

The theme of how we can work together most effectively for whānau provides the next important theme to emerge from this book. Mahi tahi is the act of collaborating, working together as one towards the same objective or common purpose. As a metaphor, mahi tahi requires true power sharing, engendering a powerful relationship of solidarity that is known to sustain itself well after the goal has been fulfilled or the project has been completed.

In Chapter 5 Kirsten Smiler reports on her doctoral study (Smiler, 2014), which examined the experiences of whānau with deaf children. Her whakataukī, "Kua takoto te mānuka" (The leaves of the mānuka tree have been laid), extends from the key metaphors she used in her doctorate to provide a Māori way of conceptualising and framing not only the experience of deafness but also a system of supports for Māori deaf children and their whānau. She discusses how these experiences contribute to whānau constructions of the meaning of deafness, and explores whether the current system design and delivery of early intervention supports need to be adapted to be more effective for Māori.

Kirsten argues that professionals who provide Māori whānau with specialist forms of support must allow whānau decision making and ongoing evaluation of the intervention. The coming together of whānau and professionals in ways that exemplify mahi tahi does not happen in a vacuum. True power sharing is built on relationships of interdependence; it respects the whakapapa and cultural toolkit that everyone brings to the table, and the rights of personal agency and self-determination that contexts such as these can promote.

Chapter 6, by Jill Bevan-Brown and Tai Walker, begins by looking at the prevalence of blindness and vision impairment among Māori in pre-European times. The writers then move on to the present time by reporting on the implications of a number of small studies of Māori and vision impairment. The whakataukī in this chapter, "E kore taku moe e riro i a koe" (My dream cannot be taken by you), refers to a person's ability to define themselves and their aspirations. This has implications for kāpō Māori as well as the professionals who work with them. Jill and Tai propose a three-step approach that includes taking collective responsibility, ensuring the right attitudinal disposition and providing high-quality services. They conclude with another whakatauākī, "He kino tokomaha ki tae kainga a kai, tēnā kia tū ki te mahi, ka aha hoki", which reminds us that "While the task may be a challenging one, working together, as in mahi tahi, has its rewards".

Whakapapa and whanaungatanga

As previously mentioned, whakapapa, as it connects to one's genealogy, is important. Undoubtedly the majority of Māori who perceive themselves as Māori and/or who are perceived by others to be Māori do not generally understand themselves to be a single homogeneous group, but rather members of separate tribal groups, each with their own ancestral stories, their own dialect and their own special association with the land (Durie, 1997). The link to the land results from the specific waka or canoe on which key ancestors first travelled to Aotearoa / New Zealand from the Pacific, and from whom all members of particular iwi descend. Therefore, waka and iwi membership, together with explicit links to the land and waterways—to tūrangawaewae and marae—provide the very foundations of a Māori person's cultural and societal identity. As understood within a Māori world view, the whakataukī "E kore koe e ngaro, he kākano i ruia mai i Rangiatea" (Do not forget, you are a seed descended from Rangiatea) enables those with Māori blood to trace their whakapapa back to the beginnings of time and to the creation of the universe (Mead, 1997).

Closely aligned to whakapapa is whanaungatanga. When one encounters new people, whakawhanaungatanga—the act of making connections through a ritual of reciprocal introductions called mihimihi—provides a formal opportunity for people to announce their familial connections, and to make connections to other people (both living and dead), and to inanimate objects such as the canoe that brought their ancestors to this country, their mountain, and their waterway. Mead (2003) maintains that making whanaungatanga connections can reach beyond actual familial relationships to include relationships to people who are not kin, but who through shared experiences feel and act as kin. This process of establishing links, making connections and relating to the people one meets by identifying, in culturally appropriate ways, whakapapa links, past heritages, common respect for places and landscape features, and other relationships or points of engagement brings with it connections but also real responsibilities and commitments.

For many Māori, knowing who you are, where you come from and what your whakapapa is, is the important, most respectful, first step. Connections are seldom made about who one is in terms of wellbeing, work or title until whanaungatanga connections have been properly established. Therefore, anyone perceived as attempting to define these things about you before they have attempted to get to know you can be perceived as rude or even insulting. Relationships of trust and respect are most useful when they are able to be defined and determined by the individual parties themselves, when they extend both ways—between Māori and the groups seeking to engage with Māori—and when they are reciprocal.

For too long, in many Western models relationships are devalued as getting in the way of the professional response. At best they are overlooked, sometimes emerging almost by accident out of the work that is done. In Māori models, relationships precede all else. More likely, the most effective work for Māori emerges out of purposeful cultural constructs such as pōwhiri, whanaungatanga and mihimihi, at which relationships can be clearly prioritised and deliberately established.

In Chapter 7, through a conversation between Huhana Hickey and Jill Bevan-Brown, we are privileged with an insight into disability from the authentic voice of a woman from Ngāti Tahinga. In their chapter the whakatauākī provided by the late Fred Kana reminds us to treasure our own uniqueness, no matter what:

> Kei tēnā, kei tēnā, kei tēnā anō.
> Tōna ake āhua, tōna ake mauri, tōna ake mana.

> (Each and every one has their own uniqueness,
> life essence and presence.)

From Huhana's generosity of spirit we can all learn, and together we can be more powerful in our work with others.

In Chapter 8, on intellectual disability, Jill Bevan-Brown's whakataukī, "E kore e hekeheke he kākano rangatira" (I will never be lost for I am the product of chiefs) also links back to the importance of whakapapa and whanaungatanga. Jill considers pre-European and contemporary Māori concepts of intellectual disability in order to better understand the implications for people who work with intellectually disabled Māori and their whānau. While acknowledging that evidence of progress in the area of intellectual disabilities has been considerable, the *IHC Submission: Inquiry into the Determinants of Wellbeing for Māori Children* (IHC, 2012) shows we still have a long way to go. The findings of Jill's research, together with findings from the health and education sectors, provide a number of implications for people who work with intellectually disabled Māori. Rather than make assumptions, professionals must understand the importance of the beliefs and dispositions they bring to these contexts, as these will often differ significantly from those of the person or people with whom they seek to engage. Again, whakapapa, cultural identity, parental and whānau involvement and support are paramount, representing huge potential, but only if intellectually disabled Māori and their whānau are provided with culturally located, relational spaces in which they are respectfully invited to and are able to contribute.

If the work is to be culturally responsive, professionals and the people with whom they seek to work would benefit from being prepared to seek relational respect and trust with these people from the very outset, then listen and learn from them throughout their work. Culturally responsive contexts must remain ongoing, spiralling and dialogic throughout the entire relationship. Furthermore, to enhance the provision being offered throughout the service, culturally relevant services should also be made available as an entitlement. These themes are consistent throughout this book.

In Chapter 9, on Māori and autism spectrum disorder, Jill again uses a metaphor that connects with whakapapa, although in doing so she is making the point that even though we have a common lineage, as individuals we are likely to be quite diverse. This point is particularly important for people with autism spectrum disorder, who argue that their different ways of processing information should be appreciated as contributing to the richness of human diversity rather than be considered a negative difference. Diversity is also important for Māori who want to be seen for *who* they are before they are seen for *what* they are: "Ko Waitaha ngā tāngata, ko kawe kē tō ngakau" (All men of the Waitaha tribe, but all differing in inclinations).

Ako

Pere (1982) describes ako as not distinguishing between the roles of teacher and learner. To teach and to learn are seen as reciprocal activities. Metge (1983) describes ako as a "unified cooperation of learner and teacher in a single enterprise" (p. 2). Ako suggests that in traditional times Māori understood the importance of learning in ways that were interactive, and where knowledge was co-constructed between teachers and learners. The writers in this book raise the important relevance of this type of two-way reciprocal pedagogy, both in and through the relationships, in special education settings, to this day.

In Chapter 10 Mere Berryman lays down a whakataukī that again calls for these relationships to be conducted with respect if we are to learn from, with and for each other:

Ko ōu hīkoinga i runga i tōku whariki,

Ko tōu noho i tōku whare,

E huakina ai ōku tatau ōku matapihi.

Your steps on my mat,

Your respect for my home,

Opens doors and windows.

Metaphorically, this whakataukī speaks of close connections and respect for our home communities if we wish to develop relationships and be invited in. This has both literal and metaphorical implications. This chapter discusses research that sought to capitalise on the strengths and knowledge available within both teachers and whānau in order to take joint responsibility for students' learning and behaviour. What emerged was a clear reminder of the strengths to be found in the students themselves, thus demonstrating the potential effectiveness of teachers, students, whānau and community to learn from one another when they work constructively and collaboratively to address their own issues. For these Māori students, their whānau and teachers, it was clear that effective solutions stemmed from activating culturally preferred values and practices for engaging school and community, and from establishing a more equitable sharing of responsibility, expertise and accountability among these groups. While the voices and experiences of these communities defined the problems, they also generated the solutions and were able to provide contexts in which all were able to learn. How power can be maintained so that collaboration and culture can be truly determined by the very communities in which the work is being undertaken is still the greatest implication for both Māori communities and for those who seek to contribute more effectively in these communities.

Mana tangata

Mana tangata is the final important theme that has emerged from the chapters of this book. Mana tangata provides a specific reference to a type of authority that is bestowed upon an individual or group by others according to the other's perception of the individual's or group's ability to develop and maintain integrity and/or skills. Sometimes these qualities are acquired through self-motivation, or through commitment and determination, and sometimes these qualities may be handed down. Mana tangata therefore affirms the demonstration of exceptional leadership, qualities and/or special skills. This concept is evident in the whakataukī Jill Bevan-Brown uses in Chapter 11: "Kīhai i taka te parapara a ōu tūpuna: tuku iho ki a koe", a whakataukī that reminds us you cannot fail to inherit the talents of your ancestors: they must descend to you.

This chapter begins with a brief discussion of terminology, the concept of giftedness, and giftedness for Māori in pre-European times. It then reports, from a Māori perspective, the results of Jill's research into giftedness. The chapter concludes with a discussion about how people who work with gifted Māori children are nurturing "sturdy kauri". Kauri is a tree that towers above all others in the forest. Metaphorically, kauri are known for their own mana or chiefly status. Today, kauri are valued not only by Māori but by all New Zealanders. Just as we protect our kauri forests for future generations, by investing in these young people we are investing in our future, for they are our future.

Conclusion

A Māori world view provides the foundation for this book and may well initiate the reader into greater insights into and understanding of how Māori traditionally acquired and used knowledge for all, and by all. Māori have a culture that is based on inclusion, and a collective, reciprocal approach to learning and teaching that values all students and takes responsibility for finding ways to meet their needs, be they intellectual, physical or spiritual, or their need for being connected and included with whānau. The research reported in this book strongly suggests that Māori communities must be able to contribute if effective solutions for assessing and meeting the needs of their own children, and for finding new solutions, are to be a reality. This means that we must not continue to impose solutions on to Māori communities. Within cultural models of whānau, power sharing and collaboration Māori must be able to largely determine who is invited and how they will participate. These practices are more likely to result in the goals Durie (2004) defined for success in education for Māori: all Māori students are able to live as Māori, are able to participate actively as citizens of the world, and have good levels of health and a high standard of living.

This book suggests that if we want to achieve inclusion then we must be concerned with recognising and respecting the diversity of all. Although some students come to school from very different situations and opportunities, schools need to support them, because these same students make a contribution that, by their very diversity, we can all learn from. Inclusion is about valuing and including all children for what they arrive with and for the families that stand beside them, not just on what we might aspire to mould them into. Recognising, valuing and being responsive to the child or young person's diversity, whatever that diversity stems from, is paramount, whether their diversity be through disability, ethnicity, culture, language, religion, gender, sexual orientation, or other. I conclude with a whakatauākī that indicates what this might look like. This whakatauākī was reportedly used by Potatau at his coronation ceremony in Ngaruawahia in 1858 (Kelly, 1949):

Kotahi te kōhao o te ngira e kuhuna ai

te miro mā,

te miro pango,

te miro whero.

There is but one eye of the needle through which passes

the white thread,

the black thread,

the red thread.

Simultaneously, this whakatauākī endorses cultural diversity and the path of one culture to determine its own destiny within a nation of others. In so doing, it challenges assimilation policies and practices that impose monocultural responses. Instead, the whakatauākī points to the integrity of separate but entwined pathways. The three threads, although entwined, remain separate and distinct. They do not *blend*, as would different colours of paint. Each strand is seen in relation to the other, representing its own unique authority and integrity, while at the same time all threads are interdependent, working relationally yet together. By recognising and respecting the diversity of Māori we are establishing the basis for a more equitable and collaborative learning and working relationships going forward, where the power to learn can be open to everyone.

References

Berryman, M. (2008). *Repositioning within indigenous discourses of transformation and self-determination.* Unpublished doctoral thesis, University of Waikato.

Bishop, R., Berryman, M., Cavanagh, T., & Teddy, L. (2007). *Te Kotahitanga: Phase 3: whanaungatanga: Establishing a culturally responsive pedagogy of relations in mainstream secondary school classrooms.* Wellington: Ministry of Education.

Bishop, R., Berryman, M., Powell, A., & Teddy, L. (2005). *Te Kotahitanga: Improving the educational achievement of Māori students in mainstream education: Phase 2: Towards a whole school approach.* Unpublished report to the Ministry of Education, Wellington.

Bishop, R., Berryman, M., Tiakiwai, S., & Richardson, C. (2003). *Te Kotahitanga: The experiences of Year 9 and 10 Māori students in mainstream classrooms.* Wellington: Ministry of Education.

Bishop, R., & Glynn, T. (1999). *Culture counts: Changing power relations in education.* Palmerston North: Dunmore Press.

Bruner, J. (1991). The narrative construction of reality. *Critical Inquiry, 18*(1), 1–21.

Bruner, J. (1996). *The culture of education.* Cambridge, MA: Harvard University Press.

Burr, V. (1995). *An introduction to social constructivism.* London, UK: Routledge.

Charlton, J. I. (2000). *Nothing about us without us: Disability oppression and empowerment.* Berkeley, CA: University of California Press.

Consedine, R., & Consedine, J. (2005). *Healing our history: The challenge of the Treaty of Waitangi.* London, UK: Penguin Books.

Durie, M. (1997). Identity, nationhood and implications for practice in New Zealand. *New Zealand Psychological Society, 26*(2), pp. 32–38.

Durie, M. H. (2004, September). *Māori achievement: Anticipating the learning environment.* Paper presented at the forth Hui Taumata Mātauranga, Taupo.

Ferguson, D. L. (2008). Instructional trends in inclusive education: The continuing challenge to teach each one and every one. *European Journal of Special Education, 23*(2), 109–120.

Foucault, M. (1972). *The archaeology of knowledge.* New York, NY: Pantheon.

Heshusius, L. (1996). Modes of consciousness and the self in learning disabilities research: Considering past and future. In D. K. Reid, W. P. Hresko, & H. L. Swanson (Eds.), *Cognitive approaches to learning disabilities* (3rd ed., pp.651–671). Austin, TX: PRO-ED.

Hokowhitu, B. (2001, October). *Māori as the savage other: Icons of racial representation.* Paper presented at the Tokyo Foundation International Forum on Social Equality, Howard University, Washington, DC.Kelly, L. (1949). *Tainui.* Wellington: The Polynesian Society.

IHC. (2012). *Inquiry into the determinants of wellbeing for Māori children* [Submission]. Retrieved from http://www.ihc.org.nz/downloadsihc188

Macfarlane, A. H. (2004). *Kia hiwa ra!: Listen to culture—Māori students' plea to educators*. Wellington: NZCER Press.

Mead, H. M., & Grove, N. (2003). *Ngā pēpeha a ngā tīpuna*. Wellington: Victoria University Press.

Mead, H. (2003). *Tikanga Māori: Living by Māori values*. Wellington: Huia Publishers.

Mead, L. T. (1997). *Ngā aho o te kakahu mātauranga: The multiple layers of struggle by Māori in education*. Unpublished doctoral thesis. Auckland: University of Auckland.

Metge, J. (1983). *Learning and teaching: He tikanga Māori*. Wellington: Department of Education.

Milne, A. (2013). *Colouring in the white spaces: Developing cultural identity in mainstream schools*. Unpublished doctoral thesis, University of Waikato.

Parker, I. (1992). *Discourse dynamics: Critical analysis for social and individual psychology*. London, UK: Routledge.

Pere, R. (1982). *Ako: Concepts and learning in the Māori tradition*. Working paper No.17. Hamilton: University of Waikato.

Shields, C., Bishop, R., & Mazawi, A. E. (2005). *Pathologizing practices: The impact of deficit thinking on education*. New York, NY: Lang.

Skrtic, T. M. (1991) The special education paradox: Equity as the way to excellence. *Harvard Educational Review, 61*, 148–206.

Smiler, K. (2014). *Ka puāwai ngā kōhungahunga turi: A study of the nature and impacts of early intervention for Māori deaf children and their whānau*. Wellington: Victoria University of Wellington.

Smith, L. T. (1999). *Decolonizing methodologies: Research and indigenous peoples*. London, UK: Zed Books.

Tooley, C. (2000). *Māori education policy in the new millennium: Policy rationality and government mechanisms*. Unpublished master's thesis, University of Auckland.

Walker, R. (1990). *Ka whawhai tonu matou: Struggle without end*. Auckland: Penguin.

Wearmouth, J. (2009). *A beginning teacher's guide to special educational needs*. Buckingham, UK: Open University Press.

Abbreviations

ACC: Accident Compensation Corporation.

ADHD: attention deficit hyperactivity disorder.

AIMHI: Achievement in Multicultural High Schools.

ASD: autism spectrum disorder.

BLENNZ: Blind and Low Vision Education Network of New Zealand.

BVI: blindness and vision impairment.

COP: chronic obstructive pulmonary disease.

CPR: cardiopulmonary resuscitation.

DSM-5: *Diagnostic and Statistical Manual*, version 5.

EBP: evidence-based practice.

ECEF: early childhood education facility

EI: early intervention.

FCEI: family-centred early intervention.

GATE: gifted and talented education.

GTI: grounded theory inquiry.

ICD-10: *International Classification of Diseases, 10th Edition*.

ID: intellectually disabled.

IEP: individual education plan.

IHC: the New Zealand Society for the Intellectually Handicapped, now known as IHC New Zealand.

MAPS: personalised plan of action.

MP: Member of Parliament.

MS: multiple sclerosis.

NZSL: New Zealand Sign Language.

PBE: practice-based evidence.

PB4L: Positive Behaviour for Learning.

PhD: doctor of philosophy.

PPMS: primary progressive multiple sclerosis.

RNZFB: Royal New Zealand Foundation of the Blind.

SE: special education.

SES: specialist education services.

UNHS: universal newborn hearing screening.

UNHSEIP: Universal Newborn Hearing Screening and Early Intervention Programme.

Glossary

Aotearoa: New Zealand.

Apirana Ngata: (1874–1950); Ngāti Porou; national leader, land reformer, politician and scholar.

Aroha ki te tangata: compassion towards people.

Aroha: love in its broadest sense.

Atua: gods.

Awa: river.

Āwhinatanga/awhi: help, assist.

Cooper, Whina: Dame Whina Cooper, ONZ DBE, was a respected kuia who worked for many years for the rights of her people, and particularly to improve the lot of Māori women.

Hā a koro mā, ā kui mā: the breath of the old men and old woman.

Haka: dance; perform the haka.

Hāngi: earth oven to cook food with steam and heat from heated stones.

Hapū: sub-tribe.

Hara: to transgress, commit a sin, violate *tapu*.

Harakeke: flax plant.

Hau: wind.

Hauā: disabled.

Hianga: mischief.

Himene: hymns.

Hinemoa: female ancestor of Te Arawa.

Hinengaro: mind; consciousness.

Hinengaro hauā: intellectually disabled.

Homai: name of the campus at the Blind and Low Vision Education Network NZ.

Hongi: traditional Māori greeting, performed by pressing one's nose and forehead (at the same time) to another person at an encounter.

Hongi Hika: a Māori rangatira and war leader of the Ngāpuhi iwi.

Hononga: connection; relationship.

Horomona Maruhau: also known as Blind Solomon.

Horowhenua: district on the West coast of New Zealand.

Hui: a gathering that adheres to Māori cultural practice.

Hui whakawhanaungatanga: a gathering of people who are establishing relationships.

Huia: *Heteralocha acutirostris*—a glossy, black bird, native to New Zealand, now extinct, which had prized white-tipped tail feathers and orange wattles.

Ihi: psychic force.

Ika: fish.

Io: supreme god; god of all creation.

Iwi: tribe.

Kai: food.

Kaiako: teacher.

Kaiārahi: guide.

Kaiāwhina: teacher aide.

Kaikōrero: speaker; orator.

Kaitakawaenga: Māori cultural liaison specialist

Kaiurungi: steerer, controller, pilot

Kaiwhakahaere: organiser; administrator; boss.

Kapa haka: Māori cultural group; performing group.

Kāpō: blind; blindness; blind person.

Karakia: prayer.

Karioi: mountain southwest of Raglan and Whāingaroa harbour.

Kaumātua: respected elder (either male or female).

Kaupapa: topic; subject.

Kaupapa Māori: Māori ideology, philosophy and principles.

Kauri: *Agathis australis*—the largest forest tree in Aotearoa / New Zealand, typically found in the northern North Island.

Kawa: protocol; customs.

Kete: basket.

Kete mātauranga: basket of knowledge.

Kia ora: hello; greetings.

Kōhanga reo: Māori-medium early childhood centre.

Kōhungahunga: be young; infant.

Kōrero: speak; talk.

Kōrero ā-*ringaringa*: sign language.

Kōrero ā-tinana: observations of action and behaviour.

Kōrero ā-tuhituhi: written language.

Kōrero ā-waha: spoken language.

Kōrero whakawhitiwhiti: exchanging of information through conversation.

Kotahitanga: unity.

Kuia: elderly woman.

Kuia whakaruruhau: elderly woman who is a mentor or protector.

Kūmara: sweet potato.

Kura: school.

Kura auraki: English-medium schools.

Kura kaupapa Māori: Māori-medium school.

Kura reo rua: bilingual school.

Kura rumaki: Māori-immersion school.

Kura whānau: school family (community).

Kurī: dog.

Mahi ā-ngākau: work done from the heart.

Mahi tahi: working as one

Mahi whakahirahira: important work.

Mahuika: the younger sister of Hine-nui-te-pō, goddess of death. It was from her that Māui obtained the secret of making fire.

Mākutu: witchcraft; magic; sorcery; spell.

Māmā: mother.

Mana: personal prestige.

Mana atua: sacred spiritual power from the atua.

Mana atua ake: ancestral link.

Mana tangata: power and status accrued through one's talents or qualities and bestowed by others.

Mana tiaki: power of protection.

Mana tūpuna: power and status through descent.

Mana whenua: power from / authority over the land.

Manaaki/manaakitanga: to support, take care of.

Manawatu: district on the West Coast of Aotearoa / New Zealand.

Manuhiri: visitor/guest.

Mānuka: *Leptospermum scoparium*—a common native scrub bush with aromatic, prickly leaves and many small, white, pink or red flowers.

Māori: the indigenous people of Aotearoa / New Zealand.

Māori atua: Māori gods.

Māoritanga: Māori culture, practices and beliefs.

Marae: cultural meeting ground/place.

Marae ātea: courtyard; public forum.

Matariki: the Pleiades (the Seven Sisters)—an open cluster of many stars in the constellation Taurus. The first appearance before sunrise of Matariki in the north-eastern sky indicates the beginning of the Māori year, about the middle of June. Matariki disappears at the end of the Māori year.

Mātauranga Māori: Māori ways of knowing.

Mau rākau: Māori weaponry.

Māui/Māui-tikitiki-a-Taranga: a well-known Polynesian character of narratives, who performed a number of amazing feats.

Maunga: mountain.

Mauri: unique essence; untapped potential.

Mihimihi: greeting; pay tribute.

Mirimiri: to rub, soothe, smooth, stroke, fondle, smear, massage.

Moana: sea; ocean; large lake.

Moko: facial tattoo.

Mokopuna: grandchild.

Motatau: town located in the Northland region of the North Island of New Zealand.

Mōteatea / ngā mōteatea: lament; traditional chant; sung poetry.

Murirangawhenua: the grandmother of Māui. Māui took her jawbone and used it as a weapon in his first expedition.

Muru: to take ritual compensation; confiscate.

Nepia, George: a Māori rugby union and rugby league player. He was an exceptional All Black fullback.

Ngā atua: the gods.

Ngāti Hine: iwi from the North Island of Aotearoa / New Zealand.

Ngāti Kāpō / Ngāti Kāpō o Aotearoa: Māori advocacy and service organisation for blind people and their whānau.

Ngāti Tahinga: tribal group of the hills between Port Waikato and Whāingaroa Harbour.

Noa: be free from tapu; ordinary; unrestricted.

Noho marae: overnight stay at a marae.

Ora: life; live.

Otaki: a town in the Kapiti Coast district of the North Island of Aotearoa / New Zealand.

Pā harakeke: flax plantation.

Paekakariki: a town in the Kapiti Coast district in the southwestern North Island of Aotearoa / New Zealand.

Pākehā: New Zealander of European descent.

Pākehātanga: Pākehā world.

Pakeke: adult.

Pākeke: adults.

Parapara: gifts.

Paritutu: guarding the eastern end of New Plymouth's harbour is Paritutu Rock; volcanic remnant.

Pepeha:

Pitomata: potential.

Pono: true; honest.

Pōrangi: crazy; insane; mentally ill.

Porirua: a city in the Wellington Region of the North Island of Aotearoa / New Zealand.

Poroporoaki: formal farewell ceremony.

Pōwhiri: The coming together of tangata whenua (indigenous people, community or host peoples) and manuhiri (visitors) for a common purpose on marae in a formal process.

Pukerewa marae: tribal meeting place of Huhana Hickey.

Pūmanawa: heart.

Puna ariki: spring (water) of the gods.

Rangatahi: youth.

Rangatira: chief.

Rangatiratanga: self-determination.

Raranga: weaving.

Raruraru: problem.

Rau: leaves.

Rongoā: Māori medicine.

Ruatōria: a town in the Waiapu Valley of the Gisborne region in the northeastern corner of Aotearoa / New Zealand's North Island.

Rumaki: te reo immersion classes in English-medium schools, specifically for te kōhanga reo graduates and/or those students who speak Māori.

Rūnanga: board; council.

Taha Māori: Māori dimension.

Taha tangata: self.

Taha tikanga: compliance.

Taha whenua: environment.

Taiaha: long, wooden weapon.

Tairāwhiti: district on the East Coast of the North Island.

Tamaiti: small child.

Tamariki: children.

Tama-nui-te-rā/Tama: personification and sacred name of the sun.

Tangata whenua: indigenous people of the land.

Tangi/tangihanga: funeral.

Tāniko: form of weaving.

Taonga: prized possession; property.

Taonga tuku iho: cultural heritage; heirloom; something of value handed down.

Tapu: sacred; restricted.

Taranaki: region in the west of the North Island in the vicinity of Mount Taranaki.

Tātau: We, you (two or more) and I/me.

Tauranga/Tauranga Moana: a city on the East Coast of the Bay of Plenty, North Island, Aotearoa / New Zealand.

Tawhaki: a close relation to Māui.

Tāwhiri-mātea: god of the winds.

Te Arawa: an iwi in the Rotorua–Maketū area.

Te ao Māori: the Māori world.

Te ao Mārama: the world of light.

Te ao tūroa: light of day; Earth; enduring world.

Te Kanawa, Kiri: a Māori soprano who has had a highly successful international opera career since 1968.

Te Kotahitanga: a research and professional development programme for teachers and school leaders of Māori students in mainstream secondary schools in New Zealand.

Te oranga: healthy lifestyle and wellbeing.

Te pūmanawa o te ao Māori: Māori world.

Te pūmanawa o te ao Pākehā: the Pākehā world.

Te pūmanawa o te whakapapa: genealogy and other connections.

Te pūmanawa o te wānanga: teaching and learning.

Te reo Māori / te reo / reo: the Māori language.

Te reo Māori me ōna tikanga: the language and its customs.

Te rito: centre shoot; undeveloped leaves of harakeke.

Te taha hinengaro: the emotional, thinking dimension.

Te taha tinana: the physical dimension.

Te taha wairua: the spiritual dimension.

Te taha whānau: the family dimension.

Te Tiriti o Waitangi: the Treaty of Waitangi.

Teina: younger brother (of a male); younger sister (of a female).

Tika: correct; right.

Tikanga/tikanga Māori: customs; correct procedures.

Tinana: body.

Tipuna: an ancestor; *Tīpuna*: ancestors

Tohunga: expert.

Tohunga ahurewa: experts in esoteric knowledge.

Tohunga taura/whiāwhia: experts in occult knowledge.

Toiora: healthy lifestyle.

Tuakana: elder brother (of a male); elder sister (of a female).

Tuakana–teina: older child, younger child relationship

Tūhoe: a tribal group of the Bay of Plenty, including the Kutarere–Ruātoki–Waimana–Waikaremoana area.

Tumuaki: head (leader).

Tupuna: ancestor.

Tūpuna: ancestors.

Tūrangawaewae: a place where one has rights of residence and belonging through kinship and whakapapa.

Turi / turi whānau: deaf; the deaf community.

Turikatuku: the blind wife of Hongi Hika (a Ngā Puhi warrior and leader); she was also an important military advisor for him.

Utu: reciprocity.

Wahine toa:

Waiata: song.

Waiata tawhito: old songs.

Waikato: a collective name for the tribes living in the Waikato basin; the name of the river from which they take their name.

Waiora: wellbeing.

Wairangi: deranged; mentally ill; confused.

Wairua/wairuatanga: spirit; spirituality.

Waka: canoe.

Waka tūru: wheelchair.

Wana: inspiring awe.

Wānanga: forum; seminar.

Wehi: a response of awe in reaction to *ihi*.

Wero: challenge.

Whaikōrero: formal speech; oratory.

Whāingaroa: Raglan—a seaside town on the west coast of the North Island of Aotearoa / New Zealand.

Whaiora: mentally ill.

Whaitiri: close relation to Māui.

Whakahīhī: boastful.

Whakahirahira:

Whakaiti: belittle.

Whakamā: shy; embarrassed.

Whakapapa: genealogy.

Whakaruruhau: to shelter.

Whakatauāki: proverb by known person.

Whakataukī: proverb by unknown person.

Whakawhitiwhiti: exchange.

Whānau/whanaunga: family; extended family.

Whānau hauā:

Whanaungatanga /whakawhanaungatanga: establishing relationships.

Whāngai: adoption; adopted.

Whare: house.

Wharekai: dining hall.

Wharepaku: toilet.

Whare tupuna: ancestral meeting house.

*Whare w*ānanga: university.

Wharekura: traditional Māori school; Māori immersion secondary school.

Wharenui: meeting house; main building on the marae.

Whatumanawa: seat of emotions; heart; mind.

Wheke: octopus.

Whenua: land.

Index

www.ingramcontent.com/pod-product-compliance
Lightning Source LLC
Chambersburg PA
CBHW080043280326
41935CB00014B/1766